Looking Like What You Are

THE CUTTING EDGE
Lesbian Life and Literature

THE CUTTING EDGE
Lesbian Life and Literature

Series Editor: Karla Jay

Paint It Today by H.D. (Hilda Doolittle)
edited and with an introduction by Cassandra Laity

Heterosexual Plots and Lesbian Narratives
by Marilyn R. Farwell

*Spinsters and Lesbians: Independent Womanhood
in the United States, 1890–1930 and 1950–1980*
by Trisha Franzen

Diana: A Strange Autobiography
by Diana Frederics
with an introduction by Julie L. Abraham

Your John: The Love Letters of Radclyffe Hall
edited and with an introduction by Joanne Glasgow

Lover
by Bertha Harris

Elizabeth Bowen: A Reputation in Writing
by renée c. hoogland

Lesbian Erotics
edited by Karla Jay

Changing Our Minds: Lesbian Feminism and Psychology
by Celia Kitzinger and Rachel Perkins

(Sem)Erotics: Theorizing Lesbian: Writing
by Elizabeth A. Meese

*Bisexuality and the Challenge to Lesbian Politics: Sex,
Loyalty, and Revolution*
by Paula C. Rust

*Passionate Communities Reading Lesbian Resistance
in Jane Rule's Fiction*
by Marilyn R. Schuster

The Search for a Woman-Centered Spirituality
by Annette J. Van Dyke

*Looking Like What You Are: Sexual Style, Race,
and Lesbian Identity*
by Lisa Walker

Lesbian Friendships: For Ourselves and Each Other
edited by Jacqueline S. Weinstock and Esther D. Rothblum

*I Know My Own Heart: The Diaries of Anne Lister,
1791–1840*
edited by Helena Whitbread

*No Priest but Love: The Journals of Anne Lister,
1824–26*
edited by Helena Whitbread

THE CUTTING EDGE
Lesbian Life and Literature

Series Editor: Karla Jay

Professor of English and Women's Studies
PACE UNIVERSITY

EDITORIAL BOARD

Judith Butler, Rhetoric
UNIVERSITY OF
CALIFORNIA, BERKELEY

Blanche Wiesen Cook
History and Women's Studies
JOHN JAY COLLEGE AND
CITY UNIVERSITY OF NEW
YORK GRADUATE CENTER

Diane Griffin Crowder
French and Women's Studies
CORNELL COLLEGE

Elaine Ginsberg, English
WEST VIRGINIA UNIVERSITY

Joanne Glasgow
English and Women's Studies
BERGEN COMMUNITY COLLEGE

Marny Hall
Psychotherapist and Writer

Celia Kitzinger, Social Studies
LOUGHBOROUGH UNIVERSITY, UK

Jane Marcus
English and Women's Studies
CITY COLLEGE AND CITY
UNIVERSITY OF NEW YORK
GRADUATE CENTER

Biddy Martin, German Studies
and Women's Studies
CORNELL UNIVERSITY

Elizabeth A. Meese, English
UNIVERSITY OF ALABAMA

Esther Newton, Anthropology
SUNY, PURCHASE

Terri de la Peña
Novelist/Short-Story Writer

Ruthann Robson, Writer
LAW SCHOOL, QUEENS COLLEGE
CITY UNIVERSITY OF NEW YORK

Leila J. Rupp, History
OHIO STATE UNIVERSITY

Paula Rust, Sociology
HAMILTON COLLEGE

Ann Allen Shockley, Librarian
FISK UNIVERSITY

Elizabeth Wood
Musicologist and Writer
Committee on Theory
and Culture
NEW YORK UNIVERSITY

Bonnie Zimmerman
Women's Studies
SAN DIEGO STATE UNIVERSITY

LIBRARY
BURLINGTON COUNTY COLLEGE
PEMBERTON, NJ

Looking Like What You Are

Sexual Style, Race, and
Lesbian Identity

Lisa Walker

NEW YORK UNIVERSITY PRESS
New York and London

NEW YORK UNIVERSITY PRESS
New York and London

© 2001 by New York University
All rights reserved

Library of Congress Cataloging-in-Publication Data
Walker, Lisa, 1965–
Looking like what you are : sexual style, race, and lesbian identity /
Lisa Walker.
p.   cm.
Includes bibliographical references and index.
ISBN 0-8147-9371-1 (acid free) — ISBN 0-8147-9372-X (pbk. : acid free)
1. Lesbians—Identity. 2. Lesbianism. 3. Homosexuality.   I. Title.
HQ75.5 .W35 2001
305.48'9664—dc21   00-012049

New York University Press books are printed on acid-free paper,
and their binding materials are chosen for strength and durability.

Manufactured in the United States of America

10 9 8 7 6 5 4 3 2 1

Contents

All illustrations appear as a group following p. 126.

Preface

Writing an academic book is a strange project. When people who do not work in the academy hear that I am writing a book, they usually think it is a novel. When I explain that it is not a novel, but a book about books, they look at me as if to say, "Why would anybody want to do that?" I often evade the issue by saying that I have to do it to keep my job. But the truth is that we are much more invested in our books than that. As soon as my parents' best friends or my students or my colleagues or someone I have just been introduced to at a party asks what the book is about, I am being called on to reveal my personal investment in my writing. Some writers' investments are less apparent than others'. Mine are obvious. I can recall the very incident that determined the focus of my research.

I have to thank the exterminator at the Villa Rose apartments in Baton Rouge for the origins of this project. In Louisiana, you never have to be reminded that insects outnumber people on this planet by a ratio of millions to one. So the exterminator came regularly to keep the bug population manageable. The exterminator was a lesbian. I knew she was, because of "gaydar," because of the way she wore her hair and her jeans, because of the way she walked, because of all the ways one lesbian will recognize another—sometimes, anyway, because she was not so sure about me.

I was often home getting dressed to teach or attend class when she came to exterminate. For me, getting dressed always means getting dressed like a girl. The exterminator saw me iron skirts, apply lipstick, and slip into pumps before I flew out the door running late. But even in my haste, I tried to communicate with her through "the look"—the one that says "I know what you are because I am one too." We never spoke much beyond greeting each other. Sometimes I left before she had finished her work. Apparently it was on these days that she perused the apartment for clues about my sexuality. I know that she did because once, when my girlfriend Catherine from Philadelphia was visiting, the exterminator came while I was at school, and they spoke. The exterminator spoke to Catherine because she recognized her as a lesbian. She began the conversation in a roundabout way, dropping a few broad hints the way Southerners will. When Catherine mentioned the name of the local women's bar, the exterminator corrected her etiquette: "You're not supposed to ask if I know that bar." The question was too direct.

But at some point the exterminator got very direct about her reading of the clues in my apartment. They were, coincidentally, in the bedroom. I decorated on a graduate student budget, but I always decorated. A huge floor-to-ceiling poster of Madonna took up one wall of the room. As far as posters of Madonna go, it was good: a sepia-toned photograph of the star dripping in the pearls, lace, and crucifixes of her 1980s look. She gazed at herself in the mirror of a vanity strewn with more extravagant accessories. I had hung my windows with lace curtains that echoed the patterns of Madonna's lingerie. On another wall was a series of black-and-white fashion photos from a French magazine, all of the same dark-haired woman, looking terrifically stylish posing at a café table in a hat with a net veil over her eyes, holding a cigarette in one hand and an espresso in the other. The numerous images of women in the room struck the graduate students who helped me move in the heavier furniture from storage as odd. They asked if I knew the model in the photo, and when I said no, they asked why I had put them up. I said, "I think she's beautiful, don't you?" That answer did not register with their expectations; they looked confused and changed the topic of conversation.

But those very images must have registered with the exterminator. Catherine's presence in the apartment, clearly as an extended visitor, and the fact that I had only one double bed, confirmed a suspicion that the photos had apparently sparked months ago—she had guessed that I might be a lesbian after all. Catherine had a long chat with the exterminator about the lesbian communities in Baton Rouge and Philadelphia. I heard all about it when I came home. Listening to Catherine, I found myself a bit put out that this woman, whom I had greeted regularly at the beginning of every month, had never really spoken to me but had taken Catherine into her confidence at first sight.

Catherine tried to explain. It made sense, she said, that the exterminator, who was clearly a lesbian, should speak to her, as she was clearly a lesbian, and not to me, who was not clearly a lesbian. I listened longer to Catherine talking about how there was a bond between women who were visibly queer, and that the exterminator, despite her inferences, could not rightly be expected to feel safe talking to someone who was not so visible, who could pass for straight, and who might be straight, after all. "The look" was not proof enough. The decor was not proof enough. Only the presence of Catherine, who was readable as butch by anyone in the know, could confirm that I was a lesbian. And besides, Catherine went on, femmes did not bear the weight of the homophobia directed against lesbians; they were not under the same kind of scrutiny and assault by the heterosexual world, and so that easy recognition and trust between the most visibly stigmatized members of the community was natural.

Putting aside that the exterminator was your jock type, not your butch type, and could have just as easily been a straight softball player as a lesbian, I gave this some thought. It was true that I was not called a dyke on the street like Catherine was. It was true that the evangelists on campus did not scream "Sodomite!" when I walked by the way they did when my friend Scott walked by in those nerdy-chic outfits that only the gay boys wore.

But then I thought back to the previous year, when I was with my first lover, ML (butch for Mary Lou). I remembered dancing with her in a straight bar, foolishly ignoring the rules for personal safety in a homophobic culture. When the bar closed, there was a group of young men outside waiting for us. "You," they said, pointing to where I stood in a checked mini and heels, "don't look like one." They dismissed me in an instant. I was not a real lesbian, probably just led astray, surely redeemable, all I needed was . . . "But you," they said, pointing to where ML stood in her jeans and button-down shirt, "we know what you are."

They wanted to beat her up, and she did not want to back down in front of me or the twenty or thirty people who lined the wall outside the bar watching. The boys goaded her, making conjectures about what we did in bed in graphic and vulgar language. I had never felt so violated before, not when I heard the word "cunt" hissed in my ear on the street, not when a man had followed me from one subway train to the next for the pure pleasure of watching my anger and anxiety heighten, not when another put his hand between my legs while I stood in line to buy a token. I remembered walking up to ML, who was moving into the tightening circle of boys, preparing to defend our honor. I took hold of her belt and led her out of that circle while I told her, loud enough for the boys to hear, that they were ignorant trash unworthy of any response whatsoever. Holding myself above it all had always been an easy way out of a fight, and it worked again this time. The boys left and the watching crowd began to mumble about how obnoxious they had been. I mentally thanked them for their support during the confrontation; they would have stood there and watched one woman get beat up by half a dozen obnoxious boys.

ML was devastated, sure that the incident would scare me away from lesbianism, sure that she had not made the world seem safe enough for me to be out in. Why she thought that particular encounter with men would turn me straight never has made sense to me, but butch girls do have their own logic when it comes to femmes. They often regard us as liable to run from "the life" into the sheltering arms of normalcy at any minute. Out of this anxiety about the femme's identity, loyalty, and ability to endure, other lesbians sometimes reflect back to me just what those boys assumed when they dismissed me and turned all their hatred toward ML—that because I did not look like a lesbian I must not really be one. Maybe that anxiety can explain the times I have walked into a lesbian bar alone, without the benefit of a butch beside me, and never been spoken to or asked to dance by anyone but straight men offering to help clear up any doubts I might have about my sexuality.

Listening to Catherine and remembering, I became angry with my own community. It was not that I thought Catherine was wrong. I agreed that I do not often bear the brunt of verbally abusive and physically threatening homophobia except when I am with other women who look lesbian, or with them in a way that looks lesbian. If I am mistaken for straight, I can choose not to correct the assumption, so I do not know Catherine's experience of being constantly under surveillance. For her, this meant that being a lesbian who looked like me was easier, because I could pass. On one level this makes sense to me. Passing can be a convenience, and not all of us have access to that convenience. But on another level, I ask myself for whom is it easier that I look the way I do? It may be easier for a relative or two. If there has to be a lesbian in the family, at least she looks like a regular girl. It may be easier for some of my colleagues and some of my students, because a femme can seem less threatening, less different than a butch. And yes, it may be easier for me when I walk down the street, when I go to the store, when I go to the "ladies'" room. No one ever calls me "Sir," no one ever looks at me like I'm in the wrong department when I shop for clothes, and no one ever screams or orders me to leave when I enter a public bathroom. On the other hand, I told Catherine, you do not know what it feels like to be shut out of your own community, to be regarded with suspicion where you most need to be accepted. You do not know what it feels like to have other lesbians assume that you are straight, or even if they know better, to assume that you are not as real, to assume that at any minute you might turn "traitor" and leave your woman for a man; to assume that you are not strong and could not possibly be smart because you paint your nails instead of playing softball. What lesbians assume about me is more important than what straight people assume. And when other lesbians assume that I am less than they are because of the way I look, they devalue me.

After the exterminator incident, I decided two things: First, that I would cling to my heels and my nail polish and not be deprived of my pleasure in all things high-femme because of anyone else's expectations about what a real lesbian looks like. And second, that I would write about how lesbianism came to be defined in a way that marginalized femmes. I begin with this anecdote as a way of situating myself in relation to the issues of visibility that interest me. It is the sensation of being invisible as a lesbian in a community where, as Pat Califia puts it so well, "butches think of femmes as straight girls taking a Sapphic vacation from serving the patriarchy," that prompted me to think about the construction of identities through the trope of visibility.[1]

I am grateful to my family, friends, and colleagues who have helped me throughout the writing of this book. Crow Cianciola has provided me with daily support and encouragement, and my parents have always given me their love. Tzarina Prater, with whom I coauthored a conference paper on Ann Allen Shockley, has been invaluable in helping me to think about Shockley's work and invaluable as a friend. I would also like to thank Elsie Michie, Patrick McGee, Dana Nelson, and James Olney for helping me to shape this project, Liz Wimberly for the insightful remark that inspired the book's title, Catherine Hennessy for con-

tributing her wonderful photographs to the project, and Sigrid
King, Scott Nelson, Mary Jane Smith, and Cathy Williamson for
their valuable comments. The University of Southern Maine has
offered me research support, which I gratefully acknowledge
here, and USM librarians, Casandra Fitzherbert, Barbara Stevens,
and David Vardeman have been enormously helpful in helping
me to gather materials for this project. Niko Pfund and Karla Jay
have been a pleasure to work with.

Grateful acknowledgment is made for permission to reprint the
following material: Photograph of Natalie Barney, with permis-
sion of George Wickes. Photograph of Alice B. Toklas and
Gertrude Stein, with permission of the Beinecke Library, Yale
University. Photographs of Gladys Bentley, with permission of
Jeffrey Sunshine.

Chapter 5 appeared in a slightly different version in *Signs* 18,
no. 4 (1993) © 1993 by the University of Chicago. All rights
reserved.

Introduction
In/visible Differences

Demanding visibility has been one of the principles of late-twen-
tieth-century identity politics, and flaunting visibility has become
one of its tactics. If silence equals death, invisibility is nonexis-
tence. To be invisible is to be seen but not heard, or to be erased
entirely—to be absent from cultural consciousness. In the face of
silence and erasure, minorities have responded with the language
of the visible, symbolizing their desire for social justice by celebrating identifiable marks of difference that have been used to
target them for discrimination. Taking their cue from the strategies of groups such as the Black Power movement, whose slogan
"Black Is Beautiful" redefines the symbolic value of skin color by
reversing Eurocentric definitions of beauty, lesbians and gays
have adopted visibility politics as one way of refusing the cultural
imperative to assimilate, if not to disappear. For example, the gay
community gives symbolic power to cross-dressing as a signifier
of homosexuality by selecting a drag queen to be "Miss Gay
Pride" for the annual June Pride march and sending her down
Fifth Avenue in a convertible (Figure 1), and lesbians outfit themselves in postpunk style and stickers to announce themselves to
the queer community, to the straight world, and to the law. (Figure 2)[1] In the 1980s and 1990s, butch lesbians and drag queens
who had been anathematized in the fifties, sixties, and much of
the seventies for contributing to negative stereotypes of lesbians
and gays, have been refigured as both the forerunners and the

vanguards of the contemporary Pride movement—the ones who refused the anonymity of the closet and stood on the front lines of the margins. The phenomenon of queer chic, which reached its peak in the early to mid-1990s, when k.d. lang appeared with Cindy Crawford on the cover of *Vanity Fair*, Madonna released her video *Justify Your Love*, and RuPaul became a spokesmodel for M*A*C* cosmetics, gave pause to critics who noted that the effort to create visible political communities might be undermined by the commodification of subcultural significations of identity.[2] But the discourse of visibility remains current among many grassroots organizations, campus organizations, and cyberspace communities that understand visibility as an essential element of Pride.

The history of visibility politics begins with the production of visible difference on the body, and the scrutiny of minorities by medical and scientific "professionals." In the late eighteenth century, natural scientists began using comparative anatomy to investigate the origin and nature of racial difference.[3] Over the next hundred years, comparative anatomy became the principal methodology employed to study blacks, women, homosexuals, prostitutes, criminals, and the insane; the body had become the primary site of both identity and difference.[4] It was during the late nineteenth century that sexologists such as Havelock Ellis, Richard von Krafft-Ebing, and Karl Heinrich Ulrichs proposed the theory of inversion, or cross-gender identification, to explain the origins of homosexuality. Today we rarely hear the term "inversion" used in anything but a historical context. But the stereotype that homosexuals exhibit characteristics of the opposite sex because they are "trapped" in the wrong bodies remains prevalent. Concentrating on the biological or congenital origins of sexual deviance enabled the medical community to "discover" manifestations of homosexual difference on the body—a presumably immutable object of study.

But the physical evidence of homosexuality has always been more stable than the literature of sexology suggests. In research on female homosexuality, the mannish lesbian has been a favorite subject of investigation because her masculine qualities seemed to mark her inversion so clearly. Frequently, however, studies of female inversion contradict themselves about whether or not lesbianism reveals itself through biological anomalies such as male secondary sexual characteristics or abnormal genitalia. For example, in *Sexual Inversion* (1897), Ellis argues that "while inverted women frequently, though not always, convey an impression of mannishness or boyishness, there are no invariable anatomical characteristics associated with this impression. There is, for instance, no uniform tendency to a masculine distribution of hair."[5] Only two pages later, he claims that "there seems little doubt that inverted women frequently tend to show minor anomalies of the piliferous system, and especially slight hypertrichosis and a masculine distribution of hair."[6] Krafft-Ebing's *Psychopathis Sexualis* (1886) is similarly hazy about whether gender-digressive dressing marks lesbianism as an extension of the already masculinized body, or as a superimposition of masculine identification onto the feminine body. In his description of case number 165, Ellis's disorientation about what might be termed figure (the masculine attire and mannerism) and ground (the female body) causes him to perceive the object of study as both a man in women's clothes and a woman in men's clothes:

> Even at the first meeting, the patient produced a remarkable impression by reason of her attire, features, and conduct. She wore a gentleman's hat, her hair closely cut, eye-glasses, a gentleman's cravat, a coat-like outer garment of masculine cut that reached well down over her gown, and boots with high heels. She had coarse, somewhat masculine features; a harsh, deep voice; and made rather the impression of a man in female attire than of a lady, if one but overlooked the bosom and the decidedly feminine form of the pelvis.[7]

Having first described her attire as masculine, Ellis concludes that she looks like a man in woman's clothes. But rather than acknowledge the difficulty of interpreting figure/ground discrepancies (which gender is ground and which is figure?), the medical gaze persisted in trying to typologize its subjects into consistent and thorough categories.

The feminine lesbian has presented doctors and scientists with the greatest difficulty in typologizing the female homosexual. The sexologists' proposition that cross-gender identification accounts for homosexual behavior presumes that the male-identified woman takes a feminine woman as her love object, and therefore establishes a need for the existence of a feminine woman who would respond to the attentions of the mannish woman. But in conflating gender inversion with same-sex desire, sexology makes the feminine invert a contradiction in terms—a deductive impossibility. If the feminine woman shows no outward signs of cross-gender identification, then she should show no symptoms of inverted object choice. Sexology justifies the "womanly" woman's involvement in lesbian relationships by designating her behavior, but not her identity, as homosexual. Krafft-Ebing, for example, implies that the feminine lesbian is drawn to the masculine secondary sex characteristics of inverts, so that while she might engage in sexual behaviors with members of the same sex, the trajectory of her desire is heterosexual.

Sexologists also accounted for the feminine lesbian by downplaying her sexual agency, casting her in the passive role of the undesiring but receptive female who will settle for a masculine woman when she cannot get a man. Underlying this theory is the assumption that sexual desire itself is masculine, so that while feminine women may participate in sexual acts, they do so as the objects rather than the subjects of desire. Ellis's often-quoted description of the feminine lesbian, in which he attributes the "womanly" lesbian's sexual deviance to her less than ideal feminine qualities (not that she is masculine, just unattractive), uses the language of marking to explain the femme's passivity, reinscribing her within the very system that she problematizes:

A class in which homosexuality, *while fairly distinct, is only slightly marked*, is formed by the women to whom the actively inverted woman is most attracted. These women differ, in the first place, from the normal, or average, woman, in that they are not repelled or disgusted by lover-like advances from persons of their own sex. They are not usually attractive to the average man, though to this rule there are many exceptions. Their faces may be plain or ill-made, but not seldom they possess good figures: a point which is apt to carry more weight with the inverted woman than beauty of face. Their sexual impulses are seldom *well marked*, but they are of strongly affectionate nature. On the whole, they are women who are not very robust and well-developed, physically or nervously, and who are not well adapted for child-bearing, but who still possess many excellent qualities, and they are always womanly. One may, perhaps, say that they are the pick of the women whom the average man would pass by. No doubt, this is often the reason why they are open to homosexual advances, but I do not think it is the sole reason. So far as they may be said to constitute a class, they seem to possess a genuine, though not precisely sexual, preference for women over men, and it is this coldness, rather than lack of charm, which often renders men indifferent to them. (My emphasis)[8]

Sexology does not solve but evades the problem of the feminine lesbian by representing her as the runt of the litter of heterosexual women—physically underdeveloped, high-strung, and plain in the face. The passage suggests that the feminine lesbian produces a collapse at the intersection of the systems of marking and visibility that underpin the theory of inversion. Her homosexual difference must be visible or "distinct" to preserve the category of heterosexuality, and yet her sexuality is "not well marked" because she doesn't present the figure/ground discrepancy that signifies lesbianism within the system of marking. If marking provides evidence of an interior, inverted gender identity and produces that identity as visible, the lesbian who is not visible as such must still be marked in some discreet or vague manner (thus she falls short of being beautiful not because she is unfeminine but because she is unfortunate), or her authenticity as a lesbian must be in question.

Efforts to establish the visibility of sexual deviance with reference to the marked body continued well into the first half of the twentieth century. As late as 1941, the American Committee for the Study of Sex Variants sponsored an inquiry into the nature of homosexuality by Dr. George Henry who, with the aid of Miss Jan Gay, selected eighty informative subjects for analysis.[9] Research methods included taking social histories, conducting psychiatric evaluations, and gathering biological and "morphological data," including photographs, x-rays of the head and pelvis, physical exams, semen samples, gynecological exams, and pen drawings of female genitalia that were reproduced from exam notes and tracings obtained by "laying a glass plate on the vulva" and outlining with a crayon.[10] The purpose of collecting such data was to correlate body form with behavior (Figures 3 and 4).

The impact of medical models of homosexuality on lesbians and gays themselves is complicated. On the one hand, they created a discourse about homosexual identity that lesbians and gays used to articulate and affirm their desires. On the other hand, they shaped the way in which lesbians and gays could define themselves. In emphasizing the biological origins of sexual deviance, sexologists often attempted to counteract moral condemnations of homosexual behavior, although moralizations surface in the language of degeneracy that characterizes their writing. Speculating about the causes of homosexuality, Krafft-Ebing suggests that "psychological forces are insufficient to explain so thoroughly degenerated a character."[11] And though doctors often expressed the hope that a scientific understanding of the issue would result in decriminalizing homosexuality, they did not advocate the dignified recognition of lesbians and gays within the dominant culture. Speaking of the publicity that accompanies the legal indictment of homosexuality, George Henry commented that "it cannot in any way be hygienic for the gen-

Introduction • 7

eral public, including minors, to have daily news of the sexual misdeeds of their most prominent citizens."[12] Thus, medical studies of sexual deviance often produced homosexual bodies as visible, but perpetuated the social isolation and invisibility of lesbians and gays.[13]

This social isolation and invisibility was to become increasingly contested in the latter half of the twentieth century. With the development of homophile movements in the 1950s and 1960s and the birth of the Gay Liberation movement in the 1970s, more and more lesbians and gays identified themselves as members of a minority group with a distinctive subculture that deserved recognition and affirmation. Like other new social movements of the seventies and eighties, including the women's movement, the Black Power movement, and the Asian and Hispanic movements, the lesbian and gay rights movement centered on remaking identity, both public and private, by challenging socially constructed images—or the lack of cultural images—that create oppressive models of identity. This focus on cultural representation put issues of in/visibility at the structural foundation of identity politics.

The emphasis on visibility within identity politics has come under scrutiny as critical theorists have begun to focus not only on social visibility as a measure of recognition and access for minorities, but also on the visible performance of difference as a locus of political agency that has the potential to deconstruct foundational categories of identity such as race, gender, and desire. For lesbian and gay theorists, drag is perhaps the quintessential performance of visibility, and has been the subject of renewed critical attention and some controversy. Whereas earlier feminist criticism often characterized female impersonation (the most commonly referenced version of drag) as misogynist, recent feminist and queer theory reads drag as a radical gender performance that destabilizes normative gender identities. Judith Butler sets up her now classic discussion of drag as a radical act when she says that gender "is performatively produced and compelled by the regulatory practices of gender coherence."[14] Those practices of coherence consist of a set of norms that "operate by requiring the embodiment of certain ideals of femininity and masculinity."[15] When the subject approximates those norms "successfully," gender identity appears to be natural because it creates the effect of what Butler terms "gender uniformity." When the subject fails or refuses to approximate those norms— for example, when the drag queen "pulls the wig" at the end of a show—gender identity becomes visible as performative because s/he disrupts the effect of gender uniformity.

As the visible performance of identity gained currency in both popular and theoretical contexts, critical attention also turned to the invisible and the unmarked. In particular, the passing subject enabled critics to ask new questions about specularity and identity. Traditionally, passing (for straight, for white) has been read as a conservative form of self-representation that the subject chooses in order to assume the privileges of the dominant identity. Passing is the sign of the sellout, and also, as Carole-Anne Tyler suggests, the "sign of the victim, the practice of one already complicit with the order of things, prey to its oppressive hierarchies."[16] Because subjects who can "pass" exceed the categories of visibility that establish identity, they have been regarded as peripheral to the understanding of marginalized identities.[17] But as Elaine Ginsberg writes in the introduction to *Passing and the Fictions of Identity*,

> passing is about identities: their creation or imposition, their adoption or rejection, their accompanying rewards or penalties. Passing is also about the boundaries established between identity categories and about the individual and cultural anxieties produced by boundary crossing. Finally, passing is about specularity: the visible and the invisible, the seen and the unseen.[18]

Ginsberg thus puts the passing figure at the center rather than the margins of the field of the visible. The reevaluation of the passing figure was accompanied by an inquiry into the politics of the visible, including drag. Though performing the visible can be politically and rhetorically effective, it is not without its problems. Within the constructs of a given identity that invests certain signifiers with political value, figures that do not present those signifiers are often neglected, even though they have much to tell us about identity formation. Further, the celebration of visible performances of difference does not always attend to issues of intent. Passing is assumed to be conservative in intent, and in the culture of the social postmodern, drag is often assumed to be parodic and ironic in intent. But where does irony lie? In the design of the performer? In the eye of the beholder? Tyler points out that impersonators are never in full command of the way their performances are interpreted "because unconscious as well as conscious impulses motivate their performances." She argues that "it is important to read each instance of drag (and its interpretations) symptomatically rather than to insist it is always radical or conservative."[19]

In relation to lesbian and gay visibility, further questions arise around aspects of bodily style and mannerism that are not properly read as "drag," because they cannot be put on or taken off at will. Richard Dyer makes a useful distinction between physiognomy and sign in discussing gay visibility. He maintains that "a major fact about being gay is that it doesn't show. There is nothing about gay people's physiognomy that declares them gay." There are, on the other hand, "signs of gayness, a repertoire of gestures, expressions, stances, clothing, and even environments that bespeak gayness."[20] Dyer describes these signs as "cultural forms [of representation] designed to show what the person's person alone does not show: that he or she is gay."[21] Emphasizing the element of design in gay signification and aligning clothing and environment with gesture, expression, and stance, Dyer implies that the subject has almost complete control over self-representation; choosing not to signify homosexuality could be as easy as avoiding the local gay bar and straightening up that limp wrist.

But are all aspects of signification equally adaptable? In the case of butch and femme sexual styles, clothing is one of the most commonly read indicators of identity: butch women are recognized by their adaptations of traditionally masculine attire and femmes are (sometimes) recognized by their traditionally feminine attire. While they may be as culturally defined as clothing—though this is not entirely obvious—other aspects of sexual style are not so easily modified. A deep voice or a high voice may not be modulated with ease. Altering body language that reads as "masculine" or "feminine" may require a high degree of vigilance, and even vigilance does not guarantee success. Witness the unease that some femmes will evidence when they sit with their knees thrown apart, in proper butch stance, and the inability of some butches to look "natural" in a dress.

The difficulty of comfortably altering such signs of gender and sexual style returns us to questions of intent: Does the femme deliberately or always style herself to look heterosexual? Does the butch deliberately or always style herself to "fuck gender"? If the subject does not have control over these apparently basic elements of self-representation, what does this suggest about identity? Elsewhere I have challenged the notion that gender identity is malleable and subject to willful change, and argued that women experience butch and femme identities as embodied, fixed, and expressive of a core or interior self—in a word, as essential.[22]

Looking Like What You Are is driven by the question of what it means to look like a lesbian, and what it means to be a lesbian but not look like one. It interrogates how the visible or marked subject is defined in relation to the subject who "passes." I argue that the passer, as a figure of indeterminacy, destabilizes identities predicated on the visible to reveal how they are constructed. Because it began as a response to revaluations of the camp aesthetic that seemed to posit the visible performance of difference as intrinsically radical, the book appears to set up invisibility and visibility as competing or oppositional discourses. However, the purpose of this study is not to adjudicate between the political and rhetorical effectiveness of either visibility or invisibility, but rather to trace how the two are mapped against each other in the construction of minority identities. I analyze both the overlap and the space of contradiction between the two coexisting models to provide a more complete understanding of the way identity is constructed around in/visibility than would an analysis which focused exclusively on either the performance of the visible or on passing by themselves.

According to my identification as a femme, I initially took the feminine lesbian as the paradigmatic figure for exclusion. Several recent books, including Terry Castle's *The Apparitional Lesbian* and Renee Hoogland's *Lesbian Configurations*, have analyzed how even when the lesbian appears in cultural and literary texts, she has been "ghosted"—silenced, dismissed, erased, and rendered invisible.[23] I would argue that this is especially true for the feminine lesbian, who, perhaps more than any other figure for same-sex desire, "haunts the edges of the field of vision."[24] During the early stages of this project, I realized that my study of specularity had to attend to the connection between racial and sexual differences. Specifically, it had to be informed by an understanding of what Toni Morrison terms "African Americanism": a discourse of "denotative and connotative blackness that African peoples have come to signify, as well as the entire range of views, assumptions, readings and misreadings that accompany Eurocentric learning about these people."[25]

Included in this pattern of reading and misreading is the historical tendency of white critics to use racial difference as a marker for illegal sexuality. This is at work in all the literary and theoretical texts I study. As a figure for both illegal sexuality and a figure who is understood to craft the appearance of a legitimate sexuality, the feminine lesbian cannot be studied in isolation from the idiom of race passing. In fact, no figure accused of passing could be considered apart from race passing and from the origins of that concept in American culture, where the sexual exploitation of black women in slavery and the ongoing practice of miscegenation (re)produced light, but not "white," bodies within the black population.[26] In turn, the visibility of any identity group is necessarily linked to the paradigm of racial visibility.

The connection between figures of racial and sexual difference calls attention to the need to theorize how racial difference, because it supposedly expresses itself *prima facie* (at first *sight*) through skin color, often serves as a touchstone for playing out issues of in/visibility for other identities. In America, the black/white binary has been foundational to the definition of both race and visibility. The racial body is the black body, and my work reflects the American equation of race with blackness. Though there are several figures of racial difference that ground the definition of sexual identity in the texts I discuss, the analogy between the homosexual and the black recurs in all the texts and is key to my interrogation of economies of the visible. Thus, I use "race" primarily as a referent for blackness. Though I make this decision in order to explore the specific analogy between the black and the homosexual more fully than I could if I were to open up the category of race to include diverse identities, I am quite aware that in doing so, I replicate the effect of the analogy that I critique throughout the book—that is, in reducing race to blackness, I fail to complicate discourses of race as I complicate discourses of gender/sexuality.

Analogy repeatedly produces an inability to question the construction of more than one difference at a time. Jane Gaines inscribes this phenomenon of shifting focus within the metaphorics of in/visibility itself when she compares the structure of race in the film *Mahogany* to the mechanisms of optical illusion: "Racial conflict surfaces or recedes in this film rather like the perceptual trick in which, depending on the angle of view, one swirling pattern or other pops out at the viewer."[27] According to Gaines, film viewers can choose to "inhabit 'looking' structures," but her metaphor also implies that various looking structures may be mutually exclusive, or that viewers can only inhabit one structure at a time. My own work reflects this problem of how to inhabit various looking structures at once in that it tends to shift back and forth between race and gender/sexuality in its analysis of the visible. Although I try to keep both race and gender/sexuality in play as contested categories, sometimes I can only mark the structural shifts from one category to the next in my textual analyses, drawing attention to, but certainly not solving, the problem of how to focus multiple categories of difference.

The Definitions

Although discourses of visibility and invisibility are widely used among minorities to discuss the mechanisms of oppression, they are not often theorized as discourses or constructs, but rather are invoked to describe feelings about being marginalized.[28] Even theory that generates an analysis of in/visibility often shifts registers away from that analysis to a different set of terms. For example, Freudian and Lacanian analyses shift away from the field of perception of anatomical difference that inaugurates the Oedipus complex to a discussion of subject constitution within the field of language/the Symbolic. In "Interrogating Identity: The Postcolonial Prerogative," Homi Bhabha shifts from theorizing invisibility (the place from which the gaze is returned) as the locus of agency, to theorizing the written and aural ("the place from which the subject speaks or is spoken").[29] And in her analysis of the closet as a trope for homosexual oppression, Eve Sedgwick shifts from the field of visibility to the field of knowledge.[30] This hedginess about locating theory within the discourses of in/visibility may indicate the difficulties of working within its terms.

The systems of marking and visibility are perhaps the two most common formulations of vision, the visual, and the visible, and the issue as to which system provides the most accurate terminology is complicated and charged. With respect to racial difference, the terms "marked" and "visible" would

LIBRARY
BURLINGTON COUNTY COLLEGE
PEMBERTON, NJ

seem to be synonyms for the condition of being visibly different from what stands for the unmarked position of whiteness, where whiteness is not conceived as a racial category. For example, in Ralph Ellison's classic discussion of race and the visible in the introduction to *Invisible Man*, he uses the phrase "high visibility" to describe the condition of being marked by skin color.[31] However, the two terms belong to different sociolinguistic traditions; though each invokes issues of representation and power, the language of marking is current in feminist and cultural theories, whereas the language of visibility is in use within minority communities.

The terms take on different values in these contexts. In its technical usages within feminist and cultural theories, the apparatus marked/unmarked designates how minority identities are constructed as marked while dominant identities are positioned as "the unmarked generic"—white, male, heterosexual.[32] For example, within Western ontology, whiteness, like masculinity, is the unmarked universal, and the term "marked" carries a negative value while the term "unmarked" carries a positive one. In its current usage within minority communities, on the other hand, the recent tendency has been to assign the condition of being marked, or "visible," a positive rather than a negative value. Similarly, the terms "unmarked" and "invisible" carry different values. Both terms suggest the unseen, but "unmarked" doesn't carry the sense of erasure implicit in the terms "invisible" and "unvisible" as Ellison uses them in *Invisible Man* and as minority communities continue to use them, because "unmarked" signifies the anonymity of privilege rather than the social and political exclusion of marginalization. Here, "unmarked" still carries a positive value, unless the position of the unmarked/dominant is under critique, but "invisible" carries a negative value. Thus the title of the black women's studies anthology *All the Women Are White, All the Blacks Are Men, But Some of Us Are Brave*, which points to the exclusion and the invisibility of black women within a white- and male-dominated culture.[33]

One response to the confusing issue of terminology is to abandon one apparatus in favor of the other. But each set of terms has its advantages as a critical apparatus. In some ways, the visibility/invisibility trope is less sensitive to power relations than marked/unmarked because it does not indicate whether the condition of visibility is a function of self-representation or of attribution, whereas marking implies both noticing and attributing. Further, because visible/invisible is in popular usage, the distinction between metalanguage, which critiques the visibility trope, and object language, which can replicate the assumptions that this book wants to question, is easy to collapse. On the other hand, visible/invisible can account for the cultural invisibility specific to the experience of marginalization in a way that marked/unmarked cannot. While visible/invisible is not as sensitive to external power relations as marked/unmarked, it accommodates an analysis of the fluidity of power relations within the economy of the gaze and enables the theorization of agency for the oppressed within that economy.

The difference between the apparatuses marked/unmarked and visible/invisible creates a "critical double bind" that may determine what we emphasize in discussing domination and marginalization: the visibility/invisibility apparatus opens one up to charges of downplaying the epistemic violence that structures the representation of difference, while the marked/unmarked apparatus opens one up to charges of negating the subjectivity of the oppressed by ignoring distinctions between self-representation and attribution.[34] But the critical double bind is itself the result of either/or thinking. Perhaps more useful than abandoning one set of terms for the other is examining the relationship between the two. For this reason, I have chosen to retain the terms visibility/invisibility, using them in conjunction with marked/unmarked in order to maintain the distinctions between what and how the two sets of terms signify. While the critical impulse to avoid visibility and invisibility because of their "messiness" is understandable, I don't find that avoiding them solves the problems that they present, or that any other set of terms presents a viable alternative. Further, the impulse to avoid the terms seems to stem from the wish for a set of politically neutral terms to discuss the issues under question. Unfortunately, other terms seem either to replicate the problems inherent in the terms in/visibility, or because one set of terms does not directly mirror the other, the substitute terms fail to account for the complexities specific to the terms visible/invisible.

Retaining the terms visibility/invisibility does necessitate some attempt to delineate their parameters. To accomplish this, I risk oversimplifying the complex relationship between external power and representation better accounted for by the terminology of marking in an attempt to address the shifts that occur within discourses of visibility. However, because theory often explains the mechanics of seeing and being seen in psychoanalytic terms, I try to align the various arenas of visibility/invisibility with the psychoanalytic functions invoked to describe them, including fetishism, identification, and the mirror-stage. This project does not attempt a systematic study of psychoanalysis. Rather, it draws on psychoanalysis as a discourse about identity to explore identity formation within economies of the visible. In turn, I look to feminist and postcolonial theories of representation to suggest how the analysis of visibility and invisibility necessitates reformulating specific psychoanalytic paradigms of subject constitution that diagram the way identity is culturally understood.

The Texts

This project reads across categories of "low genre" and "literary" fiction, literary criticism, and theory to explore how visibility structures identity formation within those texts, and by extension within the culture that produces them. In general, that culture is twentieth-century Western culture, although I make forays into the nineteenth century to consider the historical de-

velopment of twentieth-century paradigms of the visible. In three
of the five chapters, I read novels that can be situated within the
modern period. When I say that the novels are part of a modernist moment, I do not want to designate only literary modernism and its techniques of fragmentation, collage, and allusion.
Some of the novels can be located within that tradition. Jean
Rhys's *Wide Sargasso Sea*, although written after the period associated with literary modernism, clearly writes out of that moment; Rhys's fiction reflects the multiple-voiced, fragmented style
of expatriate writers such as Ford, Stein, and Barnes with whom
she was published in Ford's *Transatlantic Review*.[35] But that
more traditional understanding of modernism might be hostile to
some of the texts that this project studies, such as *The Well of
Loneliness* and *Strange Brother*, which "fail" in the category of
literariness because they are conventional, and sometimes senti-
mental, realist narratives.

When I say modernist, then, I refer primarily to modernism's
anxiety around reconfigurations of sexual and racial identity
after Freud and following the eras of empire and American slavery.[36] These anxieties cut across boundaries of genre and are apparent in the writing and reception of texts that do not fall into
the category of literary modernism. The first chapter describes
how Radclyffe Hall's *The Well of Loneliness* registers a turn-of-
the-century shift in the construction of homosexuality in relation
to discourses of in/visibility. Hall produces lesbianism as visible
in the figure of the butch, and simultaneously desires and dis-
avows the possibility of the feminine lesbian. Hall's butch protagonist becomes a focal point for anxieties about lesbian visibility within modernist literary criticism, revealing how butch
and femme identities remain associated with forms of essentialism that modernism wants to, but does not always succeed in deconstructing. This critical anxiety also suggests how modernism
itself is characterized by a cultural intensity around the categories
of visibility.

In discussing how the novel renders the femme both marked

and unmarked, this chapter begins to address the question of how racial difference functions within the construction of gender and sexual identities. The second chapter pursues that question by examining the analogy between race and sexuality, which is implied in *The Well* but more fully evident in the rest of the texts I analyze. Blair Niles's 1931 novel *Strange Brother* self-consciously invokes that analogy to explore the connection between newly emerging homosexual and African American subcultures in Harlem in the 1920s, introducing the psychoanalytic schema of fetishism as a paradigm for the construction of identity within the field of visibility. The novel thus yields an analysis of how analogy itself is structured around fetishism's enactment of both the insistence on and the refusal of difference.

Chapter 3, which examines lesbian pulp fiction of the late 1950s and early 1970s, studies how those analogies work in two novels that, like *Strange Brother*, purport to advance liberal ideologies about race. But unlike *Strange Brother*, which assumes the ethnographer's outside observer point of view, Ann Bannon's *Women in the Shadows* (1959) and Ann Allen Shockley's *Loving Her* (1974) struggle to define the relationship between racial difference and homosexuality from within lesbian and gay communities by exploring interracial relationships. The novels, published over a decade apart and written by a white woman and a black woman respectively, explore the femme as a passing figure. They deploy race differently, but each invokes a fantasy of identification based on sameness that finally negates blackness and establishes lesbian identity as white.

Chapter 4 argues that various patterns of identification are central to the way I analyze structures of visibility in the first three chapters. It focuses more specifically on the act of identification itself, and shifts attention from the moment when identification is refused, which characterizes the texts studied in the first three chapters, to the moment when identification based on difference rather than sameness is desired. I begin this chapter with a reading of Homi Bhabha's theory of the stereotype as a form of fetishism, and move into a reading of three novels—Charlotte Brontë's *Jane Eyre*, Jean Rhys's *Wide Sargasso Sea*, and Michelle Cliff's *Abeng*—which are interrelated in that the latter two rewrite the text(s) that precede them. My choice of texts here obviously departs from earlier selections. Whereas the previous chapters analyze novels that deal with marginalized racial and sexual identities, I begin this chapter with a reading of *Jane Eyre*, a novel that has until fairly recently been celebrated for its representation of Jane's development as female individualist—in other words, her development as a white, heterosexual, middle-class subject. One effect of including a canonical novel like *Jane Eyre* is to show how structures of visibility define issues of race and sexual identity in texts not explicitly about those issues.

Further, the chronology of this particular set of texts traces how issues of race and sexual difference emerge from *Jane Eyre* as a text in which those issues are barely apparent. *Wide Sargasso Sea*, which deliberately foregrounds those issues, marks the moment when racial and sexual difference have come into cultural consciousness, but are unsettling to the extent that they cannot be as fully deconstructed as they will be in *Abeng*, which is written in the context of feminist and postcolonial critiques of unitary identity. In that *Wide Sargasso Sea* marks that moment of cultural discomfort with a new awareness of racial and sexual differences, it is linked to the modernist period in which I have located the texts discussed in previous chapters. Analyzing these three novels in relation to each other also allows me to trace how changing concepts of identity influence structures of the visible. The chapter maps out the movement from a paradigm of consolidated identity in *Jane Eyre*, to a modernist conception of fragmented identity in *Wide Sargasso Sea*, to a postmodern conception of identity as multiple and heterogeneous in *Abeng*. It argues that as the novels increasingly explore the fantasy of identification, racial difference and lesbian sexuality move into the foreground as part of a developing critique of the relationship between identity formation and visibility.

I conclude the book by analyzing the status of that relationship between identity formation and visibility within current feminist criticism. The last chapter, "How to Recognize a Lesbian," explores how the putative visibility of racial difference underpins the perception of the butch as marked in current lesbian theory. It is interested in how the construction of the identities "butch" and "woman of color" as visible leads to the displacement of those who do not "look like what they are" (women of color who can "pass" for white and femme lesbians who can "pass" for straight) from the communities feminism intends to represent. Analyzing how three white feminist critics, Donna Haraway, Sue-Ellen Case, and Judith Butler, have responded to the challenge of theorizing race and gender together that has been posed by feminist of color such as Gloria Anzaldúa, Cherríe Moraga, and Audre Lorde, the chapter argues that strategies of visibility are sometimes deconstructed, but also reinscribed to underpin the construction of lesbian identity within contemporary theories of race, gender, and sexuality.

Though the chapters can each stand on their own as separate essays that perform close readings of individual texts or groups of texts, read in order they sample a by no means thorough, but still loosely chronological set of significant historical and political moments, starting with the definition of lesbianism at the beginning of the century, and moving through the formulation of the ethnic model of homosexual identity in the 1920s and 1930s, the impact of pulp fiction on lesbian representation in the 1950s and 1960s, the development of lesbian feminism in the 1970s, the critique of lesbian racism in the 1980s, and the emergence of queer theory in the 1990s. Together, the chapters point to repeated breakdowns within the economy of readable identity that occur around figures of racial and sexual Otherness that do not carry obvious signs of difference, and they interrogate the persistent connection between race and sexual identity that has characterized discussions of lesbian and gay visibility for the last one hundred years.

ONE

Martyred Butches and Impossible Femmes

Radclyffe Hall and the Modern Lesbian

But then of course all intelligent people realized she was
a creature apart.
> —Radclyffe Hall, *The Well of Loneliness*

Since its publication in 1928, Radclyffe Hall's novel *The Well of Loneliness* has provoked praise and condemnation, identification and denial for generations of lesbian readers. Twenty years of feminist criticism have brought no resolution to questions about the novel's status within the lesbian literary tradition. Though it may no longer hold its place as "the Lesbian bible"— the lesbian novel that was most notorious and perhaps most widely read between the 1930s and 1960s—it still retains its rank as a landmark publication.[1] Nevertheless, the novel remains a source of controversy, and for some, of embarrassment, on several counts: its negative characterization of the lesbian life, its questionable literary merit, its definition of the "invert" as a man trapped in a woman's body, and more broadly, its portrayal of the gendered identities, which would now be termed "butch" and "femme," that Hall helped to define.[2]

On the first count, *The Well*'s status as *the* lesbian novel is inseparable from its reputation as *the most depressing* lesbian novel ever written. Many readers would understandably prefer that a novel occupying such a central place in lesbian literary history depicted lesbianism more positively than Hall's dismal account of Stephen Gordon's social ostracism and failed loves. And the novel has been maligned as much for its literary flaws as for its content. Since the 1970s, lesbian-feminist critics have compared Hall unfavorably to modernist writers such as Virginia Woolf, Gertrude Stein, and Djuna Barnes, whose stylistic innovations, poeticism, and narrative complexity have inspired more admiration than Hall's traditional realist plots and formal prose. Not without cause, Hall's writing has been called dull, overwrought, melodramatic, maudlin, old-fashioned, and stilted, and *The Well* is often regarded as pioneering for its open representation of lesbianism rather than for its literary achievements.

But aesthetic objections to *The Well* cannot be easily separated from political and social ones, for it was Hall's choice to write within the conventions of narrative realism and within the discourses of sexology that made the book's depiction of lesbianism blatant enough to come under broad public scrutiny.[3] Though Hall was careful to depict Stephen Gordon as intelligent, sensitive, and above reproach in her chivalrous behavior toward other women, many readers have taken offense at her depiction of lesbianism—most famously, perhaps, Sir Charles Biron, the magistrate who presided over the trial at which the novel was declared obscene and banned in England. Unlike feminist critics who would later link the novel's failure to provide positive images of lesbians to its formulaic realist "narrative of damnation,"[4] Chief Magistrate Biron found the novel's literary merit to be undercut by its failure to castigate the protagonist's sexual conduct.

Contemporaneous lesbian readers were also concerned with the novel's representation of female sexuality. Many worried that the book would heighten the surveillance of women showing a preference for tailored clothes or female company, and therefore that it would make lesbians more vulnerable to public scrutiny.[5] Because Hall's novel increased the visibility of the masculine lesbian in particular, it provoked the more specific concern that

Stephen Gordon, the archetypal invert, would come to represent lesbianism as a whole. This concern was not entirely unfounded. The scandal surrounding *The Well*'s publication put Hall and her protagonist in the public eye, and the image of the lesbian as the mannish woman did come to dominate the popular imagination. A portrait of Hall published in the *Sunday Express* captured that image. The photo, which appears to have been cropped from a picture of Hall with her long-time partner, Lady Una Troubridge, literalizes the feminine lesbian's elision from the representation of the female invert. It depicts Hall from the waist up, wearing a smoking jacket with her hair slicked back and a cigarette in hand, apparently alone as she stares into vacant space. The photo was accompanied by the editor's denunciation of the author as a "decadent apostle of the most hideous and loathsome of vices" who took "delight in [her] flamboyant notoriety" (Figure 5).[6]

Hostile and sympathetic readers alike shared this distaste for notoriety. One might argue that feminist scholars' discomfort with *The Well* begins with Virginia Woolf's own ambivalent response to the events surrounding the novel's publication. Hall was brought to trial on charges of obscenity in the fall of 1928, the same year that Woolf published *Orlando*, which Nigel Nicholson later described as "the longest and most charming love-letter in literature" for its portrait of Vita Sackville-West, Woolf's lover.[7] Although Woolf was opposed to the censorship of lesbian writing and was prepared to use her status as a reputable author to defend *The Well* in court, she expressed relief when she was not called to testify at "that bloody woman's trial."[8] Woolf's diaries and letters reveal that while she did not admire Hall's literary efforts, her objections to the novel were not entirely aesthetic; she was also reluctant to be seen as defending the image of the mannish lesbian.[9] Her unease with the image of the mannish lesbian reflects the concerns of Hall's general lesbian audience and highlights questions of sexual politics that remain central to critical analysis of *The Well*.

Many of these questions revolve around how Hall's representation of the lesbian as invert seems to dictate what constitutes lesbian visibility: What does it mean to create the lesbian as visible through the discourses of inversion? Is Hall's invert a product of the medical model that marks the lesbian's pathology, or does the invert exceed the framework of sexology? Does Hall perpetuate a damaging and now anachronistic stereotype of the lesbian, or does she make public a gendered identity that represents a segment of the lesbian community? Under what circumstances does lesbianism become visible? What impact has Hall's realist style made on the literary tradition of lesbian representation?

Early feminist criticism of the novel often maintained that Hall subjects herself to the biases of the medical discourses she deploys, invoking heterosexist and misogynist models of lesbian identity.[10] It saw the mannish woman as the product of erroneous masculinist stereotypes about lesbian identity, and held that the novel did not legitimate homosexuality, but encouraged the perception of lesbians as deviant and sanctioned heterosexual masculinity as the desirable norm. In the 1980s, the revaluation of butch and femme identities within lesbian communities challenged the pervasive rejection of the mannish woman as a model for lesbian identity, allowing *The Well* to be read from another perspective. In her ground-breaking 1984 essay "The Mythic Mannish Lesbian: Radclyffe Hall and the New Woman," which has influenced many subsequent readings of *The Well*, Esther Newton contends that for women of Hall's generation Stephen Gordon stood for "rebellion against the male order and . . . the lesbian's desperate struggle to be and express her true self."[11] Discourse theory also provided strategies for revaluating *The Well*. Drawing on Foucault's notion of "reverse discourse," many critics have argued that *The Well* does not simply recapitulate the patriarchal values of sexology, but also asserts sexual agency through new discourses on lesbian identity available to Hall when she wrote the novel.[12]

But sympathetic readings of *The Well* by no means ended debate over the novel's political and aesthetic value. The interpretive split between those who want to vindicate *The Well* and those who find it problematic at best, continues to rage. Defenders of *The Well* argue that while the novel may be aesthetically embarrassing, it is at least an "out novel"—a novel that is obviously about lesbians—unlike experimental texts that are more formally radical but also more "coded" in representing lesbianism.[13] Others maintain that such arguments privilege the realist novel as more authentically lesbian than experimental fiction, and counter that experimental lesbian fiction destabilizes normative sex and gender identities that Hall seems to reify.

It is important to challenge both the equation of realism with visibility and the belief that literary experimentation aims to encode or disguise lesbianism. However, given the explosion of critical work on lesbian modernist writers such as Stein, Barnes, and Woolf, I find it difficult to accept the contention that the realist narrative constitutes the "authentic lesbian text" within lesbian literary criticism.[14] Anyone keeping up with her reading will know that she can hardly speak of modernism at all without indicating lesbian modernism's experimental writers. Further, as Rita Felski points out, there is the risk that an equation between experimentalism and modernism can lead to a "fetish of avant-gardism" in which

> the modernist text becomes the privileged bearer of epistemological authority, crystallizing in its very structure the underlying fissures that the realist text glosses over. Modernism is elevated over realism paradoxically because it is a truer realism; going beyond the superficial stability of surface literary conventions, it reveals that reality is fluidity, fragmentation, indeterminacy.[15]

Clearly, the very definition of lesbian writing is at stake in the critical opposition between realist and modernist texts. I also suspect that the controversy over literary style and lesbian visibility is deeply tied to the politics of lesbian gender identity.

Specifically, I would argue that both realism and butch/femme genders are regarded as naive forms of representation. If we understand modernist writing to deconstruct reality, including the reality of gender and sexual identity, showing it to be fluid, fragmented, and indeterminate, it is easy to see how realism might then become associated with the reflection and replication of undeconstructed, hegemonic gender roles. In the equation between realism and "roles," Hall's writing exemplifies literary realism as bad mimesis (florid, maudlin, clumsy, awkward, flawed), and butch/femme exemplifies lesbian gender roles as bad mimesis—a flawed imitation of heterosexuality that is fixed within a conventional rather than a radical embodiment of lesbian identity. In this schema, the type of lesbian visibility that Hall makes available to her readers is, like her prose, conservative. Experimental fiction, on the other hand, only *seems* to make lesbianism less visible because it expresses concepts of gender identity that are less stable and coherent and therefore less recognizable than butch/femme. It follows, then, that partisanship around literary style reflects ongoing factionalism about lesbian gender.

Gertrude Stein, whose work has recently generated a good deal of criticism, is a useful figure to study in analyzing the politics of sexuality and literary form precisely because she disturbs any easy conflation of sexual and literary styles. As an experimental writer with a distinctly masculine persona, especially in her relationship with Alice B. Toklas, Stein produces conflict for some of her most dedicated and sophisticated readers—feminist readers who first focused on how Stein's work articulated a lesbian erotics. Of the writers and their partners frequently discussed in connection with the development of "Sapphic Modernism," Gertrude Stein and Alice Toklas have been perceived as the most overtly butch/femme in their sartorial styles.[16] Like Hall and Troubridge, although in different fashion, Stein and Toklas clearly dressed along gendered lines. Stein favored plain loose skirts, flowing jackets, and "sensible shoes," and Toklas carried pocketbooks and wore more "feminine" prints, heels, and furs (Figure 6).[17]

But during their lives, both friends and the public tended not to identify Stein and Toklas as a butch/femme couple. This was partly because the couple's own code of discretion around their relationship ensured that people did not speak openly of their lesbianism until after Stein's death, but also because Stein, a large woman in latter-day Birkenstocks, did not conform to the image of the lesbian defined by the boyish figure, cropped hair, and tailored clothes that *The Well* had helped popularize.[18] Further, Toklas did not fit models of conventional female beauty that typically encourage the public eroticization of lesbian relationships. Though Stein describes her lover in traditionally gendered erotic language (Toklas is the "honey suckle" to Stein's bee, she is the "tiny dish of delicious"), biographers tend to describe her as having an elegant or lovely bearing rather than physical charm. If Stein and Toklas did not conform to the fashionable image of the butch/femme couple, their relationship, which has been variously described as being patterned after the patriarchal, Victorian middle-class marriage,[19] as sadomasochistic,[20] "Byzantine," and as "obsolete, even cannibalistic"[21] by today's egalitarian feminists, has certainly been understood to replicate butch/femme roles in their most highly codified and hierarchical form.

Attempting to reconcile the belief that Stein's writing created a radical new language for lesbian eroticism with the sense that Stein's butchness makes her undesirable as a lesbian foremother, readers have both pathologized Stein's masculine persona and excused it as the anachronistic coping mechanism of a lesbian writer in the early twentieth century.[22] Sometimes Stein's masculinity becomes the compass for everything that makes her politically incorrect. For example, Catherine Stimpson, one of Stein's most astute readers, argues that "Stein's *husbanding* of her energies shows the limits of her imagination," and implies that her psychological identification with men accounts for her republican politics, her racist comments about blacks, and her

classist comments about the servant problem.[23] The reverse side
of this argument, as Marianne DeKoven articulates it, is that
Stein's psychological identification with men may have enabled
her writing:

> [Stein's] female self-hatred was such that she was psychologi-
> cally compelled to identify herself as a man in order to be a
> happy, sexually active person and a functioning writer. . . . We
> might posit a speculative connection between this male identi-
> fication, and the concomitant suppression of her female iden-
> tity, with the shift of the rebellious impulse from thematic con-
> tent to linguistic structure, where the subversive implications
> of the writing are at once more powerful and more abstruse.[24]

Here, DeKoven transposes the power associated with masculinity from Stein's sexual persona to her work. Attempting to
describe Stein's dysfunctional masculine identification as a reaction formation predictable for a woman in a male-dominated
profession, DeKoven suggests that wanting to be male makes
sense as a strategic response to sexism and homophobia. Arguably, Stein was not a radical feminist. In effect, though, reading Stein's "masculinity complex" as a sociopolitical defense
mechanism elides the erotics of cross-sex identification by constructing it as a form of false consciousness. It assumes that if
Stein had had the advantages of a lesbian-feminist consciousness,
she would not have had to resort to such a pathological form of
identification to assert herself as a writer.

What interests me especially about Stein criticism is the equation of her more realist texts with the gendered roles that she and
Toklas assumed in their relationship. Curiously, literary critics
have paid relatively little attention to the dynamics of the Hall-
Troubridge relationship, perhaps because it is easy to assume
that they are consistent with the butch/femme roles, if not the relationships, represented in *The Well*.[25] In fact, the faithful and
selfless Stephen represents a highly idealized version of the butch
role Hall aspired to. Hall took center stage in the triangulated re-

lationships with women that characterized her romantic and domestic life, and she did not play the martyr by denying herself for the benefit of her partners. Troubridge, like Toklas, has been portrayed as both the self-sacrificing partner and the manipulative wife, but cannot be accurately compared to Stephen's weak-hearted and duplicitous lovers. Troubridge represents herself as a sexually desiring subject in her first meeting with Hall, and she has been described as persistent, shrewd, controlling, and committed. She dedicated herself to Hall, promoted Hall's public image as a brilliant writer and a spokesperson for the invert, and saw herself as part of that picture. Paradoxically, the public image of Hall has produced little critical discussion of Troubridge. Like the photograph of Hall in the *Sunday Express* that seems to be excised from a fuller shot that depicts her with Troubridge, criticism of *The Well* focuses on Hall's construction of butch identity apart from her relationship with Troubridge. Toklas, on the other hand, is often central to analyses of the gendered dynamics of Stein's work.

Stein's autobiographies, which are her most "readerly" or accessible works, pose the most difficult problems for readers invested in the notion that experimental writing foregrounds the instability of the sign. Analyzing Stein's more experimental writing, it is possible to argue that even when she invokes masculine/feminine binaries, meaning oscillates to the extent that gender is destabilized. But what about the relationship depicted in the autobiographies? The common understanding of autobiography as a mimetic and confessional genre sets up expectations that *The Autobiography of Alice B. Toklas*, in particular, will reveal the "real" relationship between Stein and Toklas—when in fact, the text makes no overt reference to lesbianism.

That the autobiographies withhold references to lesbianism is particularly frustrating because we expect that our pleasure in reading them will hinge on disclosure. The lack of disclosure about lesbianism can thus make the autobiographies seem closeted, and therefore conservative. This is an argument that

Catherine Stimpson makes in her essay "Gertrude Stein and the Lesbian Lie," where she asserts that "both autobiographies pull back from Stein's upsetting challenge to representational codes and generic conventions. Telling her comic stories, Stein writes *of* modern art . . . she does not write modern art itself."[26] For Stimpson, the autobiographies are at once too transparent and too silent. On the one hand, Stein exposes the replication of the gendered roles within the lesbian relationship; for example, Stein appropriates Alice's voice when she assumes the role of Alice's autobiographer.[27] On the other hand, the autobiographies reserve the information that the relationship was both a domestic and a sexual partnership.

Stimpson sees mimesis itself (the apparent "realism" of the autobiographies) as the vehicle for concealment. The books' seeming transparency of style and their focus on the women's "everyday" lives (collecting art, dining with the Picassos, driving an ambulance during the war) create the illusion of disclosure. What they actually reveal is Stein's "homosexual dissimulation . . . a tax that homosexuals pay in order to go on being members of a society that would abhor their honesty."[28] In this intelligent reading of the autobiographies, Stimpson openly negotiates her vexation with the "lesbian lie"—"the lie that no lesbians lie abed here"—in her discussion of literary style. She also invokes the butch as a visible signifier of the sexuality that the autobiographies conceal. Referencing a moment in *The Autobiography of Alice B. Toklas* when Stein touches Toklas in public, Stimpson says:

> When Stein put her hand on Toklas' shoulder, lesbians in Paris could not wear men's clothing unless the prefect of police said they could. Stein's public silence makes much more sense when we admit the power of the legal and social codes that governed her.[29]

Here, the butch's visibility both creates the need for and explains the dissimulation that Stimpson finds problematic. But the allusion to cross-dressing is startling given that, as Stimpson herself points out, Stein did not fit the popular icon of the cross-dressing mannish lesbian.

Stimpson's somewhat equivocal reading of Stein's persona and her work implies that the butch does not signify either modernity or modernism. The butch is anachronistic; she makes sense only as a historical symbol for homosexual oppression, where she can stand for a mode of strategic dissimulation that belongs to the early twentieth century rather than to an erotic economy not necessarily confined by historical boundaries.[30] In the final analysis, then, Stein's butch persona potentially compromises her status as a modernist writer. That status can only be preserved by coding the butch as an atavistic remainder, an anomaly within the culture of antipatriarchal modernist writing, or by splitting off Stein's most experimental writing from the autobiographies and arguing that only the more "radical" texts destabilize and transform Stein's and Toklas's gendered roles.

A troubling effect of the focus on Stein's "masculinity complex" is a tendency to either dismiss Toklas or to disparage her position in the partnership. Some critics have suggested that Toklas's status in the relationship is more complicated than that of the pathetic wife and secretary. But often the primary interest in the relationship is the "problem" of Stein's assumption of male privilege, and not Toklas's identity as femme.[31] Without an adequate theory of butch and femme as specifically lesbian identities, even challenges to the assumption that the Stein-Toklas relationship mirrored heterosexuality in its most hierarchical form can encourage the perception that the relationship simply reified heterosexual patterns of male dominance and female submission.[32]

Attempts to complicate our understanding of the Stein-Toklas relationship tend to fall back on the idea that Toklas *chose* rather than capitulated to the submissive role, or that she was submissive in public but ruled the couple's private life with an iron fist. These suppositions recode the relationship through another familiar paradigm for heterosexual marriage by casting Toklas, the "wife," as the power behind the throne. Attributing compensatory forms of power to Toklas redresses rather than disputes the notion that the butch/femme relationship is inherently inegalitarian in its imitation of heterosexual gender roles.

Thus, the association of the butch/femme couple with flawed mimesis further marginalizes the femme. Because the butch's dress and stance, read as an indication of her desire to be or to occupy the position of a man, locates issues of mimesis and gender/sexual identity more obviously than do her feminine lovers, the femme remains peripheral to the discussion of lesbian representation—or worse, she is patronized for capitulating to the patriarchal regime of butch domination.[33] Meanwhile, the butch remains at the center of the debate over literary and sexual style because she is the figure who makes visible both the attempt at and the failure of mimesis—she is the one who acts like and is not a man. Like the butch's performance of masculinity, the femme's performance of femininity can be understood as imitative, but it does not produce the readable evidence of failed mimesis that marks the couple's problematic relationship to heterosexuality. The butch is a more troubling figure because as a woman performing masculinity, she seems to enact mimicry's display of the slippage between original and copy, but she does not always clearly code her performance of masculinity as ironic. Indeed, like Stein and Hall, she may reveal her investment in occupying the dominant position of the masculine.

There is no question that *The Well* follows sexology in representing the masculine woman as the "true invert" and the feminine lesbian as improbable. The novel so vividly portrays Stephen Gordon that she has become an icon. But both Stephen's lovers, Angela Crossby and Mary Llewelyn, are depicted as wayward heterosexuals, "normal" women capable of being attracted to other women but not capable of making it "in the life." In a 1928 letter to Havelock Ellis, Hall claimed that Mary Llewelyn should, in fact, stand "as a warning to any young and thoughtless girl—a warning to think seriously before she threw her lot in with an invert. Those who accept inverts only to fail them bring unspeakable misery to the inverts. The mate of the invert must be strong unto the death—Mary Llewelyn could not."[34]

Readers have often commented that the novel's weak portrayal of the feminine lesbian does not reflect Hall's experience of long-term relationships with Mabel Batteau and Una Troubridge—both of whom were married at the time of their initial involvement with Hall but were separated from her only by death—nor that with Evguenia Souline, who chaffed under her financial dependence on Hall throughout their turbulent, nine-year-long affair, and even after she had left Hall to marry. Clearly, there is something of Hall in her protagonist, but *The Well* is not autobiographical. We must look not outside, but beyond biographical sources for Hall's representation of lesbianism.

Hall's decision to depict lesbian relationships as tragic and unstable was certainly influenced by her wish to engage the sympathies of a heterosexual audience whose tolerance she knew to be limited. But it was also influenced by her indebtedness to a medical model of homosexuality that could not accommodate the feminine lesbian because it was predicated on the visibility of homosexual difference. In both *The Well* and in the sexological discourses that inform it, the conflation of "inversion" or cross-gender identification with same-sex desire defines the lesbian as butch on the basis of her visible gender transgression and renders the femme invisible (outside the economy of lesbianism) on the basis of her apparent gender coherence. We might say that the novel specifies the distinction between mimicry (a performance of an authentic/original identity that reveals its difference from the original) and mimesis (a successful imitation of the original): the butch's *mimicry* of the masculine produces the slippage that makes her visible as a lesbian, while the femme *mimes* the appearance of the heterosexual woman so seamlessly that the distinction between the femme and the heterosexual woman becomes impossible to maintain.

Not surprisingly, *The Well* reflects the inconsistencies that are inherent to the medical discourses it invokes. Contradictions and breakdowns in the logic of visibility and marking may be most apparent in relation to the feminine lesbian, who cannot be imagined within *The Well*'s paradigm of homosexuality. But contradictions also occur around the mannish woman. As the figure for whom the systems of marking and visibility reinforce each other, the mannish lesbian would seem to be the ideal model for sexologists: because her gender difference is marked, she is visible as a lesbian, and proves that the body is the site (and the sight) of sexual "deviance." But recurrent questions about the source of the masculine woman's inversion throw her visibility itself into question. My reading of *The Well* both presumes and explores its masculinist model of lesbian identity, but moves to an analysis of what the novel tells us about constructions of identity within the field of the visible by studying both the mannish woman and the feminine lesbian.

"And the Lord Set a Mark Upon Cain": Reading Butch Identity in The Well of Loneliness

Initially, it would seem that Hall takes for granted the inescapable visibility of the invert. All the "true inverts" in *The Well* bear what Stephen terms "the mark of Cain"—the outward manifestation of her core or interior masculine gender identity.[35] This manifestation may be subtle, as in "the timbre of a voice, the build of an ankle, the texture of a hand, a movement, a gesture,"[36] or it may be more pronounced, as in Stephen's case, where her body and her clothing preferences are notably masculine from the beginning of the novel. Described as a "narrow-hipped, wide-shouldered little tadpole of a baby" (1982:13), Stephen's body is masculinized even at birth. As Stephen grows up, her likeness to her father becomes more prominent: she develops "masculine" features such as a strong jaw, a cleft chin, heavy eyebrows, and a large, unfeminine quality of movement.

But social and psychological explanations for homosexuality

run parallel to the novel's overt argument that homosexuality is congenital, especially in its account of Stephen's childhood. Most obviously, the family drama that surrounds Stephen's birth and upbringing could account for her inversion. Her parents' desire to have a son creates the environmental conditions for Stephen's male identification. Her father bestows the male name chosen for the expected son upon his daughter, and treats her as he would a boy, setting the stage for her refusal of femininity. Her mother's early and instinctive rejection of her daughter solidifies Stephen's early identification with her father. Under the circumstances, perhaps it is not surprising that Stephen pretends to be a boy, and that she detests the neighbor's daughter, Violet, whose mother delights in the childish but assiduous practice of feminine artifice that Stephen finds baffling and repugnant. Violet is vain, taking pleasure in her curls and ribbons and silk frocks, and she is "full of feminine poses: she loved dolls, but not quite so much as she pretended" (1982:47).[37]

And it is class as much as constitution that defines the gendered models of dress and comportment that young Stephen navigates. She masquerades not as any boy, but as young Lord Nelson, and she resents Roger, Violet's brother, who embodies a class-marked form of male privilege to which Stephen is forever barred access. At ten, he is "already full to the neck of male arrogance" and Stephen envies

> his thick, clumping boots, his cropped hair and his Etons . . .
> his masculine companions of whom he would speak grandly
> . . . his right to climb trees and play cricket and football—his
> right to be perfectly natural [and] above all . . . his splendid
> conviction that being a boy constituted a privilege in life.
> (1982:46–47)

Roger's male privilege is synonymous with his public school education, and Hall's equation of masculinity and class privilege with the right to be "perfectly natural" replicates masculinist ideology that many readers have found offensive.

The Antrim children personify Hall's representation of femininity as artifice and masculinity as natural. Though Stephen resents Roger, she does not disdain his posturing of upper-class manhood the way she disdains Violet's posturing of the leisured wife and mother as she plays with dolls and gives tea parties. Stephen's very desire to occupy Roger's position endorses it. As an adult, Stephen will gain the independence that allows her to approximate this masculine upper-class style, even as her attire draws attention to her mimicry of its codes. She wears men's suits, ties, and shoes, short hair, and a shrapnel scar on her face (it functions as an accessory) that she acquired driving ambulances during the war—the closest to fighting on the front lines that a woman could get.

The novel codes Stephen's masculinity as noble; the shrapnel scar blurs the distinction between body and costume, recalling Krafft-Ebing's confused description of case number 165, where he cannot determine whether it is "nature" or "culture" or both that makes his client look mannish. In fact, the Antrims' posed, heterogendered identities reveal those roles to be constructed, making young Stephen's mimicry of Lord Nelson no more or less performative than Violet and Roger's mimicry of Victorian femininity and upper-class masculine entitlement, respectively. The attention to the childrens' performance of gender roles that seem to be socially assigned complicates the etiology of homosexuality, for if gender identity is not fully innate, biology would not seem to be the sole cause of inversion. But while Hall alludes to the constructedness of gender roles, she naturalizes the masculine gender role itself.

The process through which *The Well* overtly replicates but tacitly complicates medical discourses of inversion occurs not only in relation to the origins of homosexuality and the nature of gender identity, but also in relation to the problem of how to read the marked body for evidence of inversion. Though *The Well* works within the parameters of medical discourses on homosexuality by representing the lesbian body as marked, it also reveals the medical gaze's confusion about how to read the marked body. When Stephen's father studies his textbooks on medical deviance, pausing occasionally to gaze at a portrait of his family, Hall astutely describes his confused response as an affliction of the eyes, a problem of perception:

> Reading, Sir Phillip's eyes would grow puzzled; then groping for a pencil he would make little notes all along the immaculate margins. Sometimes he would jump up and pace the room quickly, pausing now and again to stare at a picture—the portrait of Stephen painted with her mother, by Millais, the previous year. He would notice the gracious beauty of Anna, so perfect a thing, so completely reassuring and then that indefinable quality in Stephen that made her look wrong in the clothes she was wearing, as though she and they had no right to each other, but above all no right to Anna. (1982:26–27)

This passage introduces the economy of visibility simultaneously with a failure in the system of marking; Stephen's difference, which the novel has painstakingly inscribed on her body to render her visible as an invert, is suddenly "indefinable," not well marked. Sir Phillip cannot identify Stephen's masculinity as such, but only a vague "wrongness" about her appearance in contrast to Anna's reassuringly "right" presentation of femininity. The location of Stephen's difference moves from her body to Sir Phillip's eye, complicating the system of marking by implicating the viewer. What Sir Phillip reads of Stephen (inversion) in his books that blinds him (he gropes for his pencil)[38] is recorded on her body in the portrait; and what he sees in the portrait (difference) he writes in the margins of his books to corroborate their narratives of homosexuality and his interpretation of Stephen. The book and the portrait refer to each other so that seeing, reading, and writing all become parts of the same economy—an economy that reveals the constructedness of gender.[39]

Stephen later discovers her father's books in a scene that reifies medical discourse's vision of the lesbian, but also turns the production of knowledge over to her by defining her as an artist. Stephen discovers the textbooks after her father's death and, examining them, finds that her own name appears in the margins. She then realizes that her father possessed the knowledge that she was "maimed, hideously maimed and ugly" and kept it from her out of pity. The patriarchal order unfolds in front of Stephen as her father's knowledge becomes God's knowledge: "And then, before she knew what she was doing, she had found her father's old, well-worn Bible. There she stood demanding a sign from heaven. . . . The Bible fell open near the beginning. She read: "'And the Lord set a mark upon Cain. . . .'" (1982:204–5). This biblical metaphor for monstrosity must be read in terms of the text that follows the ellipses, which Hall does not include here: "And the Lord set a mark upon Cain, so that no one who came upon him would kill him."

Hall's defense of homosexuality relies on the ambiguous or double-edged significance of the mark: it is both the mark of sin and of God's protection. God's exemption of the invert from the very punishment He inflicts authorizes Hall's invert to write on her own behalf at a time when the medical community did not. Though sexologists often characterized the invert as "sensitive" and artistically gifted, this did not qualify homosexuals to theorize their own experience in defining themselves. Doctors drew heavily on the personal narratives of homosexual "patients," but diagnosis and definition were always the province of specialists rather than of their subjects, whose perversions made them unreliable except as primary sources. According to Hall, the invert has been both cursed and blessed with a "curious double insight [that allows her to] write both men and women from a personal knowledge" (1982:205). Stephen's access to a vision that supersedes the medical gaze because it comes from within (insight) suggests her resistance to the totalizing sweep of that gaze. Her mission is to reclaim the authority to define homosexuality—a mission that many would argue *The Well* attempts but cannot fully achieve.

At one point, Hall suggests that the barrier to reclaiming that authority is the homosexual body itself. In the well-known passage in which Stephen, tormented by her unfulfilled desire for Angela, contemplates her naked body in the mirror, she is stricken with the thought that it will "never be indulged . . . always repressed until it grows stronger much than my spirit because of this unnatural repression"; therefore, she reasons "I shall never be a great writer because of my maimed and insufferable body. . . . true genius in chains, in the chains of the flesh, a fine spirit subject to physical bondage" (1982:217–18). Here, Hall links desire and writing in a way that seems to anticipate Hélène Cixous's formulation of writing as a realization of the "decensored relation of woman to her sexuality": if only Stephen could be sexually fulfilled, she would realize her intellectual and artistic potential as an author.[40] But the binary system of gender and sexual opposition censors her relation to her sexuality. In her agonized scrutiny of her naked form, Stephen imagines literalizing the violence that this binary enacts on a body that both represents the blurring of the masculine and the feminine (muscles become breasts and curves become lines) and signifies deviant sexual desires:

> She hated her body with its muscular shoulders, its small compact breasts, and its slender flanks of an athlete. All her life she must drag this body of hers like a monstrous fetter imposed on her spirit. This strangely ardent yet sterile body that must worship yet never be worshipped in return by the creature of its adoration. She longed to maim it, for it made her feel cruel; it was so white, so strong and so self-sufficient; yet withal so poor and unhappy a thing that her eyes filled with tears and her hate turned to pity. She began to grieve over it, touching her breasts with pitiful fingers, stroking her shoulders, letting her hands slip along her straight thighs—Oh, poor and most desolate body! (1982:186–87)

While the violence shifts to a kind of autoeroticism toward the end of the passage, this is not the autoeroticism of Cixous's *jouissance*.[41]

In her recent book *Female Masculinity*, Judith Halberstrom takes issue with critics who read this passage as a sign of the invert's self-hatred, shame, and alienation from her own body, noting that Stephen's feelings here are "essentially contradictory"— she expresses both self-admiration for her body's whiteness, muscularity, and self-sufficiency, and self-loathing and pity at being fettered in a female body. In particular, Halberstrom calls Teresa de Lauretis to task for her psychoanalytic reading of this scene, which asserts that Stephen mourns her own lack of femininity and seeks femininity in other women's bodies. Halberstrom believes this interpretation "condemns masculine women to the pathos of male mimicry."[42] She maintains instead that the scene is not about Stephen's frustrated desire for femininity or hatred of her own body but her disidentification with the naked body. Stephen's repudiation of nakedness or the biological body as the ground for sexual identity suggests a modern notion of sexual identity as not organically emanating from the flesh but as a complex act of self-creation in which the dressed body, not the undressed one, represents desire.[43]

Halberstrom would shift the reading of this scene from an economy of marking, in which the invert's body bears the signs of her perversion, to an economy of visibility in which the invert controls the representation of her gender and sexual identities through the register of clothing. Her equation of "nakedness with binary sexual and gender codes and the clothed self with the construction of gender itself"[44] is compelling because it refuses to pathologize Stephen's relationship with her body, challenging the assumption that the masculine woman must be psychologically damaged by a culture that values gender conformity, and because it replaces alienation with agency. However, I would argue that in *The Well*, Stephen's disidentification with the female body is not entirely mitigated by the transformative power of clothing to construct gender identity. For Stephen, being embodied as female is a source of shame that provokes both a rejection of and a longing for the female body that is consistent with the psychoanalytic structures of interpretation that de Lauretis employs in her reading of *The Well*.

As she reaches puberty, Stephen refuses her own embodiment as female, a process that plays out through scenarios in which the female body is both unnatural and *too* natural, while the male body, by implication, occupies a "higher" category of the natural because it transcends embodiment. Stephen's experience of female embodiment as unnatural produces discomfort with evidence of her female body that she cannot fully discipline into masculinity despite her intense regime of fencing, weight lifting, and horseback riding. Menstruation is one of the primary marks of female embodiment that Stephen abjects:

> She was shy to primness regarding certain subjects, and would actually blush if they happened to be mentioned. This would strike her companions as queer and absurd—after all, between girls—surely everyone knew that at times one ought not to get one's feet wet, that one didn't play games, not at certain times—there was nothing to make all this fuss about surely! To see Stephen Gordon's expression of horror if one so much as threw out a hint on the subject, was to feel that the thing must in some way be shameful, a kind of disgrace, a humiliation! (1982:75–76)

From one point of view, this passage constructs the female body as natural to heighten the evidence of Stephen's unnatural masculinity—her discomfort with the "natural" function of menstruation is itself "queer."[45] This reading is in keeping with the argument that the novel problematizes a literary tradition in which women have an archetypal connection to the natural world of fertility and reproduction.[46] Stephen, already shut out of woman's oneness with that world, abjects menstruation because it signifies an order of female sexuality that excludes her.

But Stephen's discomfort with the female body also contains elements of misogyny that go beyond her psychological sense of gender displacement. As an invert, Stephen is in a sense other than female; she is like a woman but not exactly a woman, and the passage above does not simply illustrate Stephen's alienation from the feminine/natural. Her disgust also makes the other girls feel ashamed and humiliated, as if it were repulsive to be embodied as female. So in an alternative reading, the passage stresses the *too* natural aspects of female embodiment that mark Woman as impure. In the binary schema that connects women with the material world—the world of the flesh—men, who are free from the constraints of embodiment, can pursue the "higher nature" of the intellectual. Stephen accordingly perceives the girls as silly and gullible in their acceptance of myths about menstruation, and she rejects their feminine sensibilities about the body. Stephen's efforts to occupy the masculine thus seem to depend on her abjection of the feminine.

Finally, however, we might best read Stephen's abjection of femininity not as a sign of her victimization or of her misogyny, but as a critique of gender categories implied by her inability to occupy either the masculine or the feminine subject position. The shifting designation of what counts as natural is part of a dialectic of desire and repulsion around the difference between the masculine body of the invert and the feminine body of the "pure woman." The prototypical feminine body is the maternal body that Stephen is "of" but not "like."[47] Anna, whose gender identity is reassuringly unified, has "that in her body that betokened happy promise—the archetype of the very perfect woman, whom creating God has found good" (1982:11). Stephen's difference, her gender incoherence, causes Anna to reject her daughter, and Stephen longs for the approval of "this woman within whose most gracious and perfect body her own anxious body had lain and quickened." Looking at her mother, "a sense of great loss would descend upon her, together with a sense of not fully understanding just what she had lost or why she had lost it—she would stare at Anna as a thirsty traveler in the desert will stare at a mirage of water" (1982:162).

In connection with this desire for the mother, the novel reconstructs the feminine body as fitting. Stephen's expression of disgust with the "other girls" thus shifts to an expression of longing that recalls the mother-child relationship:

> While despising these girls, she yet longed to be like them—yes, indeed, at such moments she longed to be like them. It would suddenly strike her that they seemed very happy, very sure of themselves as they gossiped together. There was something so secure in their feminine conclaves, a secure sense of oneness, of mutual understanding; each in turn understood the other's ambitions. (1982:76)

Here, the language of "conclaves" and "oneness" evokes the imagery of the child in the womb. The maternal body, however, is the one that Stephen has no right to, as Sir Phillip observes when he looks at the portrait of his wife and child. Given that the system of compulsory heterosexuality refuses Stephen the maternal/feminine body as an object of desire, Hall cannot portray a feminine woman that Stephen does have a right to, and she repeatedly underscores both Stephen's exclusion from the realm of the "purely" feminine and the exclusion of the feminine from the realm of the female invert.[48]

"In Her Very Normality Lay Her Danger": Femme Invisibility in *The Well of Loneliness*

The exclusion of the feminine from the realm of the invert accounts for some of Hall's difficulty in representing the feminine lesbian. In general, these women are coded traditionally as either the "wifely partner," with a woman's financial and emotional dependence and a burning desire to darn socks, and/or as the wayward heterosexual who returns to men when "the life" becomes too difficult (when the going gets tough, the femmes go straight).[49] Stephen's two lovers, Angela and Mary, represent the bad femme and the good femme, and in both cases it is their "womanliness," their visible conformity to feminine ideals of appearance and behavior that makes them essentially heterosexual and causes them to betray Stephen. But, as I will argue later, in its representation of Valerie Seymour the novel does exceed the framework of those discourses with an ambivalent representation of a woman who is both feminine and lesbian.

Because the feminine lesbian does not present the figure/ground discrepancy that the novel has established as the mark of lesbianism, a certain lack of substance in the characterization of Mary, Stephen's main love interest, augments the temptation to read the femme as unmarked. Esther Newton comments on how this sense of absence speaks to Hall's inability to represent the femme as lesbian:

> Though Mary, in effect, seduced Stephen, Hall calls her "normal," that is, heterosexual. Even Havelock Ellis gave the "womanly" lesbian more dignity and definition. As a character, Mary is forgettable and inconsistent. . . . Despite knowing Una [Troubridge, Hall's longtime femme lover], Natalie Barney [a femme poet] and others like them, Hall was unable to publicly articulate—perhaps to believe in—the persona of a *real* lesbian who did not feel somehow male. If sexual desire is masculine, and if the feminine woman only wants to attract men, then the womanly lesbian cannot logically exist. Mary's real story has yet to be told.[50]

Here is the paradox and the dilemma of the femme in both *The Well* and in the medical discourses that inform it. The femme's desire is both present (she seduces) and not present (she merely responds to being the object of masculine desire—the more masculine, the better). The lesbian femme exists but is not recognizable as lesbian.

But being invisible is not the same as being unmarked, and in *The Well* the femme is marked by the very signifier of her invisibility: whiteness. Whiteness, usually constructed as racially unmarked, becomes a trope for racial difference when the novel accentuates it and alludes to its opposite: the darkness associated with the racial Other. Whiteness signifies the idealized qualities of innocence, purity, and naturalness on the one hand, and of corruption, impurity, and artificiality on the other. Thus whiteness functions as what might be termed an "invisible sign" of the femme's difference that sets up a tension between the economies of marking and visibility by denoting the femme's indiscernibility. The novel invokes paradigms of racial difference that replicate ambiguities about issues of marking, putting tropes of racial difference into circulation with discourses of sexuality to play out the problems of the feminine lesbian's apparently unmarked sexual style.

Whiteness or paleness signifies different qualities in each of the femme characters. In Mary, paleness signifies youth, innocence, and the feminine/maternal purity associated with Stephen's mother, Anna—a purity recalled by Mary's Celtic lineage, which she shares with Anna, and by her namesake, the Virgin Mary. But Hall also associates whiteness/femininity with a fragility that leads to betrayal; both Anna and Mary reject Stephen because they require the shelter of social convention that Stephen cannot provide. The double valence of whiteness is most explicit in Angela, in whom it indicates not only fragility but duplicity, for Stephen misreads the signifiers of artifice for signifiers of purity. In a passage structured by negatives, Hall describes Angela as "amazingly blonde, her hair was not so much golden as silver. . . . her skin was very white, and Stephen decided that this woman would never have a great deal of colour, nor would her rather wide mouth be red, it would always remain the tint of pale coral" (1982:131). Angela is also likened to "some queer flower that had grown up in darkness, like some rare, pale flower without blemish or stain" (1982:132).

But her lily-white surface at once conceals and marks her corrupt personality. Stephen buys Angela a pearl, symbol of purity, from the same jeweler who sold her father stones pure enough to touch his wife's finger. But Angela is not of Anna's good breeding. She is a cave flower or a hothouse flower, not a healthy English flower, and her whiteness represents not her purity but her bloodless, reptilian nature. She diverts herself from the boredom of her marriage to a nagging, impotent man by pretending to love Stephen when she has no intentions of giving up the social privileges of heterosexuality.

The novel accounts for Angela's sexual duplicity with reference to her "checkered" past: her mother was "the descendant of women who had owned many slaves to minister to their most trivial requirements [and who could] hardly put on [their] own stockings and shoes" (1982:178). The connection between whites and blacks elucidates how whiteness can mark difference. Contiguity between white and black women places Angela's blanched exoticism in the context of racial difference; her association with black slaves as figures for illicit sexuality both heightens and "taints" her whiteness. Discourses about sexual promiscuity and race intertwine as Angela manifests her mother's legacy in her own history of prostitution and in her ultimate betrayal of Stephen—she two-times her by having an affair with Roger Antrim and then tells Anna Gordon that Stephen has made homosexual advances to her, precipitating Stephen's exile from Morton, the Gordon family estate.

"A Creature Apart": The Sapphic Lesbian as Magical Sign

The use of whiteness as a racialized trope for the feminine lesbian's sexuality emerges again in Hall's portrayal of Valerie Seymour. Valerie does offer a competing representation of the femme in that she is not coded as a wayward heterosexual but as a true lesbian. While there is something of Ellis's feminine invert in Valerie's good figure but plain face, Hall does not describe her as "the pick of the women the average man would pass by," and her preference for women is evident. Indeed:

Great men had loved her, great writers had written about her, one had died, it was said, because she had refused him, but Valerie was not attracted to men—yet as Stephen would see if she went to her parties, she had many devoted friends among men. In this respect she was almost unique, being what she was, for men did not resent her. But then of course all intelligent people realized that she was a creature apart. (1982:243–44)

Valerie is a creature apart because she is that logical impossibility—the truly lesbian feminine woman. Further, she does not fit sexology's paradigm of female homosexuality as inversion, and she is also a creature apart in that she belongs to another economy of lesbian identity. Hall modeled Valerie after Natalie Barney, the expatriate American poet whose interest in Sappho and in the French Romantics inspired her to explore a lesbian identity based on the cult of female beauty and the "religion of love" rather than the medical view of lesbianism as inversion.[51] In Paris, at her home at 20 rue Jacob, Barney established the famous literary salon where she herself promoted the aesthetic of Sapphic lesbianism, celebrating the female body in a slim, androgynous form draped in robes like the goddesses of antiquity (Figure 7). Like Barney, Valerie embodies a vision of lesbianism more rooted in mysticism and a Romantic appreciation of beauty than in sexology and a healthy respect for English tradition.

But the problems of marking and visibility persist in representing the feminine homosexual as a real lesbian. By placing Valerie outside the paradigm of sexology, the novel seems to maintain the feminine lesbian's untenability while at the same time admitting her existence. Like Mary and Angela, Valerie is marked as Other, but in this case the alterity of Valerie's lesbian sexuality rather than her heterosexuality becomes the vehicle for differentiation. That alterity is marked through discourses of white Orientalism that invoke whiteness as a sign of the femme's duplicity and define her as decadent. In the only detailed physical description of Valerie, she is draped in furs and white gowns, she wears an oriental fragrance that mingles "with the odour of tuberoses [heavily fragranced white blossoms] in a sixteenth century chalice," and she keeps a box of Fuller's peppermint creams on her divan (1982:244). The details conjure up an image of Valerie stretched out on the couch eating bonbons and sniffing flowers with her hair tumbling down and her fox sliding from her shapely shoulders.

The equation of Sapphic lesbianism with female decadence draws on a nineteenth-century tradition established by male (often homosexual) writers who had "appropriated Sappho as a figure for concupiscence."[52] Further, *The Well* links the sensuous decadence of the oriental to homosexuality in the tradition of Oscar Wilde's *Dorian Gray*, which captures the association of leisured idleness and aestheticism with same-sex desire for which Wilde would become infamous.[53] In keeping with the conservative values of the English landed gentry, Stephen's attachments are to her ancestral estate, loyal servants, and good husbandry, with all its connotations. Valerie, on the other hand, stands for the values of a more decadent aristocracy; she is attracted to wit and beauty wherever she may find them, and Hall describes her, not unkindly but matter-of-factly, as a dilettante, a lazy woman with "no urge towards philanthropy" who does little with her talent for writing. Further, she is pagan to Stephen's Christian, and promiscuous to Stephen's chaste monogamy.

Valerie might be understood to reference what Jonathan Dollimore describes as Oscar Wilde's camp "aesthetics of artifice," which "attack the anchor point of dominant values, namely the stable, autonomous Victorian self"—the very type of selfhood to which Stephen aspires.[54] For the most part, this camp aesthetic is inimical to *The Well*, which values authenticity over artifice and earnestness over irony. Rather than refuse dominant values, Hall attempts to legitimate the invert in terms of those values. As "a creature apart," Valerie signals a break from *The Well*'s dominant methodology of legitimating the homosexual. Valerie may locate the possibility of a "reverse discourse" in which "the in-

vert is not authenticated in dominant terms but the dominant itself subjected to inversion, a perverse disruption rather than an
appropriation of its categories."[55] Valerie Seymour ("See More")
stands for a different way of seeing the possibilities for lesbians
and gays, one that suggests a critique of the social conventions to
which Stephen clings. Paradoxically, then, it is the femme rather
than the butch or the queen (who visibly announce homosexual
difference) that becomes the figure for perversity.

But the temptation to read Valerie as the "magical sign"
through which the novel constructs a reverse discourse on lesbianism must be qualified by an analysis of the way the systems
of marking and visibility limit the character's subversive potential.[56] Though Valerie threatens to disrupt the medical definition
of the true invert as cross-gendered, Hall both explores that
threat and keeps it in check. Valerie challenges the primacy of the
visible as an index for inversion, but she is marginalized more
than liberated by a system of marking that locates her outside the
novel's dominant economy of lesbian identity. In particular, the
conflation of Orientalism with the social values of a leisured
upper class separates Valerie from the novel's dominant construction of lesbianism.

The mistrust with which Stephen initially greets Valerie attests to the novel's ambivalence about the femme. In spite of
what Stephen knows about Valerie's sexual preferences, Valerie's mimesis of a traditional, if not modern style of femininity, means that she does not quite register as lesbian in
Stephen's frame of reference. Accordingly, Stephen interprets
Valerie's "appraising" gaze at their first meeting to be cataloging, like a scientist's or a freak show voyeur's; she imagines
that Valerie is "secretly approving, not because her guest was a
decent human . . . but rather because she was seeing before her
all the outward stigmata of the abnormal" (1982:245–46).
Here, Stephen does not read Valerie's approval as expressive of
one lesbian's desire for and/or identification with another lesbian, but as a morbid curiosity about difference expressed by

one who occupies an ideologically dominant position to which Stephen, as Other, is martyred. Stephen's misinterpretation reinforces the characterization of the femme as sexually passive. Stephen does not realize that Valerie is cruising her because she expects the femme to be the object, not the subject, of the erotic gaze.

Elsewhere Hall clearly aligns the appraising or cataloging gaze with a patriarchal and heterosexist subject position through the figure of Monsieur Pujol, the straight owner of a queer nightclub called the Ideal Bar. Hyperbolizing Pujol's masculinity and sexuality, Hall describes him as "the most aggressively normal of men," with six legitimate children and unnumbered illegitimate ones to attest to his heterosexual potency (1982:382). For Pujol, who collects pictures of his clients and catalogs their names in a secret leather notebook, the gaze is predatory and colonizing. The notebook recalls the kind of medical cataloging that Stephen discovers hidden in her father's bookcase, even in its use of numbers to identify individual "case studies." Thus Pujol's collecting aligns him with the ideologically dominant positions of the patriarch and scientist who see without being seen.

Stephen can preserve the suspicion that Valerie, whom she knows to identify as lesbian, occupies that same position precisely because the position of being marked as Other is not always visible—because Valerie is femme. In *The Well*, the position of the unmarked seems to shift between the heterosexual man (Pujol) and the feminine lesbian (Valerie). Technically, however, Valerie cannot assume the position of the unmarked in the same way that Pujol does because she is excluded from the unmarked dominant categories "male" and "heterosexual." Stephen can align Valerie with Pujol because what is at stake here is not the general relationship between the dominant unmarked categories and nondominant marked ones; it is the visibility of each figure's relationship to the lesbian community, or the lesbian community's ability to "read" who is marked (minority) and who is unmarked (dominant).

Although Pujol locates the position of the *unmarked* in his "normality," he is *visible* as "them"—male and heterosexual. Valerie, on the other hand, who locates a marked position as Other—female and homosexual—cannot be read so easily, because she doesn't present the "symptom" of lesbianism that the novel has established: masculinity. This creates the anxiety that she could be duplicitous, another Angela *Cross*by. Valerie's feminine appearance signifies slippage and contradiction: she might be a straight woman passing for a lesbian, a possibility that is enabled by its opposite—she is a lesbian who can pass for straight. In the economy of visibility that structures the identity "lesbian" in *The Well*, what Stephen knows about Valerie (that she self-identifies as a lesbian) and what she sees of Valerie (her mimesis of traditional femininity) contradict each other to produce Stephen's suspicion.

In spite of Stephen's distrust, Valerie is in many ways the obvious solution to Stephen's tormented relationships with heterosexual women, as the narrative itself suggests when Stephen pretends to be having an affair with Valerie to break her bond with Mary and free the increasingly unhappy girl to marry a man. Valerie agrees to Stephen's request that she play the part of the other woman in no uncertain terms: "If you want to pretend that you're my lover, well, my dear, to be quite frank, I wish it were true—I feel certain you'd make a most charming lover" (1982:433). But the novel does not pursue this narrative thread, closing it off in advance by portraying Valerie as a promiscuous and fickle woman incapable of settling down.

While this temperamental incompatibility precludes a serious romance between Stephen and Valerie, Valerie may also be untenable as a love object because she complicates the novel's dominant representation of the femme as emotionally weak and financially dependent. In other words, social inequality keeps gender identity in equilibrium. Typically, *The Well* casts the femme in the economically dependent position to explain her interest in Stephen and uses class difference to uphold gender essentialism in the representation of the femme as weak.[57] All Stephen's love interests have working- or lower-class backgrounds and respond to Stephen for reasons connected to their class status: Collins, the housemaid, Stephen's first crush, indulges Stephen's romantic overtures because she has to be nice to her employer's daughter; Angela flirts with Stephen because her opportunistic marriage leaves her bored and momentarily without access to a "real man"; and the vulnerable Mary falls in love with Stephen in a wartime situation in which women work together in isolation from men. All these women ultimately choose the economic and social protection of men.

Valerie, unlike Stephen's love interests, is financially independent, and her economic position also plays a role in defining her as "a creature apart." Rather than enabling a relationship between the two characters, Valerie's *style* of financial independence compounds her incompatibility with Stephen; the values of the leisured aristocrat and landed gentry clash and prevent a romantic liaison between the two. Valerie's work is keeping her salon, where she creates "an atmosphere of courage" for "men and women who must carry God's mark on their foreheads" (1982:352). Precisely because her tolerance extends to the "queer," Valerie's salon becomes a refuge outside the heterosexual, upper-class social set that provides Mary and Stephen with "healthy" diversions until the nature of their relationship becomes obvious. But Valerie circulates within a bohemian milieu that Stephen regards as beneath her class and social status. Stephen's only other social recourse is to the bars, but she does not entirely approve of the queens and bar dykes who flaunt their homosexuality in public and then suffer persecution, ending up "bereft of all social dignity, of all social charts contrived for man's guidance" (1982:388).

Finally, if social inequality keeps the paradox of the femme in equilibrium, it may be the similarity of economic position as much as the difference in class style that makes a relationship be-

tween Valerie and Stephen unworkable. Because her interest in
Stephen cannot be explained by economic motives, Valerie
threatens the power imbalance intrinsic to the butch and femme
relationship as Hall represents it. As the brief, sphinxlike portrait
of one of Valerie's former lovers suggests, the novel can only hint
at a femme who represents the kind of society that Stephen cov-
ets. Unlike the decadent Valerie, the Comtesse de Kerguelen is
from old money. She clearly recalls Anna, Stephen's mother, in
that she is

> dignified and reserved, a very great lady, of a calm and rather
> old-fashioned beauty. When Valerie introduced her to
> Stephen, Stephen thought quite suddenly of Morton. And yet
> she had left all for Valerie Seymour; husband, children and
> home had she left; facing scandal, opprobrium, persecution.
> Greater than all these most vital things had been this woman's
> love for Valerie Seymour. An enigma she seemed, much in need
> of explaining. (1982:351)

The Comtesse represents the puzzle of the upper-class femme
with traditional values, the "womanly woman" who has society's approval to lose for identifying as a lesbian, but the strength
to leave it all behind—in short, Stephen's ideal woman. She not
only mimes but embodies a version of traditional femininity that
Stephen desires, but Stephen cannot account for the slippage between what the Comtesse has been and what she still looks like
(a lady) and what she is (a lesbian). In the brief portrait of the
Comtesse, then, we might have the novel's fantasy of the "real
femme," a lesbian who is also a lady, in both the moral and the
economic senses of the word. That she remains an "enigma much
in need of explaining" points to Hall's inability to fully imagine
the femme in literature—an inability underscored by the way the
novel will finally marginalize Valerie. In her last appearance in
the novel, Valerie's speech to Stephen dramatizes their respective
positions with regard to dominant values:

"You're rather a terrible combination: you've the nerves of the abnormal with all that they stand for—you're appallingly over-sensitive, Stephen—well, and then we get le revers de la medaille; you've all the respectable county instincts of the man who cultivates children and acres—any gaps in your fences would always disturb you. . . . But supposing you could bring the two sides of your nature into some sort of friendly amalgamation and compel them to serve you and through you your work—well then I really don't see what's to stop you. The question is, can you ever bring them together?" She smiled. "If you climb to the highest peak, Valerie Seymour won't be there to see you. It's a charming friendship that we two have found, but it's passing, like so many charming things; however, my dear, let's enjoy it while it lasts, and . . . remember me when you come into your kingdom." (1982:407–8)

Valerie's sly mockery of Stephen's instincts toward "husbandry" and her description of their friendship as charming but passing suggests how the aesthetics of artifice send up the dominant and allude to what Dollimore describes as "a notion of self as superficial, non-existent even, or perhaps just shifting, anonymous."[58]

However, given Hall's ambivalence about the status of the femme as lesbian, to position Valerie as a subject who is superficial, nonexistent, shifting, and anonymous may be less than subversive. Indeed, Valerie's speech suggests that Hall may recognize the possibility of refusing dominant discourses rather than appropriating them, and quickly closes off that possibility by marginalizing Valerie. When Valerie encourages Stephen to use her innate desire for dignity and respectability to demand tolerance for her community, she abdicates her own power to shape the depiction, and thus the definition of lesbianism. Valerie, with all her "insight," acknowledges Stephen as the "real" invert who will lead the world to enlightenment through her art, and characterizes herself as a transitory persona who will not be there to see how Stephen ultimately represents lesbianism to the world. At most, she asks to be remembered, but without specifying how. Though Valerie gives no reason for prophecizing her own absence, the logic of gender inversion grants the "kingdom" of lesbian representation to Stephen. As someone who can "pass" in and out of the lesbian community, the femme cannot be as committed to that community as the butch. Finally, then, Valerie's alliance with the decadent homosexual male via the discourses of white Orientalism marks her yet again as an unsafe object of sexual desire, allowing the novel to keep the economies of Sapphic lesbianism and inversion separate and to ensure that inversion prevails as the model for lesbian identity.

Conclusions

My reading of *The Well*, in which the butch's mimicry of masculinity is so tied to class privilege that it cannot be read as parodic, and the femme's mimesis of traditional femininity is so seamless as to be invisible, would seem to support criticism of the novel that finds it overly invested in dominant ideologies. Clearly, *The Well* is invested in a sex/gender system that excludes the mannish lesbian precisely *because* she threatens to disrupt its ontological status as natural. And although Hall invokes contradictory discourses on sexuality, attributing Stephen's inversion to congenital, social, and psychological causes, she ultimately asserts the inversion theory and suppresses the feminine lesbian's challenge to that theory. My argument about *The Well* is not that Stephen Gordon is a figure for the disruption of traditional roles, nor that Hall should be read as an experimental modernist writer who parodies traditional roles. But neither would I maintain that the book is only valuable as a historical curiosity, a documentation of early theories of homosexuality, or a cautionary tale about the perils of false consciousness.

Hall documents how the lesbian enters the field of vision in the early twentieth century, and illustrates how lesbian visibility was codified through signs of masculine identification, dress, desire, and behavior. She shows how the feminine lesbian is marginalized in the emergent definition of the "real lesbian" as invert, as opposed to the "real woman" as heterosexual, or at best bisexual, and demonstrates how the masculine woman becomes the primary figure for lesbian visibility because the femme does not fit the paradigm of the marked lesbian. Hall's novel remains significant and controversial because it raises questions about what a lesbian looks like, about the distinction between "real lesbians" and "real women," and about the place of butch and femme "roles" in modern lesbian identity, questions that are still on the table in current debates about sexuality.

Despite the proliferation of criticism on *The Well of Loneliness*, there is still work to be done on Hall's representation of the feminine lesbian. While readers have repeatedly noted the novel's failure to adequately represent the femme, a fuller discussion of how much and in what ways she might constitute a site of resistance is in order. Though some critics have commented that Valerie stands for an alternative, and perhaps more "modern" paradigm of lesbian identity, one that refuses medical models for homosexuality and the roles of the chivalrous butch and the dependent femme, and some critics have argued that Mary's initial sexual agency in her relationship with Stephen is sacrificed in order to privilege the aristocratic butch's experience as the authentic lesbian experience, this work, like my own, is still preliminary, especially in its study of the femme's relation to other figures of difference.[59]

Recalling that white Orientalism is crucial to the way *The Well* separates Valerie's representation of Sapphic lesbianism from the dominant medical model of inversion, we see how meaning changes with shifts in systems of representation, so that a character who signals sexual subversiveness may not necessarily signal subversiveness in the register of racial difference. Thus, those who appear to be unmarked within the constructs of one field of representation, such as sexuality, can carry secondary signs of difference associated with other systems of marking, such as race. Typically, the secondary signs of difference go unexamined in the initial field of representation, serving to mark the passing figure with reference to another, more familiar and apparently fixed register of difference. Because those secondary signs belong to another register of difference, they serve to exclude the "unmarked" figure from the initial field of representation.

There is much left to be said about the femme's connection to figures of difference such as the effeminate homosexual in the character of Jonathan Brockett; the African and the Latin in the characters of the locals at Oratavia, where Stephen and Mary honeymoon; and the African American and the Jew in the characters of Valerie Seymour's friends, Lincoln and Henry, who sing African American spirituals; and Adolphe Blanc, the wise and learned Jew. All these figures represent shared affliction and suffering. Here, Hall draws a connection made as frequently today as it was in the heyday of race science and sexology, and one that other authors of her period explored at greater length.

TWO

Debutante in Harlem

Blair Niles's Strange Brother

"We can none of us be as natural about sex, can we, as
the Latin? Or the Negro?"
—Blair Niles, *Strange Brother*

Nightclubs, cabarets, chitterlings, the blues, the "real Harlem."
In the 1920s white people went to Harlem in search of the exotic
and the primitive. The "soul" of black culture was an antidote to
white society's perception of itself as overcivilized. *Strange
Brother*, a white-authored Harlem Renaissance novel published
three years after *The Well of Loneliness*, makes slumming the occasion for testing the new sexual ideologies of the late nineteenth
and early twentieth centuries. Like *The Well*, *Strange Brother* ad-
vocates tolerance for homosexuality by using scientific research
to explain its origins and by illustrating the effect of prejudice on
Mark, the novel's central gay male character. It also makes a direct comparison between the "primitive" black and the homosexual, an issue to which Radclyffe Hall alludes but which she
does not explore. In *Strange Brother*, Blair Niles, a heterosexual
female author, records the emerging group consciousness of
lesbians and gays who conceptualized themselves for the first
time as a minority group like racial and ethnic minority groups.
They compared themselves to African Americans in particular,
imagining that as homosexuals living in a heterosexual world
they experienced oppression not unlike that of blacks living in a
white world.[1]

58

Strange Brother is a novel of historical importance because it synthesizes an early and self-consciously liberal use of this analogy between blacks and gays in defense of homosexuality. In doing so, it reveals how the analogy by which homosexuality is understood to be "like race" replicates the logic of racism, positing blackness as a fixed, biological difference that is always marked by skin color. As the primary term in the analogy, race facilitates the goal of explaining homosexuality. Race itself goes unexamined, and the process through which blackness is constituted as visible and natural is obscured. Thus, Niles can explore questions about the relatively unstable category of homosexuality by comparison with race as a presumably stable category: Is homosexuality, like race, a biological and fixed difference? Or is it, not like race, a product of psychological conditioning? Is it like race, visible and marked, or is it not like race, invisible and unmarked?

Because Niles will find homosexuality to be both like race and not like race, she reveals how the analogy is structurally parallel to fetishism, which simultaneously represses and insists on difference. In the Freudian scene of fetishism, castration anxiety is symbolically about the loss of masculine identity accompanying the recognition of (female) sexual difference. Fetishism masters this anxiety by substituting another object for the threatening/desirable signifier of difference, an object that both conceals difference and acknowledges it through the very need for concealment. Like the fetish, analogy suppresses some forms of knowledge and creates others according to its needs because it recognizes difference and sameness selectively.[2] Although in *Strange Brother* the like-race analogy seems to establish the similarity between blacks and gays as oppressed minorities who have no choice about their minority identities, whenever the distinction between blacks and gays threatens to collapse, skin color is reasserted to affirm the homosexual's difference from the black. Thus, Niles reinforces Homi Bhabha's analysis of the function of the stereotype in colonial discourse, in which he argues that the primary fiction supporting the association of "race" with skin color is the narrative of fetishism.[3]

But why would Niles need to maintain the distinction between blacks and gays to begin with? The answer lies in the recognition of a second pattern of analogy that underpins the novel: the analogy between the New Woman and the homosexual. Though *Strange Brother* and *The Well* appear to have the same polemical aim, unlike Hall, Niles is not fundamentally invested in the plight of the homosexual. Her primary interest is in the fate of the New Woman, who emerged at the turn of the century and was defined in the popular imagination as defying Victorian convention through her insistence on her economic independence and her social and intellectual equality with men.[4] Specifically, Niles is concerned with the ideal of the companionate marriage, which emphasized both personal intimacy and female sexual fulfillment over motherhood and reproduction. Male homosexuality offers biological evidence that sex and reproduction need not be equated either with each other or with marriage. Thus, homosexuality functions as the paradigmatic term in this second analogy that allows the novel to explore the nature of female heterosexuality.

Niles does represent the New Woman as confronting the racial and sexual orthodoxies of her time, and in this regard her interest in the black and the homosexual is not trivial. However, contextualizing the novel in the historical moment when the New Woman, the homosexual, and the primitive emerge as figures that challenge the supposed repressiveness of the Victorian era exposes how both blacks and gays become screens in the novel for exploring the shifting status of female heterosexuality in the 1920s. Blacks are the site of projection for fantasies of sexual freedom; they stand for both sexual plenitude, where all sexualities are affirmed, and lack, where only white heterosexuality is affirmed. Gays are the site of projection for fantasies of sexual fulfillment within the nonreproductive relationship, but they also represent the lack associated with being outside the economy of heterosexuality. Finally, as emblems of non-normative sexualities, both blacks and gays allude to another figure, the lesbian, who appears briefly in the novel but signals a muted, flickering anxiety that lesbianism might emerge as a viable alternative for women should both traditional heterosexuality and the companionate marriage fail them. One index of Niles's anxiety about lesbianism is that though Niles uses white male homosexuality as a model for the companionate marriage, there are no white lesbian characters in the novel. Ultimately, she affirms the fulfillment of same-sex desire only in relation to the black female body, which she fetishistically constructs as the site of both plenitude and lack.

This chapter connects Niles's relatively overt projection of sociosexual fantasy onto the black and the male homosexual with her less explicitly articulated anxiety about lesbianism, showing that both rely on similar constructions of visibility and difference. Mapping out this correlation necessitates a multilayered analysis of the novel: in order to get to the "latent" narrative of lesbian panic and eroticism, I first move through a series of readings that examine how the shift in gender and sexual politics brought about by feminism influences the "liberal" representation of homosexuals and blacks. Linking the novel's twin projects of exploring homosexual identity via black identity and examining the status of the New Woman, these readings use the "like-race" analogy to focus on the variable representation of the white male homosexual as both visible and invisible, and the bracketed representation of the black lesbian as both contained and subversive. Finally, the chapter ends with a discussion of the novel's lesbian "subtext," examining how the white, upper-class, heterosexual woman repeatedly consolidates her own subject position in relation to both marked and unmarked bodies, insisting sometimes on the visibility and sometimes on the invisibility of the Other, but always normalizing her own identity in the process. To lay the groundwork for this textual analysis, I begin by placing the novel within the context of primitivism and the new sexual ideologies of the 1920s.

Blair Niles was the daughter of a Virginia plantation owner whose acquaintance with her father's black tenants gave her what one biographer describes as "a sensitivity to alien cultures"—especially the ones in her own backyard. Presumably, this sensitivity enables her exploration of Harlem as a homosexual enclave in *Strange Brother*. One of the earliest American novels to depict an openly gay character, the book was first published in 1931 and was out of print for nearly sixty years. The main characters are June Westbrook, a rebellious socialite looking for adventure, and the ironically named Mark Thornton, a tortured homosexual artist who is, in fact, unmarked, passing for straight except in Harlem where he seeks refuge and acceptance. The two meet by chance in a Harlem nightclub, and the novel tells the story of their friendship during a hot New York summer in 1927, when, as Langston Hughes put it, "the Negro was in vogue." The novel has two intersecting story lines, one that revolves around June's relationship with a distinguished, older, high-society businessman, Seth Vaughn, and another that revolves around Mark's efforts to come to terms with his desire for social respect and long-term companionship in a world that regards homosexuality as a perversion. The story ends abruptly with Seth's death in a plane crash and Mark's suicide, but these tragedies are not preceded by a traditional plot with rising action, crisis, and resolution. Rather, a series of social events such as evenings on the town, parties, and house calls creates opportunities for Niles's detailed descriptions of the Harlem nightlife and lengthy deliberations on the natures of the homosexual and the primitive.

The book was one of a cluster of gay-themed novels published between 1931 and 1934. Although widely discussed among gay men, the mainstream press regarded the novel as rather seamy in its "faintly disreputable exoticism" and its sympathy for the "panorama of abnormality" it depicted.[5] Though it has never been proclaimed for its literary merit, contemporary overviews of Harlem Renaissance fiction and of gay-themed fiction often note the book's value as a period piece. *Strange Brother* is in many ways a sequel to Niles's 1928 novel, *Condemned to Devil's Island*, a fictionalized account of the lives of white convicts in French New Guinea's infamous penal colonies that anticipates *Strange Brother*'s interest in the primitive and the homosexual. In her introduction to *Condemned*, Niles discusses how her work as a journalist lets her observe the contrast between the "civilized" Frenchman turned criminal and New Guinea's population of "savage" blacks descended from African slaves. She says:

> I selected the notorious Devil's Island Penal Colony as the place where I would make my investigation, because there the drama of the criminal is staged against a background of tropical jungle, where descendants of escaped negro slaves live the jungle life of Africa; dancing the African dances and worshiping the African gods. While, locked behind the bars of prison, are criminals sent from highly civilized France. The Devil's Island Colony thus offers a startling contrast between the primitive and the civilized.[6]

Here Niles articulates the primitivist aesthetic of the 1920s, when the modernist reaction against industrialization counterbalanced the fear that civilization was becoming destructive and evil.[7] Exploring the contrast between the primitive and the civilized, she uses the regimented penal system to symbolize civilization's dehumanizing qualities, and the jungle surrounding the prison, where the Bushmen dance and sing at night, to symbolize freedom. Although she avoids overt references to homosexuality in her introduction to *Condemned*, rather coyly stating that she wants to examine "what happens to a man when suddenly woman is taken from life, and stripped of all, he stands starkly forth," Niles is fascinated with the homosexual subculture of prison life—especially with the way relationships that begin as a form of prostitution in which men exchange sex for food and protection are transformed by a passion "[that] flares up into a holy flame . . . something beautiful [that] grows out of the filth of prison."[8] In that they fulfill basic needs for love and physical desire, Niles associates these affairs with the liberating and instinctive sexuality of the natives who populate the jungle surrounding the prisons. The analogy between the homosexual and the black, though not fully developed in *Condemned*, lets Niles use the idea of the natural that is intrinsic to primitivism to establish the "naturalness" of homosexuality, a strategy that she employs more extensively in *Strange Brother*.

Niles naturalizes homosexuality by analogy with racial difference, positing them both as biological conditions, but the naturalness of the homosexual and the black are not synonymous. The connotation of the term "natural" modulates throughout the novel, designating genetic constitution, artlessness, atavism, and instinct. Because its meaning shifts with reference to the construction of whiteness and heterosexuality as *normal*, what counts as natural depends on who is being counted. In general, blacks are associated with the natural as a primordial state with which whites have lost contact, while homosexuals exemplify the natural occurrence of mutation from that primordial state. In its various formulations, the preoccupation with the natural respecting both race and sexuality was characteristic of discourses of primitivism in the 1920s.

Primitivism was not, of course, new to the 1920s. Arthur O. Lovejoy, author of *Primitivism and Related Ideas in Antiquity* (1935), defined cultural primitivism as "the discontent of the civilized with civilization," and imagined that the cavemen themselves "discoursed with contempt upon the cowardly effeminacy of living under shelter."[9] Historians frequently argue that primitivism crystallized in the twenties because World War I trench warfare had revealed the self-destructive capacity of machinery and weaponry supposedly created to defend and advance civilization.[10] But changing discourses about sexuality also made primitivism the cultural force of the moment in the twenties. Freud's visit to Clark University in 1909 lent authority to America's growing reaction against "civilized" sexual morality. To young American doctors and intellectuals, Freud's theories seemed to call for unleashing repressed sexual instincts to promote a new and healthier society.[11]

Sexologists such as Havelock Ellis and Edward Carpenter, who were widely read in America, reinforced this belief in the liberating potential of sexual expression by equating sex in its original, natural form with purity and simplicity. By the end of World War I, anthropologists conducting comparative studies of sexual relations among "primitive" races were depicting tribal peoples as unashamed of their own bodies and their relations with one another, evoking a world of sexual innocence lost in the rush toward civilization and progress. In the 1920s, then, the idea that the "lower" races had access to a more authentic and healthy experience of sexuality counteracted the white bourgeoisie's sense that overcivilization was producing "moral impotence and spiritual sterility" within its class.[12]

This fear of "impotence" was literalized in the nation's response to the rise of European immigration and the migration of southern blacks to northern cities. Between 1892 and 1919, Theodore Roosevelt expressed his alarm over the declining fertility of the "higher" races and classes in his developing theory of race suicide. Roosevelt worried that "Americans of old stock" were choosing to have small families, or worse, selfishly refusing to have children at all in order to afford themselves luxuries and leisure time. This decadence put them in danger of being overrun by proliferate immigrant and black populations, who were thought to be immune to the influences of civilization and therefore of impotency.[13]

Roosevelt was not the only one calling for sexual reform. By the twenties, modern discourses of sexuality emphasized the importance of female pleasure apart from reproduction and the recognition of diverse sexual identities, particularly of homosexuality.[14] This new sexual morality established the link between the homosexual and the primitive that Niles explores in her novels.

Just as primitivism underwrote new models for heterosexual freedom, sexologists sought to decriminalize homosexuality by pointing to its well-tolerated existence within primitive and ancient societies. But Anglo-European and American societies did not uniformly accept the new sexual morality, especially as it was influenced by feminism and the more liberal strands of sexology. The late nineteenth- and early twentieth-century cult of masculinity also created the conditions for refusing homosexuality as the worst form of effeminacy.[15] The more radical implications of the new sexual morality, including female sexual autonomy and the acceptance of homosexuality, were eventually supplanted by a reformulation of the ideal of sexual freedom that attacked feminism and homosexuality and advocated sexual liberation for women only insofar as it reinforced heterosexual monogamy.

In representing alliances between women, gays, and blacks, *Strange Brother* signals its liberal interest in the new sexual morality of the twenties. But Niles also dramatizes the failure of heterosexuality, symbolized by the specter of white male sterility, suggesting that the cost of sexual liberation may be the white woman's successful marriage. Consequently, the very alliances that Niles promotes turn out to threaten the fabric of the social order, and the novel reflexively contains or omits the figures that most obviously jeopardize that order. Niles spends some time rendering portraits of the effeminate white homosexual and the masculine black lesbian, who are visible representatives of the Harlem subcultures that June tours.

Notably absent from a book that documents Harlem's gay nightlife are the black male homosexual and the white lesbian. As potential objects of desire, each of these figures threatens the social status of the main characters; Mark's involvement with the black homosexual would mean the loss of his unmarked status as a white, middle-class man, and June's involvement with the lesbian, white or black, would mean the loss of heterosexual status. Perhaps because the image of a black woman and a white woman together is more remote than that of two white women together, Niles gives us the safer character of the black lesbian and avoids depicting the white lesbian. Though the novel does not represent the black homosexual or the white lesbian, it explores the potential breakdown of social order that they represent through two other figures who auger the perils of boundary crossing: the immigrant Italian homosexual and the light-skinned black lesbian.

The Normal Abnormal: Companionate Marriage and Homosexuality

In the first of a series of close readings that follows, I show how Niles constructs her representation of homosexuality in response to a perceived crisis in the heterosexual status quo of marriage and reproduction, and a concomitant fear that men would reject feminist calls for the reform of traditional gender and sexual roles. June, the novel's white, upper-class protagonist, is at the center of this crisis. June's refusal of traditional gender roles begins in her childhood, when her fondness for catching toads and riding horses perplexes her conventional family. As an adult, June enacts the emergence of modern love from the outmoded sexual ideologies of the nineteenth century. The one socially correct action she takes is to marry well at a young age. But after ten years of wedded boredom, she divorces her rich, well-connected husband to seek a romantic relationship that will meet her needs for both companionship and sexual satisfaction—a relationship that she hopes to find with Seth, the quite eligible bachelor she meets when interviewing him for a women's column in the newspaper.

June clearly represents the new sexual morality of the 1920s, especially as it was encoded in the ideal of companionate marriage. But the success of companionate marriage depended upon men's willingness to adapt to women's new social and sexual equality, and the difficulty of finding a willing man threatens June's ability to achieve fulfillment and intimacy. Seth, who is alternately affectionate and aloof, substantiates the fear that the cost of abandoning traditional heterosexual relationships might be virility itself, leaving women unable to find satisfactory mates. Seth is not openly hostile to the New Woman's social and sexual ambitions, but he remains attached to reproductive heterosexuality. When his daughter gets married, Seth affirms the equation between marriage, sex, and reproduction, feeling assured that his daughter's marriage and the offspring she will inevitably produce guarantee him a "kind of immortality denied to the childless." [16]

June associates the very traditional wedding with death rather than immortality. When the rector says "till death do them part," she suddenly sees each face in the wedding party "as though it had been a dead face, upturned and infinitely still" (1991:224). Confronted with the image of Seth and his daughter, June considers that the body undergoes a cellular change every seven years, and she imagines that the body of Seth as her would-be lover (the sexual body) and the body of Seth as progenitor of the bride (the reproductive body) are not the same. After Seth's tragic death, she discovers that they never became lovers because he had been concealing "the impotence of his approaching age," brought on prematurely by his ambitious pursuit of financial and social success (1991:339). Seth's impotence suggests that the sexual body is used up in the reproduction not only of children, but also of wealth and social status. He embodies both the conviction that virility's proper place is within the heterosexual, reproductive marriage, and the fear that it is depleted there.

Theoretically, at least, homosexuality offers a model for the kind of relationship June wants—one in which sexual intimacy does not presuppose reproduction. If Seth fails to appreciate June's modern ideas about love, June's gay friend Mark understands them intimately. As Mark himself points out, gays and lesbians "by their very existence, in a way prove that there's no real connection between sex and reproduction" (1991:203). Niles also uses the homosexual in the figure of June's ex-husband, Palmer, to expose the lack of connection between traditional marriage and reproduction. Throughout her own childless marriage to Palmer, June is ignorant of his homosexuality. When she recognizes him at a drag ball in Harlem, his presence there would seem to compound the anxiety that men will not be available for the companionate marriage; he substantiates the fear that "all the good ones are married or gay," or worse yet, married *and* gay.

Though Palmer is one of many minor figures in the novel, his role is significant. Within the white upper class, he destabilizes signifiers of sexual identity, raising the question of how to distinguish the straight man from the gay man passing for straight. June's contained response to discovering Palmer's homosexuality seems to belie any anxiety about misreading the passing homosexual for straight. She checks her friendly impulse to greet him out of an instinctive sense that he would not want to be recognized at a drag ball. Niles describes June's discovery of her former husband's homosexuality as a moment of enlightenment rather than shock: "seeing the truth, June saw also, the infinite plot complications of life, its complexities revealed in the searching light of fact" (1991:220).

But Palmer is not the center of the "plot complication" in the narrative of upper-class, white heterosexuality. In fact, Palmer legitimates June's desire for the companionate marriage and its attendant sexual satisfaction for women. Relying on the notion that homosexuality is innate to a certain percentage of the population, Niles uses Palmer to show that in a culture of intolerance, gay men will be forced to pass and heterosexual women will unwittingly marry them. Social constraints against homosexuality backfire, and the traditional, heterosexual social order is already compromised or infected by the very forms of sexual deviance that it fears the new sexual morality will encourage.

Palmer is not only a product of the very social order that he threatens, but in his lack of virility and his acquisitiveness he symbolizes its decay. He conforms to the stereotype of the homosexual aesthete who mercenarily amasses collections of European art, decorates his house in opulent period styles, and regards a wife as one of his trophies. The youthful, naive June initially sees Palmer as the strong, silent Byronic type who cuts a dashing figure in the romantic setting of his "Italian room" on the night he proposes to her. Later June discovers that Palmer does not have the strength that she takes for granted in a man, and that he is "indolent and absent-minded" (1991:117).

But it is not until she sees her ex-husband at the drag ball, where homosexual difference is on display, that June recognizes the signs of that difference on Palmer. Palmer's sexuality must be invisible enough to let him pass for straight and yet marked enough to make him legible in the correct context. At the drag ball, Palmer wears an antique Venetian gondolier costume that he had purchased on their honeymoon, and his lack of virility and his taste for exotic beauty take on a new dimension; the signifiers of aestheticism and homosexuality finally converge. Although the Venetian gondolier costume is not necessarily feminine, Palmer's interest in art, fashion, and decor now read as effeminate, not just effete. Further, the Venetian costume registers as a form of gay drag because, as George Chauncey explains, "by the late nineteenth century, southern Italian men had a reputation in northern Italy and in the northern European gay world for their supposed willingness to engage in homosexual relations."[17]

This reputation, which extended to the Italian immigrant community in America, allows *Strange Brother* to position the Italian as an intermediate figure when it uses racial difference to underpin the construction of homosexuality as visible. Moving from the Social Register to the drag ball, the invisible fact of Palmer's homosexuality becomes evident; suddenly it is clear to June that for him, the romance of Italy was never heterosexual. Reread in the correct framework, Palmer recalls Roosevelt's paranoia about "race decadence" and clarifies how the discourses of sterility and decadence are linked to the homosexual. Palmer is the type of sensuous, effeminate aristocrat against which "normal robust manhood" defined itself by the turn of the century.[18]

Niles does not vilify Palmer, but she uses him to encode the stereotypes she will reject in portraying Mark as a sympathetic character with whom June can identify. Palmer is a sociological problem, an anachronistic type who shows not that homosexuality is a product of overcivilization, but rather that homosexuality takes a certain form in the environment of overcivilization. Niles must depict homosexuality in another form if it is to suggest a model for the heterosexual companionate marriage. But what does it mean to compare the heterosexual woman with the homosexual? And what does it mean to take "deviant" homosexual relationships as a model for "normal," if not traditional, heterosexual relationships? Such correlations clearly have the potential to destabilize the white woman's subject position, constructing her as deviant by analogy with the homosexual, and through the homosexual, by analogy with the black. They potentially put her in competition with the gay man for the desired love object—heterosexual white men—or worse, raise the specter of the white woman's own lesbianism as a response to the failure of heterosexuality. The novel guards against these possibilities by deploying the codes of visibility and marking to protect June from both the difference and the threatened sameness of the Other.

It would appear that June's most "significant Other" is Mark, an art teacher at a settlement house for immigrants who becomes her entrée to Harlem. White, middle-class, educated, and not obviously homosexual, Mark is probably the most sympathetic character that Niles could create for readers likely to resist her defense of homosexuality. Perhaps more importantly, as the character who articulates the ideals of companionate marriage, he is the most "normal" and least threatening of the homosexual types that Niles portrays. Niles carefully distinguishes Mark from Palmer, the effete, aristocratic homosexual, and from the flamboyant street fairies who frequent the Harlem nightclubs.

To protect June from her own identification with this "strange brother" who understands her hunger for love, Niles renders Mark the unmarked deviant. If homosexuality is the obvious model for a relationship in which sexual desire is not linked to procreation, then this desire must be naturalized so that June does not become deviant by association. Naturalizing Mark's desire means naturalizing his identity, keeping him as close to the white male norm as possible by ensuring that his masculinity, his class status, and his racial purity are not compromised. But how can Niles stabilize these apsects of Mark's identity while putting him in connection with the black, working-class, and queer inhabitants of Harlem, the only place where he finds refuge from the straight world? And more to the point, how can homosexual identity be naturalized without threatening to infiltrate the upper-class white society where June hopes to find the man of her dreams who is man enough to fulfill her dreams?

First, Niles contains the threat of similarity implied in the analogy between the New Woman and the homosexual by proposing a model of homosexual origins that ensures Mark's *appearance* of normality. Second, she guarantees Mark's appearance of normality by asserting that homosexuality is *not* visible like race; in fact, male homosexuality is only visible in its unnatural manifestation as the product of an abnormal psychological environment. At the most obvious level, Niles bars Mark access to the status of full normality by positing that it is his sexuality itself that separates him forever from the truly normal man, who is "entirely masculine . . . strong, keenly intelligent." This kind of man, Mark says, "could only feel loathing for me, or at best nothing more than pity" (1991:154). Mark's proximity to the norm that he must approach but cannot fully achieve is also circumscribed by the discourses through which Niles defines his homosexuality.

Because it is driven by different aims, the politics of visibility are different in *Strange Brother* than in *The Well*. Rather than conflating homosexuality and gender identity to produce the homosexual as visible, *Strange Brother* separates same-sex desire from gender inversion. Niles uses the analogy between race and sexual orientation to establish homosexuality as biological but not necessarily visible. According to the popular science of the nineteenth century, homosexuality was like race in that its difference from (and inferiority to) the norm of white, male, heterosexual monogamy was perceptible on the body. But in the ethnic model of homosexuality that Niles deploys, racial difference and sexual orientation occupy opposite ends of the field of visibility: where race is always marked by skin color, homosexuality can pass unmarked and undetected.

There are several competing models of homosexual identity that circulate within the novel. But in portraying Mark, Niles is most heavily indebted to Edward Carpenter's concept of the "intermediate" sex, which serves to explain the difference between the masculine homosexual and the "truly normal" heterosexual man. The person of the intermediate sex is, like the gender invert, defined by a combination of masculine and feminine qualities. But unlike the theory of gender inversion, which conflates same-sex desire and gender identity to produce the homosexual as visible, the notion of the intermediate sex does not make visibility the condition of homosexuality. Aligned with the Whitmanesque aesthetic of male "comradeship," this "gender-separatist" model of homosexuality emphasizes sexual desire based on sameness—the man's love of the masculine.[19]

Clearly, the gender-separatist and gender-inversion models impinge upon each other; Mark's sexual desire for men is a feminine quality that distinguishes him from the heterosexual man. But Mark's "feminine" desires are not fully correlated with female identification—he is not a woman trapped in a man's body. Because he is not cross-gendered, June cannot discern any traces of his sexual orientation in the "Hellenic beauty of [his] profile" or in his slim but strong figure (1991:200). The reference to classical

Greece here emphasizes the gender-separatist model of homosexuality by invoking a culture in which manly love, ranked
above heterosexual relations and seen as the highest expression
of physical and emotional intimacy, solidified patriarchal society.

The movement away from inversion as the explanation for
Mark's homosexuality guarantees that he is not marked by any
signs of gender "abnormality." Niles also establishes both the
naturalness and the invisibility of Mark's sexual orientation by
analogy with racial difference. This analogy contains the threat
of homosexuality by establishing that, like race, sexual orientation has biological origins. For "liberal" sexologists, the primitive encompassed both heterosexual potency and the naturalness
of homosexuality. Ellis points to the "primitive indifference" to
homosexuality among the "lower" races and classes and among
criminals, arguing that in the absence of cultural interdiction,
there existed among a small percentage of the population "a
strong natural instinct impelling man toward homosexuality."[20]
By claiming that homosexuality was a defect of only 2 percent of
the population, he could assert that "civilized sexual morality"
produced an unnecessary intolerance of an essentially natural,
and fortunately limited, phenomenon.

Through the character of Irwin Hesse, a Jewish scientist from
Vienna whose work on lab animals and insects was leading to
"the recognition of more than two hard and fast sex forms in
man, even some day perhaps to the control of sex forms," Niles
implies that the biological explanation for homosexuality was
cutting-edge (1991:172–73). In fact, the idea that homosexuality
was environmentally or socially produced was more prevalent by
the twenties.[21] It makes sense, however, that *Strange Brother*, like
The Well of Loneliness, relies on congenital explanations for deviancy to create sympathy for its homosexual characters. Sociological explanations opened up questions of environment and
choice, letting homosexuality emerge as an alternative pattern to
failed heterosexuality, while the congenital explanation made homosexuality more fixed by grounding it in biology.

Dark Princes and Fairy Queens: The Limits of the Like-Race Analogy

To establish the biological origins of homosexuality through analogy with race, Niles must posit race as a category that is self-evidently biological rather than socially constructed. Race is a fixed difference, a "natural" function of seeing, demanding what Homi Bhabha describes as "the occlusion of the preconstruction or working-up of difference" so that "the difference of the object of discrimination is at once visible and natural—colour as the cultural/political sign of inferiority or degeneracy, skin as its natural 'identity.'"[22] In *Strange Brother*, this relationship between visibility, identity, and knowledge applies differently to the black and the homosexual. Though Mark's description of the sympathy and freedom he finds in Harlem assumes a similarity between two minority groups, homosexuality is invisible in opposition to the putative visibility of blackness.

The opening scenes of the novel establish the parameters of the "like-race" analogy by comparing the gay man's ability to pass for straight with the black man's inability to conceal the facts of racial identity. The story begins with June's visit to the Magnolia Club (modeled on the famous Cotton Club), where black entertainers perform for white audiences. Mark is seated at the back with two black friends, Caleb and Ira; club policy forces them to watch the show from a discreet corner of the room. The black men are discussing this segregation, when Mark interjects that if anyone understands segregation it is he, who has to pass for straight in order to keep his job. His pain and frustration contrast with Caleb and Ira's acceptance of their inability to escape the condition of being marked. As one of the men explains, "If you're black, everybody's got to know it. Can't wash yourself white, nor powder yourself white either. Even if you're light complected, somewhere there'll be something to give you away. Maybe behind your ears, or maybe the color of your fingernails" (1991:28). Mark expresses his desire for the same kind of indelible visibility, suggesting that if everyone knew he were gay he would be spared the humiliation of having to pretend to be something he is not. This conversation reveals how the like-race analogy flattens the complexity of both African American and gay experience; it suppresses the possibility of race passing and abjects gay visibility.

By privileging African American visibility, the novel trivializes the experience of racism, rendering all blacks, not just the passing black, invisible as social and political subjects. In his introduction to *Invisible Man*, Ralph Ellison explains the paradoxical relationship between marking and visibility when he says that "despite the bland assertions of sociologists, 'high visibility' actually rendered one *un*-visible—whether at high noon in a Macy's window or illuminated by flaming torches and flashbulbs while undergoing the ritual sacrifice that was dedicated to the ideal of white supremacy."[23] But unlike Ellison's narrator, Caleb and Ira are depicted as too naive to develop a critique of their own oppression. They insist that it is possible to forget even racism in Harlem, whereas Mark portends that the white invasion of Harlem will lead to the debasement of the black race. Admonishing Mark to forget his troubles, Caleb and Ira inspire Mark to proclaim that "the wonderful thing about you black people [is that] nothing hurts so much that you can't forget, and laugh . . . even laugh" (1991:28).

Niles's recourse to the stereotype of the happy-go-lucky black reveals her lack of interest in the lived experience of racism. Her physical description of Mark in comparison with Caleb and Ira metaphorically illustrates the degree to which the analogy between gays and blacks generates knowledge of sexuality at the expense of knowledge about race. From June's perspective at the Magnolia Club, Caleb and Ira blend into the shadows; each is literally like H. G. Wells's invisible man, an empty suit of clothes. June thinks that they "seemed scarcely to have faces at all" and that "above their white shirt fronts there seemed only shadows, blacker and more tangible than the shadows of the corner." Between these two invisible figures is Mark, whose "face and hair stood out so extraordinarily fair . . . like a pale oval moon in a dark sky" (1991:15). The black men are the background that renders whiteness, which is usually unmarked, "remarkable" so that it can reveal the true aspect of Mark's difference, his homosexuality. In other words, the novel makes homosexuality visible not in and of itself, but visible against the background of blackness through its opposite: whiteness.

Here, as in *The Well*, whiteness functions as an invisible sign of difference. For Mark, however, the link between homosexuality and whiteness is not indicative of his deviance or duplicity; rather, it preserves his status as the normalized homosexual. The description of Mark's relationships with other men reveals how the novel's liberal impulses are at odds with the need to separate him from the "shadow world" of sexual deviance that is the underside of sexual freedom. On the one hand, Niles represents both blacks and gays "sympathetically," positing an identification between the two minority groups. But even as Mark identifies with blacks on the basis of a supposedly shared experience of oppression, he maintains the racial binaries that guarantee his position as the unmarked subject.

Mark's eroticization of darker-skinned men as objects of desire is part of the mechanism through which he consolidates his own identity in relation to the Other. It is notable that these dark-skinned men are never black, even though Mark seeks out Harlemites because he feels free to reveal his sexuality with them. In fact, Niles carefully excludes relationships between whites and blacks from the sexual revolution she documents. Ira and Caleb's sexual orientation is unclear, although Ira seems to be Glory's boyfriend, and there is never any hint of attraction between Mark and his Harlem friends. Caleb, in particular, is domesticated, desexualized, and contained. When he visits June's apartment to break the news of Mark's death, he soothes her by reminiscing about the good old days on his Virginia plantation home. Playing the "happy darky," he neutralizes any suggestion of personal intimacy between the two.

Peter Burton, who wrote the introduction to the 1991 edition of *Strange Brother*, suggests that Niles avoids depicting sexual attraction between blacks and whites because "she probably didn't want to add miscegenation to the list of taboos she was trying so valiantly to bring down."[24] Using the term miscegenation, which is historically associated with concerns about the offspring of interracial unions, in reference to homosexual relationships, Burton may not be employing the most precise vocabulary. But the word resonates accurately if we see Mark's homosexuality as a paradigm for the companionate marriage, in which case the analogy would raise the specter of miscegenation for June. Specifically, allowing Mark a black love interest would compromise his status as the "normal abnormal," making him too much a part of the shadow world that he reveals to June. June's identification with Mark is predicated on their shared understanding of love. For this identification to be sustained, it is essential that Mark and June desire the same type of man *and* that they not be in competition for him—thus, Mark's eternally unrequited love. Giving Mark a black love interest would not put him in competition for the heterosexual white man, but it might imply that June's sexual inclinations, like Mark's, could cross racial boundaries.

The novel sidesteps the issue of cross-racial desire between men by inserting ethnicity into the equation of "race" with blackness. Mark's first crush, Luis, whose mother was South American, "wasn't like any of the other boys. The first day he went to school the boys yelled 'Eyetalian' after him. He had dark hair and skin like an Italian" (1991:142). Here, as with Palmer, the Italian becomes the figure for homosexual desire. However, in contrast to June's effete ex-husband, Luis is virile and dark like the young, princely black stallion that roams in an alfalfa field near the pond where the two boys swim. Luis concretizes the association of the immigrant with manliness, which was part of the discourse of overcivilization that eschewed homosexuality as part of the cult of masculinity within white middle-class homosexual subculture. Luis is desirable because he embodies an essential, natural masculinity that seemed diluted in white American culture.

Replicating the mechanisms of fetishism, Mark's desire for the swarthy immigrant threatens as well as consolidates his middle-class white identity. On the one hand, Luis is the dark, masculine Other who completes Mark. Mark says, "I can't remember having any emotions before Luis came. . . . I can't see myself before that" (1991:143). Here, as in the Magnolia Club, Mark becomes visible against the background of darkness. Luis acts as the mirror for Mark's recognition of his own desire, and through that desire, his identity. On the other hand, Luis portends the disruption of race and class position that allows Mark to represent the "normal abnormal." The tenuous status of the white middle-class homosexual becomes more explicit with the introduction of Rico, the Italian fruit vendor who has a stall outside the settlement house where Mark teaches. Openly expressing his interest in Mark, Rico confirms the association between the Italian and the homosexual.

Though Mark admires Rico's "exotic beauty" and "animal happiness," as an adult he has transferred his desire for the dark Other to a safer love object: a white man with darkened skin. Mark is smitten with Phil, June's cousin, an upper-class white man who can carry the signs of darkness and masculinity: "I like his color. I wonder where he's been to get deep tanned that way . . . he's as strong and as tanned as the life-savers you see on the beaches" (1991:46–47). Later Mark will learn that Phil gets his tan when he goes to the jungle to study insects and comes into contact with the primitive. Phil can thus satisfy the fantasy of difference without endangering Mark's race and class position. Rico, to the contrary, will eventually act out the danger of crossing those boundaries. Rico's family fled Italy because they displeased their Mafia bosses, and the criminal element of his Sicilian origins manifests itself when he confronts Mark with his feelings. Jealous of a downtrodden queen that Mark has befriended in an effort to come to terms with the effeminate homosexual, Rico threatens Mark with blackmail, and Mark commits suicide rather than suffering the loss of middle-class status and social respectability that blackmail would bring.

If the swarthy immigrant represents the desirable but dangerous masculinized homosexual, the effeminate homosexual poses another kind of threat to the middle-class gay male. In *Strange Brother*, this figure is portrayed by Nelly, whom Mark encounters at the Lobster Pot, an after-hours bar that he visits with June when they leave the Magnolia Club. Nelly, the fairy with plucked brows, marcelled, blondined hair, painted nails, and powdered face, is the white working-class counterpart to the immigrant. Whereas Luis and Rico physically embody Mark's ideals of "manly love" à la Walt Whitman, Nelly is the type of effeminate man that Mark loathes because he "makes a mockery" of the more staid, less flamboyant men who pass for straight. Nelly's femininity is the vehicle through which Mark rejects class differences that he fetishizes elsewhere. In speaking to Caleb and Ira at the Jim Crow Magnolia Club, which exudes middle-class respectability, Mark deplores his ability to pass for straight, but when Nelly enters the Lobster Pot, the working-class after-hours club where Harlemites do their real socializing, the fairy's visibility throws Mark's ability to pass into question by exhibiting that homosexuality can, after all, be visible on the body like racial difference. Mark's disgust for the effeminate homosexual reflects a historically specific form of class antagonism between the middle-class "queers" and working-class "fairies" that George Chauncey describes succinctly:

The style of the fairy was more likely to be adopted by young and poorer men who had relatively little at stake in the straight middle-class world, where the loss of respect the fairy style entailed could be costly indeed. Most men who were involved in that world sought to pass in it by adopting the style of queers, who typically displayed their homosexuality only in more private settings. . . . [Middle-class queers] believed it was the flagrant behavior of the fairies on the streets that had given the public its negative impression of all homosexuals.[25]

Dismayed at the thought that June might "class" him with Nelly, Mark expresses this antipathy among homosexuals. As Mark uses the term "class," it refers to the act of classification; he does not want to be associated with the effeminate homosexual. But the term carries a more literal meaning as well, in that Mark's own class position could be more secure. He is marginally middle class, teaching at a settlement house where the discovery of homosexuality would get him fired, in which case he too would be on the street. As Rico proves, his status as an underpaid professional leaves him subject to blackmail—as a richer man would be, but without the money to buy his security.

Niles dramatizes the dangerous consequences of gay visibility when a plainclothes cop entraps and arrests Nelly for solicitation. At June's request, Mark follows up on Nelly's trial and sentencing to Welfare Island. The court scene demonstrates the Law's surveillance of homosexuals, and Nelly's effeminacy incriminates him on the stand: "He raised his hand, and with an unmistakably feminine gesture he patted into place his blondined waves. When he lifted his hand his cuff slipped back and revealed a gilt bangle" (1991:98). Nelly's whiteness magnifies Mark's perception of effeminacy as threatening because with Nelly, racial difference cannot function as a buffer between Mark and the working class as it does with Luis and Rico.

At the Lobster Pot Mark uses the language of racial difference metaphorically to distance himself from Nelly, describing him as belonging to the "tribe" of homosexuals that Mark loathes. However, in this scene where Niles specifies the racial identity of most of the patrons and staff, down to the precise racial composition of the waitress with "the hair and high cheekbones of a North-American Indian, the nose and mouth of an Ethiopian, and the skin of a mulatto," the initial description of Nelly is curiously uncoded by any literal reference to race. He and his companions are not racially identified until "the Law" threatens to disrupt the easy and tolerant atmosphere of the bar. In the grip of the police, Nelly blanches under his makeup, "leaving the outline of the rouge clearly marked, like a hectic fever spot" on his white skin. Later, in the courtroom, his rouge and powder are washed off, leaving him "with the plucked eyebrows and marcelled, blondined hair remaining to testify against him" (1991:66, 97).

Nelly's arrest destabilizes Mark's sense of security in being the unmarked subject because Nelly himself destabilizes the invisibility of sexual identity in opposition to the supposed visibility of racial identity. The references to Nelly's powdered and then washed face recall Ira's earlier argument that blacks cannot wash or powder themselves white; neither scrubbing nor makeup will change the fact of blackness. Similarly, whether Nelly wears his powder or washes it off, he looks like a homosexual. Indeed, scrubbed clean of his powder and rouge, he looks "much more like a girl in man's dress than like a boy with shaped eyebrows, waved blondined hair and a gilt bangle" (1991:99). In this scenario, race and sexual preference are no longer "constituted as binary opposites in a visual economy of readable identity."[26] The "truth" of Nelly's femininity and his sexuality are evident, and perhaps even exaggerated, without cosmetic enhancement.

What threatens the invisibility of the passing homosexual is like the vague "something" that gives away the race passer—the color of the fingernail (race) or the inflection of the voice (sexuality). For both passing figures, the mysterious signs of difference are indefinite because they are established not so much by concrete similarity with another marked body, but by the impossibility of becoming what one seems to be—the unmarked, "purely" white and/or "purely" male subject. Thus, the evidence of homosexuality on the *white* male body, in particular, upsets Mark's assurance that he can pass for straight and avoid being subjected to the Law's gaze.

Mark's apprehensive response to Nelly's exposure is immediate and tangible. When Mark leaves the courtroom, he stops before a mirror in a shop window to inspect himself for signs that might reveal him to the Law. Though he sees none, he fears that he might be deceiving himself, and wonders "How does the Law read anyway?" (1991:105). He goes to the library and finds that according to New York Penal law on "Crimes against Nature," he is not considered any less deviant than Nelly. Here, the Law might be understood as the psychoanalytic "Law of the Father" that prohibits incest and thus regulates both gender and sexuality, ensuring a correspondence between sex and gender identification and consequently, heterosexual disposition toward the opposite sex. The Law establishes the legitimacy of heterosexuality and therefore the illegitimacy of homosexuality. The Law reads all homosexuality as criminal and does not distinguish among homosexual types—none are exempt. Mark can only console himself with the hope that the Law does not see him because he looks "just like anybody else" (1991:131). But can he be sure?

When the "like-race" analogy fails to guarantee Mark's invisibility, Niles returns to sexology to shore up the distinction between Mark and Nelly as homosexual types. By invoking conflicting narratives about the origin of homosexuality, Niles establishes that Mark's Whitmanesque version of "manly love" is natural, while Nelly's effeminacy is not. Nelly explains his "pathology" to the demanding judge in the most reductive version of the Freudian narrative of homosexuality—his mother had wanted a girl when Nelly was born, and she let him dress like one and play like one, so he turned out to be gay. By giving Nelly's homosexuality a psychological rather than a biological etiology, Niles dispenses with the problem of the truly deviant homosexual, one whose sexual expression and social values do not lend themselves to the model of the companionate marriage. Mark is duly outraged at Nelly's sentencing to "The Island," but he also understands that prison fosters the kind of homosexual subculture to which Nelly belongs. That Mark, with his desire for a noble and devoted "comrade-alliance" and his investment in social approval, would not survive in such an environment is proof that his homosexuality is a more natural aberration than Nelly's. The necessity of exorcizing Nelly because he disrupts the process through which Mark is naturalized by comparison with blacks reveals how the supposedly liberal analogy between race and sexual orientation, like the analogy between homosexuality and the companionate marriage and the analogy between gay men and women, actually maintains the categories of difference that uphold the status quo.

Black Bulldaggers and Lesbian Brides: Lifting the Veil to the Shadow World

So far, this chapter has dealt with the way male homosexuality functions as a trope for the companionate marriage. One might expect that Niles would find the lesbian to be another figure of interest in exploring alternatives to the traditional reproductive marriage. But in the context of the backlash against feminism in the 1920s and the "reform" of marriage in the interest of ensuring harmony within the marital bond, the lesbian may prove *too* interesting for close inspection. Niles does not introduce any lesbian characters who might divert June's erotic energy away from men. The only lesbian characters in the novel are Sybil, a black nightclub singer at the Lobster Pot, and Amy, her lighter-skinned and feminine "wife." They do not embody the ideals of the companionate marriage, but according to the popular stereotype of the butch/femme couple, they seem to replicate the patterns of the traditional heterosexual marriage that June rejects. Further, as a black couple, their sexuality does not demand a narrative. Neither the butch's gender inversion nor the feminine lesbian's attraction to the butch require the scientific, psychoanalytic, or sociological analysis to which white characters such as Nelly and Mark are subjected. "Racialized sexuality," unlike the sexuality of the white homosexual, is produced through what Abdul Jan-Mohamed terms the "condensing discursivity" of the symbolic, in which a set of allegorical discourses or stereotypes replaces the analytical imperative of pseudoscientific methodologies like sexology.[27]

This condensing discursivity allows for a proliferation of contradictory images of black sexuality as simultaneously innocent and bestial, primitive and sophisticated, that is typical of the stereotype as a structure that "is curiously mixed and split, polymorphous and perverse."[28] This proliferation of contradictory images is also, as Marianna Torgovnick observes, consistent with primitivism, which makes of the primitive whatever it needs at the moment, and usually defines the primitive in opposition to the present: if the present-day culture is sexually repressed, then the primitive is sexually liberated; if the present is decadent, the primitive is wholesome and temperate.[29]

In *Strange Brother*, the "primitive" black obviously represents sexual liberation, but Niles's ambivalence about the consequences of sexual liberation results in proliferating images of the black woman in particular as both artless and excessive, natural and perverse. A character who strikingly illustrates the concentration of such disparate images in a single figure is Sybil, the entertainer June watches at the Lobster Pot. Eric Garber suggests that Sybil is probably modeled after singer Gladys Bentley, who "personified the one identifiable black lesbian stereotype of the period: the tough-talking, masculine acting, cross-dressing, and sexually worldly 'bull dagger.'"[30]

Ironically, however, in *Strange Brother* the analogy between racial difference and homosexuality is least examined in the figure of the black lesbian. Like Nelly, Sybil marks the visibility of a specific homosexual subculture, but she does not provoke the same anxiety as the white queen. The figurative language that describes her, the attention to her physiognomy, and the repetition of her name like a mantra all reinforce Sybil's status as the symbol of a type—the primitive—that June finds charming:

> "She looks like the heart of Africa . . . the heart of darkness! And the way she's dressed!" . . . For Sybil's big feet wore old, down-at-the-heel, black oxford ties. Sybil's legs were in gray cotton stockings. A short tight black cloth skirt was stretched taut about Sybil's heavy thighs. A white blouse and dark coat clothed Sybil's shapeless torso. And set close to her shoulders was Sybil's head; with its protruding lower jaw, its flat receding brow, and its hair, oiled and brushed to an unnatural straightness, as though the hair were Sybil's one vanity. (1991:41–42)

Because Sybil symbolizes the heart of darkness, her sexuality does not require analysis. She articulates, not verbally but inchoately in song, a primal sexuality that June associates with both the fecundity of the jungle and with heterosexuality. Sybil's cry is "universal, the very birds and beasts cry for each other like that," and it makes June remember how her lover Seth touches her (1991:43). Here is the condensing discursivity of the symbolic at work: Sybil stands for the affirmation of all sexualities subsumed under the sign of heterosexuality. The black lesbian can ratify both heterosexuality and homosexuality precisely because she incites no analytical imperative. She sustains the contradictory logic of the stereotype wherein the construction of blackness as natural takes precedence over the construction of homosexuality as unnatural, and the association of blacks with perversion makes black homosexuality paradoxically natural. In other words, any perception of Sybil's lesbianism as unnatural is canceled out by her race, because within the primitivist discourses of the novel, blacks symbolize the naturalness of all sexuality.

Paradoxically, by describing Sybil from June's point of view as a "naive reader," Niles *desexualizes* Sybil to make her represent lust as a universal urge, so that she becomes a racist type more than a sexual persona. Just as June overlooks the signs of Palmer's effeminacy, she will divest Sybil's masculinity of sexual significance, coding it purely in terms of class and racial difference. Playing off the correlation of masculinity with the natural that we have seen in the representation of Mark as opposed to Nelly, the novel posits Sybil's masculinity as a lack of artifice rather than as a sexual style that is as constructed as Nelly's effeminacy. June sees Sybil as "just an untidy fat woman" who sings out her soul and is not vain about her appearance; Sybil's oxfords and shapeless jacket are not indications of mannishness but of her "simplicity" and working-class status. Her straightened hair, the one token of her "vanity," does not signify a specific sexual style, as does Nelly's blondined, marcelled hair.

Whether we read it as the adaptation of a "white" hairstyle by an African American or as the adaptation of a "masculine" hairstyle by a woman, Sybil's hair is an anomalous sign of artifice that is supposed to look out of place and to heighten our perception of her as primitive; it is the one mark of culture on a figure that is otherwise completely uncontrived. Photos of Bentley at the time show her both in the oxfords and jacket that Niles describes here (Figure 8), and also dressed up in a dinner jacket and tie, with her hair straightened and smoothed back perfectly. Garber reports that Bentley performed at the Clam House in white tie and white tuxedo; in this photo, perhaps a publicity shot, Bentley appears dapper, the picture of the suave, gentlemanly type, and not at all "untidy" (Figure 9). In describing Sybil, Niles seems to collapse these two images, emphasizing the "untidiness" of the one over the polish of the other, but retaining the reference to straightened hair as the signifier of artifice to force the contrasting perception of Sybil as the natural black.

To represent Sybil as a butch with sexual power would suggest threatening alternatives to the failure of white heterosexual relationships in the novel. First, it would invest the black body with masculine sexual potency, something that Niles is very careful not to do. Second, it would give lesbianism an overtly erotic presence in the novel. Though Sybil is quite clearly a figure for the butch, Niles only alludes to lesbian sexuality in the most bracketed fashion. When Sybil's song stirs June's memory of sexual pleasure, she quickly transfers sexual potency from Sybil, who invokes it, to Seth, who cannot provide it.

This bracketing is perhaps most obvious in the description of Amy, Sybil's light-skinned "wife," who embodies the threat of both interracial relationships and lesbianism. Another ghostly femme, Amy is an absent presence, framed and contained by structures of representation; she appears only as a frozen image in Mark's reference to a picture of the two women at their "imitation marriage ceremony." Mark describes Amy as "a beauty— what they call 'high-yellow' in Harlem. In the photograph, she's in a bridal veil and orange blossoms. Sybil is in a tuxedo" (1991:156).

Unlike Sybil or Mark, the light-skinned, feminine lesbian symbolizes the threat of passing on more than one level. As the bride in orange blossoms, Amy blurs the distinction between black and white; the white flowers and veil heighten her near-whiteness through proximity to her light skin. Here, miscegenation becomes the symbolic but unarticulated paradigm for the disruption of the social order that homosexuality explicitly bespeaks. Whereas Mark's masculinity is reassuringly normal, Amy's wifely femininity disturbs the boundary between reproductive heterosexuality and homosexuality. Amy demands monogamy and plans to adopt a child to complete her marriage. Her feminine appearance coincides with a commitment to traditional "family values," but she is not straight, and her lesbianism is not reduced to the matter of sexual object choice, but takes on the dimensions of marriage and child rearing that are supposed to be the purview of heterosexual relationships.

In Mark's account of "the life," he explains his sense of being "a half-man," expresses his desire for an "entirely masculine" partner, and analyzes gay male promiscuity. But it is his description of Amy that makes June dizzy with the realization that homosexuality is "real" and "everywhere." Niles transposes the image of the veil in Amy's wedding photo to the description of June's vertigo, and uses metaphors of darkness that conflate the threats of racial and sexual differences:

> It was a dark place into which the tide of Mark's emotion had borne June. She felt also, for the first time, an impulse to close her eyes on the facts and to go away to some bright light place where she might forget. For it seemed to her not only tragic but sinister. She felt mentally upside-down, as she had sometimes felt when waking in the night, she had not known for one dazed moment where she was, or which way she lay in her bed, or where to locate familiar doors and windows. . . . She sat silent now, feeling as though she had been ushered into a mad-house, whose inmates contradicted all that had been most firmly established in the social order. . . . No, it was not a dream of madness, June realized. It was all fact. Quite suddenly the veil which separates the normal from the shadow world had been lifted, to let her pass in. (1991:157–58)

In effect, it is Amy rather than Sybil who symbolizes the real heart of darkness because she betokens the horror of the black lesbian appropriating white heterosexual privilege. June "passes" into the shadow world, but Amy proves that the shadow world might also pass into hers. We might recall that this has already happened in June's marriage to Palmer, and that Niles contains the threat posed by the gay man passing for straight by casting him as an anachronistic homosexual type who legitimates June's transition from trophy wife to New Woman. Unlike Palmer, however, Amy could cross multiple boundaries of class, race, and sexual difference.

Further, Amy represents a specific threat to June, who must realize that if class, race, and sexual difference may not keep Amy from occupying the position of the white heterosexual woman— if there is nothing to separate the positions of the lesbian and the heterosexual—then June might already occupy the position of a

lesbian. And finally, Amy represents a more radical disruption of
the social order than does Palmer because she is not, in fact, passing—she does not conceal her real desire to occupy the positions
of wife and mother *as a lesbian*. The novel balances the unsettling possibilities that Amy represents through the narratives of
heterosexual "normalcy" that make her dizzying to begin with,
discursively familiarizing and containing her the way she is
framed in the wedding photograph. It is as if Niles asks, "If they
want marriage and a family, doesn't that mean that homosexuals
are just like us?" But a liberal answer of "yes" reveals that likeness can be both reassuring and threatening.

Familiarizing the Other by establishing similarity suggests not
only that the Other is like us, but that we are like the Other. This
begs another question, then, of who "we" are in the novel, and
how we are like "them." In *Strange Brother*, where June shapes
the exploration of difference, "we" is the white heterosexual
woman. Niles consciously proposes that June's tolerance of homosexuality is based on her understanding, as a heterosexual
woman, of Mark's feminine desire for the masculine and not on
any lesbian sexual desires she might harbor. On another level,
though, the novel subverts its conscious intention with a subtext
of lesbian sexual desire that structures the narrative even before
June meets Mark and is officially introduced to the world of male
homosexuality.

Slumming as Phallic Power: The Lesbian Subtext of **Strange Brother**

To read *Strange Brother* for a lesbian subtext is to ask what constitutes lesbianism. On the one hand, the novel represents lesbian
characters in Sybil and Amy. On the other hand, the protagonist's
lack of female friendships is conspicuous. This subtext, then, is
not a palimpsest, a real or original story of lesbian love waiting
to be revealed. Borrowing from Judith Butler's reading of Willa

Cather, we might best understand the "lesbian" of *Strange Brother*'s lesbian subtext to be

> constituted in and through discursive sites at which a certain transfer of sexuality takes place, a transfer which does not leave intact the sexuality that it transfers . . . it is not some primary truth awaiting its moment of true and adequate historical representation and which in the meantime only appears in substitute forms. Rather, substitutability is the condition for this sexuality . . . it is the historically specific consequence of a prohibition on a certain naming, a prohibition against speaking the name of this love that nevertheless and insistently speaks through the very displacements that prohibition produces, the very refractions of vision that the prohibition on the name engenders.[31]

Given the presence of black lesbian characters and the absence of white female relationships, we might name the prohibition in *Strange Brother* as *white* lesbianism, and place that prohibition in the historical context of the changing sexual ideologies of the 1920s. The fear of lesbianism that was quite prevalent in the twenties and thirties was based on the idea that lesbian relationships might emerge in the absence or failure of heterosexuality. Because heterosexuality does fail in the novel, representing June's relationships with other women might uncomfortably raise that fear of lesbianism. June's friendship with Mark provides her with an entrée into the gay life without threatening to absorb her into that life, because it takes the place of friendships with other women. June and Mark are "friends without any complication of sex . . . closer than any which had ever existed between her and a woman friend, and more serene . . . than would ever be possible in any equally close relationship with a normal man" (1991:193).

The logic through which Mark is constructed as neutered in relationship to "normal men" is predictable, but exactly what

"complications of sex" prevent June from having close relationships with women? The parallel between "woman friend" and
"normal man" implies that it is the same complication—erotic
attraction. And though June has no women friends, the novel
opens with a scene that creates the discursive condition for "lesbianism" when June's identification with a black nightclub singer
defers the very fantasy of heterosexual fulfillment that it seems to
anticipate, in effect substituting a lesbian phallic economy for
heterosexuality. This process is mediated by race, because the
substitution of "lesbianism" for heterosexuality coincides with a
"refraction of vision" in which June substitutes the racialized
body for her own.

As June watches the show at the Magnolia Club with Seth
and Phil, she meditates on Glory, a black cabaret singer. Glory
performs "The Creole Love Call," made famous in 1927 by
Adelaide Hall, who probably serves as a model for Glory just
as Gladys Bentley serves as a model for Sybil.[32] The club scene
makes Glory the site of woman's desire for the phallus and of
her concomitant signification of phallicism.[33] Glory stands
"straight and slender" under a "brilliant shaft of light" and her
voice rises from "the dark column of her throat"; she is a girl
who can "make a man know joy" (1991:9). As June watches,
she wonders whether Glory "possess[es] all that she seems to
have" (1991:10); in other words, she asks if Glory is really
able to represent masculine desire well enough to fulfill it. She
projects herself into Glory's body to see "how it would feel . . .
to give yourself to life . . . completely," playing out the primitivist fantasy of the black female body as the site of sexual
plenitude. In her reverie, the phallic signifiers shift from Glory
to Seth, June's lover; June becomes aware of his presence, ob-
serving how big he is and the length of line from his hip to his
knee (1991:10). June refigures her daydream about being
Glory, waiting for a lover, as a fantasy about having Seth. But
consider the erotics of the following passage, in which June
imagines herself to be Glory:

She saw herself inhabiting a lithe brown body. She was wearing a scarlet negligee of soft chiffon; trailing, and with great transparent sleeves. She was lying back among heaped up pillows, with her brown arms raised, and her hands clasped behind her head. The sleeves floated away from her bare arms. Red silk mules dangled from her toes. She felt her whole body relaxed; her face relaxed; especially her lips relaxed.

She was waiting . . . for a lover who was certain to come. And nothing else mattered.

She felt languorous, and at the same time was aware of deep fires burning within her, waiting to leap into flame. (1991:11)

In June's vision, Glory's lingerie and slippers emphasize a hyperfemininity attached to the woman of color that signifies heterosexuality through its "being for" the masculine subject. However, the phallicism of this scene also feels as if it excludes the masculine by its intense focus on female sexual desire. June's identification with Glory is eroticized in a way that does not seem entirely heterosexual. The fires ostensibly burn at the thought of the male lover, but it is Glory's clothes that caress June; they set up a sort of contiguity between the two female subjects, a contiguity of touch in which the clothes rather than the penis are the fetishized representative of the phallus.

Both the structure and the language of this passage recall a similar scene from Nella Larsen's 1929 novel *Passing*, which has been read as a narrative of suppressed lesbianism.[34] *Passing* tells the story of two women, Irene and Clare, girlhood acquaintances who meet by chance at a tearoom atop an exclusive Chicago hotel where they are both passing for white to escape the summer heat and crowded streets below. Though Irene is passing for temporary convenience, having secured her position among the New York's black bourgeoisie through her comfortable if passionless marriage to Brian Redfield, a successful Harlem doctor, Clare has passed out of the black community completely by marrying a rich white man who can afford her the social and class status she lacked as a child. The novel steadily builds up the tension between the two women as Clare insistently attempts to renew her friendship with Irene to satisfy her need to return to the black community and still maintain her white identity at home, while Irene struggles with her simultaneous attraction to Clare and her resistance to Clare's dangerous disregard for the conventions of marriage and the color line. Critics have argued that while Irene's simultaneous attraction and resistance to Clare is overtly about her discomfort with Clare's racial passing, it also signals a conflict of lesbian desire produced by Irene's sexual desire for Clare. Clare, like Glory in *Strange Brother*, is hypersexualized, and Irene's descriptions of Clare are highly eroticized: she is described as "exquisite, golden, fragrant, flaunting"; her "tempting mouth," "arresting eyes," and "seductive smile" give Irene the sense of being "petted and caressed."[35]

The scene that I want to focus on here in comparison to *Strange Brother* occurs toward the end of Larsen's novel, when Clare invites herself to a party with the Redfields. Irene begins to nurse a suspicion that her husband, Brian, and Clare are having an affair—a suspicion that coincides with her own intensified attraction to Clare, so that Brian seems to mediate female homoeroticism at this point in the novel.[36] Brian's function as mediator and signifier of desire takes on a tangible form as the three walk to the party, and Irene feels "something in the air, something that had been between those two and would be again. It was like a live thing pressing against her."[37] The phallicism here is unmistakable; this "live thing" is the erect penis, the signifier of sexual desire that is absent from the Redfields' marriage.

But as in the scene from *Strange Brother*, where Seth serves as a pretext for June's erotic identification with Glory, phallicism does not necessarily signify heterosexuality. Both scenes can be said to invert, if you will, the common literary structure that Eve Sedgwick describes, through which "male-male desire bec[omes] intelligible primarily by being routed through triangular relations involving women."[38] In this inversion of the homosocial triangle, man serves as a token of heterosexuality between women. In both *Strange Brother* and in *Passing*, the main character *seems* to see another woman as a rival for possession of masculinity (the phallus). At the same time, she eroticizes the other woman as the embodiment of a hyperfemininity that signifies both heterosexuality and another erotic economy—one that occurs between women and does not require men to provide the phallus. Metaphorically, at least, we might think of this as a lesbian phallic economy. The production of this lesbian phallic economy could then be said to realize the fear that, given the inability of white men to provide the phallus in this novel, lesbianism would present itself as a viable alternative to the failure of heterosexuality.

I don't want to suggest here that the lesbian phallic economy is utopic. The phallic economy set up in these scenes depends on the contrast between Glory's excessive performance of femininity and June's more "natural" (that is, white, upper-class) femininity. Glory's "hyperfemininity" is embodied as race and class difference and constructed as lacking. In *Strange Brother*, the emergence of lesbianism depends on a process of substitution in which an erotic identification with the black female body momentarily displaces the white woman's heterosexual desire for the white man. Making race a condition for lesbianism, Niles guards against lesbian panic here as she guards against Mark's panic over gay visibility elsewhere—by enacting forms of race and class privilege that mark the Other's sexuality as performative.

Drawing on Carole-Anne Tyler's feminist analysis of mimicry and masquerade, we can read June's fantasy about Glory as enacting a form of power in which the white woman refuses lack (here the lack evoked by the prospect of a lesbian phallic economy) by "fetishistically projecting it on to the class, ethnic, or racial other, from whom [the middle-class white woman] distances herself through a dis-identification that takes the form of an apparent identification." White women can "distinguish themselves from 'other women' even as they assimilate the latter by romanticizing them, assuming the 'other' has a critical knowledge about femininity because of her difference from what counts as natural femininity: white, Anglo, bourgeois style."[39]

We have already seen how the novel romanticizes Glory as the site of sexual plenitude and gives her the knowledge of "how to make a man know joy," precipitating June's erotic identification with the black woman. Here, the distinction between June's femininity and that of the other woman reveals this apparent identification to be a form of disidentification. June's femininity appears effortless and seamless because it is white, upper-class, and tastefully chic. The novel describes her as

> aristocratic in appearance . . . [with] small delicate features, a Dresden China complexion, and straight dark brows above eyes of the quality of Concord grapes, Blue-black and lustrous, veiled by quite incredibly long, dark lashes.
> Her hair was blonde, pale and shimmering gold; she wore it cropped, and carried her head triumphantly, as though she defied Dresden China ladies. (1991:18–19)

June is white perfection updated; she is the bohemian New Woman of the twenties with the genetic inheritance of a beautiful Gilded Age debutante. Glory's femininity, on the other hand, is repeatedly marked as performative; she is orientalized, exoticized, and linked to the primitive through a series of costume changes. Watching Glory perform in a "white tulle and silver lace gown which [foams from her] chocolate brown shoulders down to her silver slippers," Seth, June's lover, and Phil, the insect specialist, imaginatively undress and redress her as the "native woman" who isn't "wearing anything more than a strip of calico around her waist, a string of beads and some bracelets" (1991:10–11).

The transformation suggests that on Glory the evening gown is drag, much as Nelly's lipstick and powder are drag. Black women can only mimic "real" femininity, so that blackness becomes the ground against which femininity can be seen as gendered performative. Take, for example, the following scene, in which June watches Glory's second performance at the cabaret:

> The second revue came on. There was Glory again, this time in red and gold, with a great Spanish comb, and a mantilla of black lace. She was surrounded by a group of chorus girls, wearing striped silk scarves, like parti-colored wings, with a strange strip of violet among the simple red and blue and green, a single wide band of violet on each of the brilliant scarfs which waved and fluttered in a circle about the figure of Glory.
>
> The revue moved quickly.
>
> A beautiful young dancer revolved around Glory. His crimson velvet trousers burned under the spotlight, and as he whirled the lining of his black cape undulated, like flame blown in the wind.
>
> Tap dancers followed the vivid spectacle of the scarf dance.
>
> A grotesquely made-up negro, with abnormally long shoes and abnormally exaggerated red lips, sang a song about jail, and while he sang he held under one arm a live white rooster with bright red comb and wattles.
>
> The negro was in turn replaced by a chorus of almost entirely nude girls, with great gorgeous feather head-dresses and feather wings. They entered slowly in single file; walking with majesty under their towering head-dresses, the golden flesh of their legs stepping forth against the background of their long feather trains. Flamingo pink girls. Red and yellow bird-of-paradise girls. Snow white swan girls. Bluebird blue girls.
>
> [At this point there is a break in which June meditates on Seth's desire for her. Then the final revue comes on:] a group of laughing, prancing girls with loin cloths of iridescent metallic fabric. They did a wild dance to the blare of the great bass horn and the wail of saxophones. (1991:31–33)

Here the black dancers perform racial difference as a range of exotic female sexualities; Glory opens the show as Spanish dancer/harem girl, and other performers succeed her as bird girls and jungle savages. The implication is that all racially marked styles of female sexuality are appropriate to dark-skinned women, and that the only style of femininity not proper to them is the Western, Anglo-Saxon form that is the province of white women. Glory appears first in her evening gown only as an invitation to undress and redress her as various exotic Others. And the novel even manages to contain the threat of that exoticism, the threat that it might represent masculine desire too enticingly, by giving us the man in black face who sings with a rooster under his arm. His performance presumably allows the girls time for costume changes so that they can vary the spectacle of exotic eroticism, but it is also a more domesticated representation of sexual otherness that belongs to the comic, burlesque tradition of the minstrel stage and renders the threat of the Other harmless through buffoonery.[40]

Even when Glory makes her appearance at the Lobster Pot after hours, the novel maintains a continuity between her performance costumes and her own clothes, emphasizing that her tastes are in keeping with her race and class position. She is "perfect," but not in the manner of June's perfection:

> Glory was in a robin's-egg blue dress, very simple, and so thin that the molding of her small pointed breasts showed distinctly. She had a string of big round white pearls close about her throat; the sort of necklace that hangs in shop windows labeled, "Choker, $3.75." There were heavy gilt hoops in her ears and a plain, close-fitting felt hat—robin's-egg blue, like her dress—was pulled down over her brow. Beneath the hat, the whites of her eyes showed like bright crescents against her dark skin; with, between them, the apex of a nose, set on her face like a triangle in low bas-relief. But it was her lips, in shape and color like segments of ripe pomegranate, that were her chief distinction. (1991:40)

Glory's brightly colored dress recalls the "bird girls" of the revue in its color, and her jewelry is gaudy and cheap. The description of her face and breasts evokes *National Geographic* photos of bare-breasted tribal women and Gauguin's paintings of island women, and works to maintain the depiction of Glory as the exoticized Other. As in the case of Gladys Bentley, photos of Adelaide Hall, the model for Glory, reveal how the novel emphasizes Glory's racial difference by emphasizing one version of Hall's style—in this case, the performative version—over others. An early photo of Hall in the Broadway show "Blackbirds," the year after she recorded her famous, wordless song "The Creole Love Call" with Duke Ellington, shows her in a cabaret costume of the kind Niles describes at such length here (Figure 10). But other photos from the period show Hall performing in classically tailored white suits and sight-seeing in London wearing stylish fox furs draped over her wool coat and perfectly proper patent leather pumps.

Niles also uses class difference to construct white femininity as performative in relation to class when June channels the thoughts of the white working-class woman at the Magnolia Club whose date has passed out in front of her. The girl touches up her makeup over the collapsed body of her date, and of course she has on too much of the wrong color and commits the unforgivable faux pas of plastering it on in public. To top it all off she returns her vanity case to a cheap rhinestone bag. Watching her, June imagines out loud, for Seth's benefit, the girl's excitement at finding the bag on special for $2.95 at Sterns and how she thinks to herself that she can carry the bag often because "rhinestones go with anything" (1991:25–26). These passages featuring Glory and the girl with the vanity case draw attention to the way the working-class and black woman too obviously commodify their sexuality by revealing the fact that they use makeup, costume, and mannerism to produce and perform their femininity. June, on the other hand, has an apparently unstudied, elegant sexual style, characterized by an artlessness that she has the material resources to produce.[41]

One paradigm for this manufactured artlessness would be the

"natural look" that cosmetics companies promoted in the late 1980s, selling products to create flawless complexions, bright eyes, and smooth lips that looked bare of makeup. In fact, it took lots of makeup to achieve a look of unadorned polish. This was the era of clear mascara—a product that women have actually found a use for, appropriating it to fix groomed brows into place. Another more academic paradigm would be Marx's optic analogy for commodity fetishism. To explain how commodities take on value apart from their use-value, their functional status as products of labor, Marx describes how the moment of perception elides the physical process that produces it. When we look at an object, we perceive it "not as the subjective excitation of our optic nerve, but as the objective form of something outside the eye itself."[42] In the very act of perception, we fail to see how objects are produced, constructed by the gaze. Similarly, commodities conceal themselves as products of labor.

June, then, successfully packages herself as a commodity because she conceals the labor that produces her as a valuable object of exchange in the sexual marketplace. The novel makes no reference to June's use of makeup, and describes her clothing as making her look like a jonquil at one point and a violet at another. She is the essence of natural beauty as symbolized by the fresh spring garden. Glory and the working-class woman are unsuccessful versions of "the real thing" because they draw attention to their own commodification. In Strange Brother, the visibility of gender as performative is predicated on assigning racial and class difference a phallic significance that invests the white woman with relative power. While Glory's ability to be the phallus seems powerful as the novel opens, closer analysis reveals that June is never divested of white privilege, and that this privilege takes the form of phallic power. June "has" the power of the phallus, or takes up the power of the phallic posture when she makes other women represent the phallus, and thus lack, for her.[43]

June's assumption of phallic power in the opening scenes of

the novel indicates what a reading of the novel as a whole supports—that ultimately Niles upholds the boundaries she seems to want to cross in her infatuation with difference. Niles certainly conceived *Strange Brother* as sympathetic to homosexuals and large-minded about Harlemites, and reviewers saw her work as "less a novel than a special piece of pleading" for homosexuals. And in a sense, her interest in the plight of her "strange brothers" is not disingenuous. Because the analogy between blacks and homosexuals that drives her representation of both groups derives from the historical moment when lesbians and gays were adopting the ethnic model of homosexuality, Niles's liberalism appeared to have a legitimate source outside the New Woman's immediate agenda—she saw herself, in today's vocabulary, as an "ally."

But what is also at stake for Niles is gaining acceptance for new modes of sexual expression for white heterosexual women without compromising their social status. Niles's use of the "like-race" analogy is intimately connected to the need to posit women's desire for nonreproductive sexual relationships as natural, particularly in that it allows her to construct the gay male as a paradigm for the companionate marriage. In this regard, she cannot interrogate the discourses of primitivism and deviance that inform her characterization of blacks and homosexuals. She fetishizes the black as hypervisible in opposition to the invisibility of the homosexual, and pathologizes gender inversion when it disrupts that opposition by threatening the unmarked homosexual's ability to pass.

Mapping out how Niles uses the analogy between racial difference and sexual orientation to further the agenda of the New Woman reveals not only that analogies are based on reductive and partial forms of knowledge, but that they enact culturally violent forms of specularization and erasure to maintain stable categories of difference. By the late twentieth century the analogy between racial difference and homosexuality became increasingly contested, because it replicates the logic of racism.[44]

Broadly speaking, this analogy subsumes the specificity of racist oppression under the banner of marginalization. With relation to visibility specifically, the analogy replicates the logic of racism in two ways. When the analogy establishes similarities between the way the visibility of racial and sexual minorities targets them for discrimination, it does not account for how those groups experience and are defined by visibility in different ways. But just as frequently, when the analogy establishes differences between the way those two groups are defined regarding structures of the visible, it reifies racial difference as an uncontested category. The readings in chapter 3 continue to explore the use of the "like-race" analogy in fictions of the 1950s and 1960s, when color-blindness emerges as the liberal discourse on racial difference.

THREE

Lesbian Pulp in Black and White

Like the unforgettable SPRING FIRE, here is an urgent young first novel of emotions running wild—beyond the pale into the dark country of love that should never have been.   —Cover blurb, *Odd Girl Out*

Though *Strange Brother* was one of many gay-themed novels to appear during the early 1930s, it was not until the mid-1950s that the exploding paperback industry made lesbian novels available to a large number of readers. Cover blurbs for titles such as *Twilight Lovers* (1964), *Stranger on Lesbos* (1960), and *Women's Barracks* (1950), announced stories of strange lusts, unnatural love, and perverse relationships in worlds of women without men. Much of this fiction was male-authored and as part of a larger market for erotic paperbacks, its aim was to titillate. A handful of lesbian writers, including Ann Bannon, Paula Christian, Vin Packer, and Valerie Taylor tried to treat lesbianism sympathetically. But the majority of these novels were homophobic in the extreme, and for many readers looking at the covers, it was difficult to tell which novels were written by lesbians and for lesbians and which were written for a male heterosexual audience.

It was in the context of this sensationalized genre that the feminine lesbian achieved real "literary" visibility for the first time. With butch and femme "roles" an established part of lesbian subculture by the 1950s, the femme was a staple character in pulp. Her presence in the bar, the school room, and the dressing room, and her frank sexual initiative with other women lent her more substance than she had in *The Well of Loneliness* and in much lesbian fiction of the 1930s and 1940s. Given the homophobic social climate of the 1950s, it is not surprising that increased visibility did virtually nothing to correct prevailing stereotypes of the feminine lesbian. Pulp novels typically depict the femme as manipulative, tyrannical, and predatory, or clinging, desperate, and weak, and she often fails the test of social pressure to direct her attentions toward men. In an era when publication standards practically guaranteed that lesbianism would end in separation, alcoholism, or death, the femme was likely to be instrumental in causing one or more of these tragedies. But as Joan Nestle, a self-identified "fifties femme," recalls, purchasing and reading lesbian pulp was an act of courage for women with little other access to public representation of lesbian lives.

Pulp fiction was recognized as an important element of lesbian literary history at least as early as 1957, when Barbara Grier, a librarian and collector of lesbian fiction from a young age, began annual surveys of lesbian literature that appeared in *The Ladder* under the pseudonym Gene Damon. These surveys expanded into Grier's later publications of *The Lesbian in Literature: A Bibliography.* The changing content of Grier's bibliographies reveals growing judgments about pulp's literary and cultural value, especially as other kinds of lesbian fiction became available. The first edition of *The Lesbian in Literature*, published in 1967, contains over three thousand titles marked "T" for "trash" that compilers of the third edition subsequently eliminated. Most of these entries were pulp novels of the 1950s, 1960s, and 1970s. As Grier explains in the introduction to the 1981 edition of the bibliography, they were deleted not only to make room for new, presumably better titles, but also to "acknowledge the changing consciousness of the world" about what counted for quality lesbian reading material.[1]

For the most part, these books are now unavailable, except in lesbian and gay archives that collect pulp. But recent books and archives-sponsored shows on pulp cover art demonstrate a resurgence of popular and scholarly interest in pulp fiction. Several academic essays have been written on the work of Ann Bannon, whose novels became the most accessible of the vintage pulp titles when Naiad Press reprinted the Beebo Brinker series in the 1980s.[2] Focusing on how the novels navigate sexual ideology in the conservative social climate of the 1950s, these essays seek to revaluate pulp fiction by arguing that in spite of the genre's limitations, lesbian writers such as Bannon are able to complicate stereotyped representations of lesbianism.

So far little work has been done on lesbian identity in pulp fiction that includes a consideration of racial as well as sexual ideologies. In part this may be due to the fact that pre-Stonewall lesbian novels usually feature white protagonists, presenting race and class as a "neutral background" against which to dramatize their emergent lesbianism.[3] There is a subgenre of lesbian pulp that sought to heighten titillation, adding racial taboo to sexual taboo by featuring black lesbian characters as partners in interracial relationships. But it was not until the 1974 publication of *Loving Her,* by the African American author Ann Allen Shockley, that we see a lesbian novel self-consciously attempting to address issues of race and lesbian subjectivity. The minimal conversation about race in what is hopefully only the beginning of critical work on lesbian pulp can be seen as part of a pattern around the recovery of neglected or "rediscovered" lesbian texts. Typically, critical attention to issues of race tends to emerge after and in response to earlier feminist readings that focus on lesbian subjectivity where "lesbian" is presumed to be white, or where minor or peripheral nonwhite characters do not enter into the discussion of white lesbian subject constitution.

Two novels that lend themselves to the beginning of a dialogue about race and sexuality in lesbian pulp are Bannon's *Women in the Shadows* (1959), the fourth installment in the Beebo Brinker series,[4] and Shockley's *Loving Her* (1974). While scholars often acknowledge *Loving Her* as a milestone in lesbian literary history, it has not gained even the minimal critical attention that

Bannon's novels have received. Published over a decade apart—
the decade marked by Stonewall and the emergence of the gay
liberation movement—and written by a white woman and a
black woman, respectively, the two novels do have common
threads. Both provide the opportunity to study the feminine lesbian and the black lesbian as focal points for questions about the
origin, nature, and visibility of sexual orientation within the context of changing discourses on race and homosexuality in the
1950s and 1960s.

Structuring race passing and sexual passing as parallel narratives (and here I use the term "passing" to indicate a character's
movement from a marginally defined community to one more
closely aligned with the dominant culture, as well as to indicate
passing *for* a member of a dominant identity group), the novels
repeat the gesture that Niles makes in *Strange Brother*, using
racial difference as an analogy for sexual orientation. Whereas in
Strange Brother, Niles uses the "like-race" analogy to define sexual identity by reasserting the essential difference of race, Bannon
and Shockley ultimately neutralize racial difference in order to
"solve" the problem of sexual identity. In both novels, racism becomes a symptom of homophobia and interferes with the
progress of the lesbian romance. Shedding or escaping racism
leads to the consummation of the lesbian relationship and the affirmation of lesbian identity, while the failure to transcend racial
difference leads to the repression of lesbian identity. Though each
novel deploys the rhetoric of "color-blindess," suggesting that
race does not matter, they are written out of different historical
moments and conditions that shape the way the authors represent race and sexuality. ⬩

Fifties Femmes Fatales: Ann Bannon's
Women in the Shadows

Ann Bannon's novels, unlike the bulk of 1950s pulp, are sympathetic to lesbians. Bannon wrote her first lesbian novel when she

was a young married woman living in Philadelphia. On secret weekend excursions to New York City, she visited gay bars in the Village. Her novels document an increasingly visible lesbian and gay subculture, and explore issues of sexual identity in ways that both reflect and resist the 1950s moral and medical understanding of homosexuality, which was heavily influenced by a popularized version of Freudianism. In its more liberal variations, the ideology of the 1950s defined homosexuality as a disease of biological and psychological origins; in its more conservative moments, it defined homosexuality as a dangerous perversion.

Bannon's novels often broke with the conventions of both "literary" lesbian fiction and of lesbian pulp by creating happy endings for women who were true to their sexual preference for other women. Even in *Women in the Shadows*, probably the bleakest novel in the Beebo Brinker series, the marriage of the feminine lesbian to a gay man rather than a straight man compromises a full reconstitution of the heteropatriarchal family, and pushes the envelope of credibility in a genre notorious for unlikely plots. More than her other novels, though, *Women in the Shadows* validates the heterosexual status quo as it moves toward closure, and not coincidentally, it is the novel in which the feminine lesbian most explicitly embodies the dilemma of sexual identity. She appears here in the character of Laura, whom we first meet in Bannon's 1957 novel *Odd Girl Out*, and in the character of Tris, a black dance teacher who is passing for Asian Indian when she and Laura meet. The narrative suspense hangs on the question of whether Laura, the novel's white femme protagonist, is willing to leave her lover, Beebo, and marry their mutual friend Jack, who sees no future for himself in the homosexual world.

Briefly, the plot is as follows: Beebo and Laura's relationship, promisingly established at the end of *I Am a Woman* (also published in 1959), is on the rocks. Laura falls hard for the exotic, feminine Tris. A series of events leads Laura to discover that Tris is a married black woman who is already familiar with the gay scene in the Village and is attracted to Beebo, not her. Disappointed in her affair with Tris and frustrated in her relationship with Beebo, Laura allows Jack, a gay male friend and confidante, to persuade her to flee the gay life in the Village by marrying him, bearing his child, and passing for a straight couple in a nice uptown neighborhood. She bases her decision on the conclusion toward which Jack has been pushing her all along: that same-sex relationships have no purpose beyond the satisfaction of an almost atavistic physical desire that inevitably wanes, and that there is more comfort and more future in a platonic marriage to a gay man than in a romantic relationship with a woman.

The difference between the femme, who has the option of passing, and the butch, who does not, is made painfully clear when Jack proposes to Laura. Beebo, who is a "freak" by virtue of her boyish appearance even in the gay territory of the Village, cannot offer Laura either financial security or protection from homophobia. Urging Laura to marry him, Jack makes the economic and social consequences of not doing so clear by painting a picture of her future if she chooses to stay with Beebo:

> "Have you seen the pitiful old women in their men's oxfords and chopped-off hair, stumping around like lost souls, wandering from bar to bar and staring at the pretty kids and weeping because they can't have them any more? Or living together, two of them, ugly and fat and wrinkled, with nothing to do and nothing to care about but the good old days that are no more? Is that what you want? Because if you stay here, that's what you'll get."[5]

Jack's homophobic and misogynist speech underscores the reality that many women, especially those who are marginalized on more than one count, do not have the economic resources to live well independently of men. His repeated marriage proposals set up a triangle in which Jack and Beebo compete for Laura, and position the butch as the figure who potentially disrupts the heterosexual institutions of marriage and childbearing to which

Jack wants access. Beebo is at a disadvantage, even against a man who cannot fully align himself with patriarchal power as long as he might be identified as gay. An engineer, Jack does have the potential for upward mobility that Beebo, as an elevator "boy," does not. Jack also has the power to legally legitimate his union with Laura in the eyes of the "normal world," a fact which Beebo laments.

Indeed, the primary weapon that Beebo has to rival Jack's male privilege and social power is her own sexual power. In the lesbian popular imagination, Beebo's sexual power makes her the quintessential butch. Over 25 years after Bannon created the character, Jennifer Levin wrote, "Beebo is still passionate, sexual, hot, honest rough and tough and utterly herself in the face of a brutally homogenizing world. Furthermore, she aggressively goes after love—and, more often than not, she gets it."[6] But in *Women in the Shadows,* unlike the other novels in the series, Beebo's sexual power is fading; after two years of domestic routine, her animal magnetism displays itself as jealous violence more than irresistible butch allure. Emotional and erotic factors appear to subsume the economic and social reasons for Laura's decision to leave Beebo. When Laura tries to return to Beebo after a year with Jack, she finds that even Beebo's jealous rage has dissipated. Admitting that their "crazy, beautiful love affair" is over, Laura recognizes that it is time to "grow up" and return to Jack. Growing up also means growing out of a phase and making a transition toward the "real" experience of womanhood that only marriage (even to a gay man), motherhood, and middle-class comforts can provide.

In *Women in the Shadows*, the femme's decision to pass out of the lesbian community overlaps with the light-skinned woman's decision to pass out of the black community. Though issues of visibility, authenticity, and oppression are associated with the idiom of race passing, what is really at stake for Bannon is the status of the femme's sexual identity, and race is part of a figurative strategy for negotiating among oppositional discourses of homosexuality that converge in the figure of the feminine lesbian.[7] The femme represents the possibility of multiple and indeterminate causes of homosexuality, and it is this that makes her unstable as a lesbian. Throughout the Beebo Brinker series as a whole, Bannon tends to offer more varied representations of the femme than she does in *Women*. Her other novels portray femmes who are "real lesbians," femmes who bring home the money, and femmes who stand by their women, as well as femmes who are weak and wayward. In *Women* the femme is selfish, needy, childish, and worst of all, married.

Bannon makes the most overt analogy between racial difference and homosexuality in a short scene in which Laura discusses whether or not she has any choice in the matter of sexual identity with Milo, Tris's husband. The issue of choice is central to Laura's passing. Milo, whose dark, satiny skin makes him the only obviously black character in the novel, provides Laura with a literal body of evidence against which to test the issue. When Milo asks Laura whether she was born gay, Laura responds by saying she was "made that way," and lists her father, her first lover, herself, and "fate" as causes for her sexual orientation. Her reply suggests multiple possibilities: that her homosexuality is psychological in origin because she was incested by her father; that she was "seduced" into lesbianism by her first lover, Beth; that she chose her sexuality herself; and that she was biologically and/or psychologically destined to become a lesbian. But when she turns on Milo and demands, "Do you think I live this way because I like it? Would you live like you do if you could live like a white man?" Laura suggests that her ability to choose identity is as limited by her innate homosexuality as Milo's is by his skin color, and that she is in some sense "born that way." However, Bannon has already established the feminine lesbian's ability to choose social position, if not sexual identity, by structuring the plot around the question of whether Laura will pick Jack or Beebo. Thus, Laura clearly makes a false analogy between her own situation and Milo's, eliding the fact that visible marks of difference do not fix her subject position or her identity the way they do for Milo.

Laura's position is closer to that of Tris, the light-skinned black woman through whom Bannon plays out the consequences of moving between multiple worlds (black and white, gay and straight, working-class and middle-class) without penalizing her main character, Laura. Tris is a minor character in Bannon's work. She only appears in one novel, whereas other characters such as Beebo, Laura, and Jack recur throughout the series. In *Women in the Shadows*, Tris plays the role of the "other woman" in the central love relationships between Beebo and Laura, and Laura and Jack. However, Tris is central to the novel as "a narrative device of mediation"—a function that Hazel Carby points out is common for the mulatta in American fiction.[8] Here, she is a vehicle for exploring the geography of passing as it relates to lesbian identity. Because Bannon splits the passing narrative between a black character and a white one, Tris can bear the negative consequences of passing so that Laura can be allowed to benefit from its privileges. Laura will cross the bridge of Tris's back, making the transition into the "uptown," middle-class, heterosexual lifestyle, fully understanding her decision to pass, and passing without fully renouncing her lesbianism. That is, Tris will represent the construction of passing as a pathological act that denies "true" identity, while Laura will represent passing as a healthy choice, given the difficulties and limitations of the gay life.

As the mulatta character, Tris fits within a specific tradition of literary representation. Discussing nineteenth-century literature, Judith Berzon argues that antislavery fiction in particular emphasized the mulatta's nobility, intelligence, and courage. In the twentieth century the old stereotype of the tragic mulatta persisted, but to it were added the exotic mulatta, the villainous mulatta, and the light-skinned "dicty" who holds herself above darker blacks.[9] Tris plays all these roles. She is the beautiful, duplicitous villain who is capricious and dishonest with Laura and cheats on her husband, but she is duplicitous because she is tragically torn between identities. Tris is caught between two worlds on more than one level; she fetishizes whiteness and refuses blackness, and she cannot fully accept her lesbianism.

Tris gives voice to the novel's own conflation of sexual and racial undecidability by hedging her answer to Laura's question about whether or not she is gay. Tris's response to Laura's insistence that she must be either gay or straight implicitly challenges Laura's understanding of identity as fixed by invoking the rhetoric of choice and by employing the double entendre: "'If you force me to choose between black and white, I'm white,' . . . and Laura thought she heard a double emphasis on the word 'white.' 'I like men. More than women'" (1986:45–46). On the surface, Tris uses the words "black and white" as a metaphor for the way Laura has presented heterosexuality and homosexuality as mutually exclusive and as polar opposites. But the double emphasis on the word "white" indicates that the term also refers to race. With skin that is "three parts cream to one part coffee," Tris cannot pass for white, but the word resonates with the idiom of passing, destabilizing the precise nature of both her sexual and racial identities.

Ostensibly, Laura's own identity as a lesbian is not in question; even when she marries Jack, it is with the understanding that she will continue to have female lovers. I would suggest, though, that Tris represents the fear that white femmes are duplicitous like mulattas; they are not real lesbians in the same way that Tris is neither a real Indian nor a real black woman. The parallel between Tris and Laura, established through the conflation of race passing and passing for straight, becomes most evident when Tris mirrors Laura's sexual desires. In literature about race passing, passers often seek to return to a culture which they knew in childhood, but Tris repeatedly returns to the lesbian community—the community from which Laura has passed and to which Laura wants to return—indicating where Bannon's investments lie in her use of the passing narrative. Tris delineates Laura's relationship to the lesbian community, and also marks the trajectory of Laura's desire for butch women.

When Laura finally discovers that Tris has never been sexually attracted to her and has only used her to get closer to Beebo, Laura is sitting in a lesbian bar admiring the women. She reflects that it is really the masculine women who excite her the most. Here, Tris's attraction to Beebo causes Laura to recognize the "truth" about her own desire for butch women. This recognition in turn suggests that Laura was only drawn to Tris because she had mistakenly replaced one form of difference—gender difference between lesbians—with another: racial difference. Laura has misguidedly equated the attraction of Tris's "fragrant tan skin" with the attraction of Beebo's masculinity.

In addition to delineating Laura's desire for the butch, Tris also personifies Laura's need for the social privileges of heterosexuality. But while Tris will remain torn between the butch as an object of sexual desire and the social legitimacy that her husband provides her, following Beebo like a puppy only to be returned to Milo when Beebo is tired of her, at the end of the novel Laura will anticipate the experience of what it is "to be a woman," as opposed to a lesbian. Finally, Tris's pitiful, and perhaps most significantly, her *failed* attempts to repress her lesbianism and to transcend her racial identity and her working-class status in an effort to become "normal" will establish her as the marked subject. For Bannon, the marked subject is often literally scarred not by her deviancy itself but by her self-hatred and internalized homophobia.[10] The butch is not necessarily constructed as the marked lesbian in this sense; she may carry the visible signifiers of lesbian desire without bearing the mark of shame.

The narrative of race passing in *Women in the Shadows* complicates the construction of marking as a signifier of self-hatred because it registers Tris's internalized racism and homophobia through skin color as a "natural" sign of difference. Tris evinces racial self-hatred from her first appearance in the novel, where the bindi on her forehead denotes her attempt to recode signs of blackness using a mark of Indian femininity, and thereby to assume a racial identity that she associates with class and cultural status denied to African Americans. Later, her internalized racism will be linked to her internalized homophobia. When Laura accuses her of being sick for denying her lesbian desire, Tris goes "a strange ashy color" (1986:92). In other words, Tris's sexual "sickness" manifests itself through the signs of racial difference—Tris *blanches*, and her skin both reflects the sickness of wanting to be white and reveals her as black through its sudden "ashiness."

Race indexes the truth about sexual identity, becoming the register for what can and cannot be detected about sexual identity. As in other passing narratives, Bannon's novel foregrounds the insider's ability to read the "telltale signs" of marginal identity, but here the double layers of passing interfere with readability. Laura, who "prides herself on being able to identify other lesbians," is so hypnotized by the spectacle of Tris's racial difference that she is blind not only to the clues that Tris is passing for Indian, but also to the evidence that she is only pretending to be inexperienced with women. Because Laura is reading for signs of Tris's suppressed lesbian identity, she does not pay attention to the strangeness of Tris's accent, which is "very precise and softly spoken, but not noticeably British or anything else" (1986:40), or to Tris's slips into English that is "clear and plain, like Laura's own" (1986:48). Nor does she attend to Tris's persistent, curious questions about Beebo. Bannon implies that the breaks in the illusion of Tris's Indianness should cue Laura in to Tris's interest in Beebo, in spite of her assertions that she likes men more than women.

Race passing and passing for straight are also narratively linked. Laura's discovery that Tris is passing, which occurs when Milo arrives at the beach house where the two women are vacationing, not only signals the end of the women's badly consummated "affair," but directly precedes Laura's decision to marry Jack. Confiding in Jack, Laura speculates that Milo's arrival at the beach house may not have been coincidental: "I think myself she needed a man just then, to make herself feel normal. And protected" (1986:99). Laura will seek the same protection in her marriage, though unlike Tris, she does so without the burden of self-hatred that marks Tris. Laura's decision to marry Jack also proves that femmes are the weak point in the economy of lesbian identity. When Beebo finally turns both women out of her apartment and over to their respective husbands, Bannon implies, like Hall, that even femmes who acknowledge their lesbianism and actively seek sexual contact with other women rightfully belong to the heterosexual world because they need male protection. At the end of the novel, Laura, ensconced in Jack's arms, feels "more comfortable . . . and more safe than she had ever been," and the two actually exchange a "real" kiss, signaling the completion of Laura's transition into the heterosexual life that she and Jack have created (1986:176).

Laura and Jack's sudden discovery of not just the social benefits but the romantic pleasures of their heterosexual contract is certainly too abrupt to be convincing, and Bannon does not belabor the idea that the two are "cured" of their homosexuality. But Laura's move away from the lesbian community does structurally stabilize her subject position, while Tris remains caught between worlds, unsure whether she is gay or straight, black or white. Clearly, hers is not the story that demands resolution. It would be another fifteen years before the black lesbian was more than a peripheral, if not pivotal, character in the discussion of lesbian identity.

Liberal Feminism and the Black Lesbian Subject of Ann Allen Shockley's Loving Her

Ann Allen Shockley's 1974 novel *Loving Her* is a landmark in black lesbian literature.[11] Until the publication of Audre Lorde's *Zami* and Michele Cliff's *Abeng* in the 1980s, it was the first novel written by a black woman to depict a black lesbian as a central character, and Jewelle Gomez recounts that reading *Loving Her* was "for many Black lesbians . . . like reading *The Well of Loneliness* for the first time and realizing there were 'others' out there."[12] In spite of the novel's reputation and Shockley's own commitment to black women's writing in her activities as a librarian and as the author of numerous short stories published since the 1940s, Shockley is a writer who is referenced more than she is read. To date, there has been little serious critical attention to her work, and currently SDiane Bogus's 1988 dissertation, "Theme and Portraiture in the Fiction of Ann Allen Shockley," is the only extended study of her writing.[13]

Like *Women in the Shadows*, Shockley's *Loving Her* narrates the protagonist's transition from a marginal community to one more closely aligned with the dominant culture.[14] Bannon and Shockley both invoke the analogy between homosexuality and racial difference, but whereas Bannon tends to use race figuratively to indicate the social condition of lesbians and gays without exploring the social condition of blacks, Shockley's main character experiences and analyzes institutional racism. *Loving Her* is not, however, unproblematic in its representation of race and racism. If *Women in the Shadows* fails to represent any black community at all, *Loving Her* represents the black community as the site of poverty, homophobia, and violence against women. Ultimately, Shockley does not put forth a specifically black lesbian identity as much as a lesbian identity that is configured as white.

The mixed critical reception of *Loving Her* is a measure of Shockley's difficulty in representing the black lesbian. While some critics praise the novel for its historical significance, giving the impression that it has been unanimously received as an affirmation of black lesbian identity, response to the novel upon its publication was uneven.[15] For example, Jean Cordova's 1974 review of *Loving Her* acknowledges Shockley's "nobility of purpose and theme," but criticizes the book's inferior literary style and its inadequacies in "presenting the complicated politics of white liberalism, anti-lesbian prejudice, black hatred of whites, and black matriarchal sociology," and Beverly Smith criticizes the novel's message that love conquers all adversity, and that lesbian love, in particular, can triumph over the external forces of racism and homophobia.[16]

The mixed reception of *Loving Her* may point to critical dilemmas about how to evaluate black lesbian fiction.[17] *Loving Her* presents distinct problems for feminist critics, because, as Bogus points out, it "was written before the formulation of the lesbian-feminist aesthetic" by which it is often judged.[18] Though it was published in 1974, well into the feminist movement, Shockley confirms one reviewer's suspicion that *Loving Her* was actually written between 1960 and 1969.[19] Thus, reviews of *Loving Her* frequently hold the book to literary and political standards that do not take into account its position on the threshold between "the golden age of the lesbian paperback" that preceded its publication (which Grier dates between 1950 and 1966) and the advent of post-Stonewall lesbian fiction that followed its composition.[20] In fact, though the novel contains a feminist critique of black macho and of homophobia, it is most appropriately read with the conventions of pulp fiction rather than lesbian-feminist fiction in mind. The narrative, although unique in featuring a black protagonist, follows the typical lesbian pulp romance plot: a woman comes to awareness of her lesbian sexuality, experiences that awareness as a form of freedom, and is then punished for her transgressions.

As the story opens, Renay, the protagonist, is preparing to leave her black husband, Jerome Lee. The two got married in college when she became pregnant after he raped and impregnated her on the way home from a fraternity dance. During the marriage, Jerome Lee becomes increasingly irresponsible and abusive, and Renay struggles to support herself and her daughter by playing the piano at a supper club where she meets Terry, a wealthy white lesbian. When Renay finally flees Jerome Lee with her young daughter Denise, she finds love and protection with

Terry until her husband pursues her. Furious that Renay would leave him for a "bulldagger," Jerome Lee beats Renay and threatens to sue for custody of their daughter. Renay sends Denise to her mother's house in Kentucky, but it is not long before Denise is killed in a drunken car accident with Jerome Lee at the wheel. Devastated by the death of her daughter, Renay abandons Terry in despair, only to return to her months later. The lovers are reunited at the end of the story, but Renay's near-fatal beating and Denise's death put the novel within the conventions of earlier pulp fiction that ends in punishment for the lesbian couple. In addition to the tragic ending that is so typical of earlier lesbian fiction, Shockley conforms to pulp conventions when she shows the lesbian and gay social life, specifically the bar culture, as deviant—made up of working-class, role-playing, promiscuous alcoholics who cheat on each other, cat fight, and fist fight.

However, *Loving Her* also diverges from the conventions of earlier pulp in ways that characterize it as a sixties' novel. Shockley flatly rejects the medical and psychoanalytic explanations of lesbianism that Bannon tests but does not fully abandon. By the 1960s, the emerging discourse of "deviance theory" within sociology provided alternatives to traditional interpretations of homosexuality that authorized Shockley's refusal to construct lesbianism as a sickness. Though it did not displace traditional interpretations of homosexuality, John D'Emilio explains that because deviance theory developed out of a "radical relativist perspective," it did allow for a revised understanding of the homosexual "problem" as one caused by social intolerance rather than the lesbian and gay individual.[21]

If, in keeping with some of the conventions of earlier pulp, Shockley pathologizes the lesbian subculture insofar as it deviates from middle- to upper-class values and behavior, she also identifies the "problem" of homosexuality as a social rather than an individual one when she dismisses medical and psychological explanations for lesbianism. For example, Renay's "bad experience" with heterosexuality, though it is the pretext for her discovery of lesbianism, is never offered as the *cause* of her lesbian-ism. Shockley emphasizes Renay's lack of interest in men before her marriage to Jerome Lee, and after Renay comes out, Shock-ley reconstructs the narrative of her latent erotic attachment to her childhood piano teacher, Miss Sims, who is herself a re-pressed lesbian. Further, Shockley offers a pointed rejection of lesbianism-as-pathology through Terry, the more experienced and worldly lesbian, who says of herself:

> I'm not going to blame my inclination on the [girls'] schools or a mother's rejection. I simply like my own sex and that's that. I've come to accept it . . . and I've stopped wasting money try-ing to change myself and conform to what society thinks a fe-male should be. . . . Why should I? People aren't made alike, don't all think alike, and aren't pigmented alike. Why should our sex penchants have to be the same?[22]

That Terry compares her lesbianism to racial difference for the purpose of rejecting society's expectations about sex roles and sexual orientation indicates the political shift in the homophile movements of the sixties from an accomodationist/assimilation-ist position to a more militant refusal of "professional" opinions about the origins of homosexuality. This was accompanied by a demand for lesbian and gay rights consciously patterned after the strategies of the civil rights movement.[23]

To recognize *Loving Her* as a pre-Stonewall text requires us to place the novel not only in the context of pulp fiction conven-tions and the emergent gay rights movement, but also in the con-text of black feminist discourses that were developing when the book was written. Though contextualizing this novel appropri-ately cannot address complaints about the quality and politics of Shockley's more recent work, it does suggest that in *Loving Her*, Shockley was attuned to cultural anxieties about lesbianism, in-terracial relationships, and black masculinity that were specific to the 1960s and 1970s.[24] Clearly, *Loving Her* invokes these anx-ieties better than it critiques them. Still, the novel does anticipate the analyses of racism, sexism, and homophobia that black feminist and lesbian feminist activists would develop in the decades after Shockley wrote *Loving Her*.

Locating the novel at the juncture of various movements in the U.S. discourses of race and feminism demands a revision of recent overviews of the lesbian literary tradition that frame *Loving Her* as an affirmative representation of the black lesbian and overlook the historical controversy surrounding the novel's reception. In responding more fully to the salient criticisms of the novel's rhetoric of individualism and racial integration, my aim here is not to engage in the kind of critique that often labels earlier feminisms "wrong." Rather I am interested in the way the novel dramatizes and genders the tension between two modes of race discourse characteristic of the 1960s and 1970s—the "race-cognizant" discourses of black nationalism on the one hand and the "color- and power-evasive" rhetoric of color-blindness on the other hand.[25]

Whereas many black feminists were refusing the rhetoric of color-blindness by the mid-1970s, Shockley, writing when color-blindness was commonly deployed against earlier forms of race essentialism, offers it as an alternative to the separatist politics of black nationalism that she associates with the ideology of male supremacy. But the rhetoric of color-blindness does not so much facilitate as impede the effort to create a discursive space for the black lesbian subject. Since the early 1980s, feminists of color have challenged the assumption that claiming a lesbian identity means leaving their communities of origin.[26] *Loving Her*, composed during the 1960s, enacts the anxiety that claiming a lesbian identity necessitates losing one's black identity. Shockley's protagonist does find strength in her connection with other black women when confronted with racism. For example, when wrongly accused of stealing money, Renay "search[es] for her mother's strength and the strength of all other black women who had taken such malicious accusations with courage and composure" (1986:52). But Renay is also prepared to give up her connections with the black community to preserve her relationship with her white lover, "even if it mean[s] losing her identity in Terry's world" (1986:37). And as the narrative of the interracial romance unfolds, the novel divests its protagonist of any connection with black culture, which becomes the site of both the homophobia and the sexism that she must escape in order to assume a lesbian identity.

The novel establishes the black community as the site of compulsory heterosexuality through Jerome Lee, Renay's husband, who embodies the hyperheterosexual, predatory, posturing, macho black male: "big and brown and handsome . . . he swaggered with a hip-dip walk, hugging and kissing everybody lightly in passing, calling all baby and doll and honey" (1986:13). After he marries Renay, he takes a job selling products to black beauty parlors but squanders his money drinking and womanizing, stays away from home for long periods of time, and returns only to abuse his wife and ignore his daughter. Jerome Lee personifies the black father depicted in the Moynihan Report, one who is "either not present, is unemployed, or makes such a low wage [that] the Negro mother goes to work."[27] Shockley represents Jerome Lee in sympathy with the black feminist critique of the macho ethos that marked black nationalism, pride, and power in the 1960s—a critique that Michele Wallace popularized in her controversial book *Black Macho and the Myth of the Superwoman.*[28] Jerome Lee literally embodies the black man's anger at black women in general. Before Shockley describes him in any detail, she metonymically portrays him as "the back of a large black hand striking out in angry rebuttal against [Renay] and all the other black women before and after her" (1986:2). Here the book represents sexist hostility that Wallace argues the Moynihan Report brought to the surface in depicting the black man as the sexual victim of a matriarchal tyranny.[29]

Shockley reverses the stereotype of the castrating black woman by casting Renay as the victim of domestic abuse, and satirizes the masculinist rhetoric of black nationalists such as

Amiri Baraka and Eldridge Cleaver, who fetishized the black phallus as part of their attack on white racism. For example, the narrative voice explains that Jerome Lee perceives Renay's leaving him more as an affront to his manhood than as a loss of a companion:

> His sexual narcissism was wounded—the steel armor of black men, the one and only form of manhood the white man had given them in slavery—the myth of their sexual prowess which black males had come to believe and somehow had made black women believe. The black man was the superstud. The bed was his kingdom, the womb his domain, and the penis his mojo hung with black magic. (1986:44)

But in positing Jerome Lee's macho posturing as a response to Moynihan's "emasculation" theory, Shockley recapitulates Moynihan's argument that black male deviance is the result of a historical emasculation that began with slavery, and she invokes racist stereotypes of black men, ultimately casting Jerome as the quintessential black rapist. Toward the end of the novel, Terry and Renay retreat from the city to a secluded country cottage. Jerome Lee finally discovers Renay, and the novel magnifies his brutality. When Renay is alone, he breaks into—or penetrates, if you will—the lesbian home, returning as the repressed image of the "wild black savage" (1986:130). He is described as a "hulking brown shadow," and as "a black giant whose Afro bush was too long and wildly matted. He was growing, by design or laziness, a beard which was ragged and hid most of his lower face like a mask" (1986:127). Shockley uses Jerome Lee's assault on Renay to establish the presence of domestic violence within the black community, and to respond to the negation of black women that developed partially out of black nationalism's focus on possessing the white woman as a symbol of conquest in the contest over power with white men. In a sense, Shockley addresses the way the focus on white women as the objects of black male violence elides sexual violence against black women.

But her satirical protest against black macho collapses into an exaggerated version of the black nationalists' own reclamation of black masculinity through the myth of the black man as rapist. Despite what Frank Lamont Phillips says in his infamous review of *Loving Her* to offend—and he does offend by articulating his complaints about the novel within the context of a diatribe against lesbian and interracial relationships—it is hard not to agree with his assessment that Jerome Lee embodies an offensive stereotype about black men:

> Jerome Lee is *so* insensitive, so purely physical and stupid . . . [he] grunts, beats his breast (and Renay), parades his penis, until one wonders why the author didn't just dress him in black: black cape with red lining, top hat, have him twirling his black handlebar mustache wickedly.[30]

Phillips is correct to observe that Jerome Lee's villainous behavior is juxtaposed with Terry's near saintly benevolence. Terry, a version of Stephen Gordon—the rich, noble-spirited, white writer—is a better provider, a better lover, and a better "father" than Jerome Lee.

Connected to *Loving Her*'s critique of black macho is the characterization of the black community as intrinsically homophobic. Shockley aligns black women's homophobia with the myth of black macho and its militant heterosexuality. Throughout the novel, Shockley represents heterosexual black women as gratifying the black male ego, "spoiling their men," and conspiring against other black women. Their devotion to black men is the source of a homophobia that runs deeper in black women than in white women. Black women are tolerant of social and moral ills such as illegitimacy and adultery, but are "vehement" in their opposition to black lesbianism, which they blame on white women (1986:31). Shockley also suggests that most black men are homophobic in the extreme as a result of their over-investment in their own masculinity. For example, one of the two black gay men who make brief appearances in the novel,

Clarence Wigginstone III, explains his presence in the white gay community as a form of exile. He feels isolated from the black community, but his one experience with a black male lover reaffirms the pervasiveness of black macho. Describing his ex to Renay, he says:

> "Dearie, the guy was big and ugly-looking as Sonny Liston". . . . "And treated me like *shit!* I suppose the black superstud image making it these days can't be tarnished. . . . And because of it, I don't believe there can or ever *will* be gentleness among black men." (1986:75)

Invoking Sonny Liston, the boxer infamous for his sexual appetites, his drug habits, and eventually for his violent death emphasizes the destructiveness of the macho ethos to which Shockley returns almost obsessively throughout the novel. Her reliance on this testosterone-driven image of black masculinity reinforces the characterization of the black community as homophobic by illustrating that there is no room for Clarence, the feminized black man, in a world that fetishizes "the black superstud image."

This representation of the black community as homophobic can be read as a response to black nationalism's formulation of homosexuality as a white man's disease. Baraka's description of the white man's impotency and effeminacy is perhaps the most infamous instance of such rhetoric:

> Most American white men are trained to be fags. For this reason it is no wonder that their faces are weak and blank, left without the hurt that reality makes—anytime. That red flush, those silk blue faggot eyes.[31]

Cleaver, in his discussion of James Baldwin, defines black homosexuality as a form of emasculation produced by submission to white power:

> The white man has deprived [the black homosexual] of his masculinity, castrated him in the center of his burning skull,

and when he submits to this change and takes the white man for his lover as well as his Big Daddy, he focuses on "whiteness" all the love in his pent up soul and turns the razor edge of hatred against "blackness"—upon himself, what he is, and all those who look like him, remind him of himself.[32]

In a 1970 letter "To the Revolutionary Brothers and Sisters about the Women's Liberation and Gay Liberation Movements," Huey Newton challenges such rhetoric, calling on black male revolutionaries to overcome their sexism and homophobia and to form alliances with both women and homosexuals:

> Sometimes our first instinct is to want to hit a homosexual in the mouth and to want a woman to be quiet. We want to hit the homosexual as soon as we see him because we're afraid we might be homosexual and want to hit the woman or shut her up because she might castrate us or take the nuts we may not have to begin with. . . . I don't remember us ever constituting any value that said a revolutionary must say offensive things toward homosexuals or that a revolutionary would make sure that women do not speak from their own particular kind of oppression. . . . there is nothing to say that a homosexual can not also be a revolutionary. And maybe even now I'm injecting some of my prejudice by saying "even a homosexual can be a revolutionary." Quite the contrary, maybe a homosexual could be the most revolutionary.[33]

His letter appears in an ephemeral pamphlet series published by Gay Flames, a group of male homosexuals active in New York's Gay Liberation front. His message never received the kind of publicity that might have helped to counter the predominant image of the black nationalist movement as homophobic and sexist. Given that image, Shockley's assertion that the black community is more homophobic than the white community may be seen not only as a reaction against the overt homophobia of black nationalism, but also as a strategy for shifting the rhetoric

of disease from homosexuality to homophobia, so that homophobia becomes a sign of sickness.

The blanket generalization that the black community is homophobic has come under fire since Shockley wrote *Loving Her*.
In the 1980s, black feminists began to reject "accusations of homophobia hurled at the black community by many gay men and
lesbians, as if the whole black community were more homophobic than the heterosexist culture we live in."[34] Shockley, writing
well before the 1980s, represents the black community's homophobia as psychically disruptive to the formation of a black lesbian identity. Consequently Renay must leave the black community in order to embrace her lesbian identity. Shockley's response
to black macho becomes a fantasy about escaping patriarchy,
sexism, and compulsory heterosexuality by crossing lines of
color and class into a utopian lesbian relationship. Terry's class
and race status are critical to Renay's "discovery" of her lesbianism; her wealth and whiteness allow Renay to escape the world
of poverty and brutality that Jerome Lee embodies. With Terry's
financial support, Renay leaves the dingy, cramped rooms that
she shares with Jerome Lee in a neighborhood of "crumbling,
low-rent apartment houses inhabited by struggling blacks and a
few blue collar white immigrants who had not yet saved enough
money to move away . . . [where] the streets were narrow and
crowded, inflamed with wasted grown-up faces and too-old ag-
gressive children" (1986:7).

Terry's apartment, in a fashionable building on "the edge of
the city where the streets were broader and cleaner and well-kept
lawns graced neat houses," is the site of Renay's attempt to
reestablish a home. In this white, upper-class milieu, the super-
markets themselves, clean, well-lit, and stocked with delicacies,
are more conducive to the production of domesticity than the
empty refrigerator in Renay's old apartment. Terry's money pur-
chases Renay's new identity; not only can Renay be a better wife
and mother under Terry's protection, but Terry buys her a piano
to replace the one that Jerome Lee sold to pay the rent. The piano

FIG. 1. *Miss Gay Pride 1988. Credit: Catherine Hennessy.*

FIG. 2. *Houston ACT UP march. Credit: Catherine Hennessy.*

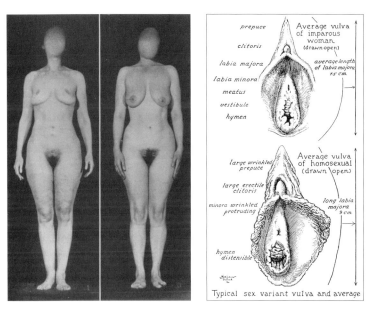

FIG. 3 *(left). Sex Variants, Figures 1 and 2. From George Henry,* Sex Variants. FIG. 4 *(right). Typical Sex Variant Vulva. From George Henry,* Sex Variants.

FIG. 5. *Radclyffe Hall and Lady Una Troubridge, August 1927. Photo:* © *Hulton Getty / Liaison Agency.*

FIG. 6. *Gertrude and Alice in the 1920s. The Beinecke Rare Book and Manuscript Library.*

FIG. 7. *Natalie Barney. Credit: George Wickes.*

Fig. 8 *(left). Gladys Bentley and friend. Estate of Eric Garber.* Fig. 9
(right). Gladys Bentley. Estate of Eric Garber.

FIG. 10. *Adelaide Hall in "Blackbirds." Photo: © Hulton Getty / Liai-son Agency.*

triggers Renay's reconstruction of the narrative of her own lesbian identity, which was always there but just unrecognized: "As she reflected on her life with Terry, whose gift of the piano had stirred the well of memories, she wondered about Miss Sims. She hadn't thought of her old teacher in years. Yet it was impossible to completely forget some segments of the past, especially when they fit in so neatly with the present" (1986:11). Miss Sims fits neatly into the present not only through the gift of the piano, but because looking back, Renay recognizes herself in Miss Sims. But when Renay returns home for a visit and meets Miss Sims's new "roommate," a woman with "a warm attractive smile and inscrutable dark eyes" (1986:148), she wonders if "Miss Sims faced the real reason for her new-found happiness? She and Miss Tremaine might live together for years in a close but sterile companionship, never understanding just why they were satisfied with each other" (1986:150).

By describing the relationship as a romantic friendship in which women deny and repress their sexual feelings for each other, Shockley implies that black homophobia precludes not only the existence of a black gay community, but even the existence of individual lesbians within a black community. Renay's discovery of her lesbianism, then, demands her move away from the black community. *Loving Her* is not so much a novel in which the black lesbian subject emerges as it is a novel in which the black lesbian subject gets subsumed into the white lesbian community.

The process of Renay's migration from one community into another depends upon representing her as light-skinned and feminine. If "commonsense" knowledge equates the racial body with blackness and the lesbian body with masculinity, Renay's femininity and her light, but not white skin, enables the perception of her racial and sexual difference to shift repeatedly as her relation to both the black community and the white lesbian community changes. To begin with, according to the conventions of the coming out narrative, which typically posit the butch as always having known about her sexual difference while the feminine lesbian comes to an awareness of her "true" sexual identity later in life, Renay's femininity enables her "discovery" of lesbianism. In turn, in American culture, where whiteness has been one of the conditions of femininity and the "mulatta" has been thought to approximate white standards of female beauty more closely than darker-skinned women, Renay's light skin enhances her femininity. Further, within the racial economy of lesbian representation, to describe Renay as dark-skinned might invoke the stereotype of the black "bulldagger," who is both dark and masculine. If Shockley does represent the black lesbian as feminine in order to resist the stereotype of the black bulldagger, then she seems forced toward the literary convention of the tragic mulatta. That is, because dark skin and femininity are at odds with each other both within dominant heterosexual and lesbian corporeal schemas, there is little precedent for depicting a lesbian who is both dark-skinned and feminine.

On the other hand, one might argue that the figure of the mulatta enables Shockley to create a character that can cross lines of color and class in ways that allow her to explore black lesbian identity within the context of a lesbian subculture that is predominantly white. The mulatta is characteristically indeterminate in terms of social position. As Barbara Christian argues, her racial background alienates her from "the upper-middle class society to which, by virtue of shade and taste, she rightfully belongs."[35] And as Lauren Berlant points out, she also has the capacity to "wear [her] gender according to a particular class style" that gives her access to the privileges of whiteness.[36]

Renay's ability to cross over into the white lesbian community lets Shockley explore the in/visibility of the black lesbian within that world, for Renay's movement into the white lesbian community is not without its own complications. The novel does not solve the problem of Renay's marginality as a lesbian within the black community through her move into the white community, where her racial difference perpetuates her position as outsider. When Terry introduces Renay to a white friend who exclaims, "For the first time in my life, I've met a black Lesbian!" (1986:72), the comment evokes the layered issues of visibility for the black, feminine lesbian. First, Renay is highly visible as black within the white lesbian community because of her skin color. The woman's comment calls attention to the equation of lesbianism with whiteness, and the cultural invisibility of the black lesbian—an invisibility that Shockley seems to perpetuate by suggesting that there is no black lesbian community, and that there are very few black lesbians in the white world. Simultaneously, the comment precipitates a crisis about the visibility not of race but of sexual orientation. Renay quickly determines that there is nothing to mark her lesbianism except for her association with Terry:

> The word [lesbian] staggered her as much as if the girl had called her a nigger. She was appalled at herself. How could she equate the two terms? The Lesbian as the nigger of sex? And was it noticeable now? She knew of no visible changes in herself. She still talked, looked and acted the same. (1986:72)

Renay's response highlights the connection between racial and sexual visibility. Not only does Renay struggle with her own equation of the words "Lesbian" and "nigger," but her paranoia about whether she shows any evidence of her newly discovered sexual orientation recalls the race passer's anxiety about "telltale" signs of blackness, revealing her desire to maintain a degree of invisibility in relation to lesbianism. Renay's visibility as a lesbian would seem to depend on the way Terry's body, not hers, signifies sexual deviance. Though the novel does not dwell on physical descriptions of Terry's butchness, she has the lean, small-hipped physique of Hall's invert.

But for the most part, Shockley minimizes questions of lesbian visibility. Terry contemplates the stigma of invertedness only briefly when she compares the oppressions of racism and homophobia, and decides that "her burden wasn't as visible, which made it easier to conceal" (1986:61). The most obvious homosexuals—the butches and drag queens who flaunt their sexuality in ways that irritate Terry and scare Renay—belong to the working-class milieu of the bars and parties that the couple increasingly avoids as they discover each other and try to create a world where differences of class and race present no obstacles to their union.

Fade to White: The Integrationist Ethos and the Fantasy of Racial Indifference

In *Loving Her*, the rhetoric of color-blindness is crucial to the interracial couple's success in transcending difference. As Renay moves away from the black, working-class world and into Terry's white, upper-class one, this rhetoric proliferates, intersecting with the ideology of liberal humanism that pervades the novel, and becomes totally intertwined with lesbianism. If color-blindness downplays racial difference, and liberal humanism assumes the universality of human nature, then the intersection of these two discourses allows Terry and Renay to avoid attaching any significance to superficial differences of race and class and to focus on the "real" person beneath the skin. Note, for example, how Shockley renders the dichotomy between inside and outside in the passage when Renay contemplates what it means to be in an interracial relationship. Renay tells Terry that as a black woman she is already toughened against oppression; her skin is "a hard dark shell to hide and protect all the hurts to come" (1986:37). She draws attention to her difference from Terry, but in language of interiority and exteriority that enables her to move past that difference immediately to seek what is "underneath" it: "Funny how she could love Terry so deeply that she did not see Terry's white skin—only knew of Terry's heart and the love in it" (1986:37).

However, the ideology of color-blindness in *Loving Her* does not so much preclude as displace the critique of racism that Shockley asserts. Unlike Bannon's work, which tends to regard racism almost purely as an individual pathology, examples of white racism pervade the novel to the extent that it must be recognized as a social institution. Even Terry and Renay's relationship is not devoid of the power dynamics ingrained in hierarchies of race and class difference. For example, while Beverly Smith astutely points out that Shockley doesn't address the fact that Renay's domesticity "meshes perfectly with the traditional black servant role," Shockley does suggest that racial difference complicates the dynamic of traditional butch and femme "roles" as they are played out in courtship, before Terry and Renay set up house.[37]

The couple's first meeting is fraught with tension. As a patron of the supper club where Renay works, Terry requests that Renay play Debussy. Renay assumes that Terry is making fun of her because of course "a nigger knows nothing but blues and jazz" (1986:19). But needing the twenty dollars that accompany the request, Renay plays "Claire de Lune." The room falls silent as all watch "the sad black girl in the bargain basement black dress with dime store accessories" (1986:19–20). When Terry later reveals her lesbianism, the suggestion that she can buy Renay is even more explicit: "I'm wealthy. I'm used to getting what I want, even if it means buying it. You've probably guessed what I am by now, or else you're terribly naive. I'm one of those women who prefers her own sex and I want you" (1986:22). Here Terry positions Renay as both prostitute and Cinderella.

I would argue that it is the pattern through which Shockley consistently undercuts her own observations about the significance of race and class differences that many readers find disturbing. Generally, the novel depicts Terry as innocent of prejudice and innately sympathetic to Renay's experience of racial oppression on the basis of her own experience of homosexual oppression. When Renay joins Terry at her table following the performance of "Claire de Lune," she discovers that Terry did not ask for Debussy to humiliate her by requesting something she would be unable to play. Rather, Terry likes Debussy and senses that Renay is gifted enough as a musician to do justice to the piece. So Renay's suspicion turns out to have been wrong after all, implying that she is guilty of "reverse racism."

Further, the novel represents love as salvation, revealing what Beverly Smith describes as Shockley's

> belief that it's [un]necessary for her characters to participate in consistent political struggle in order to change the conditions of their lives. Instead Renay and Terry's love for each other is presented as an individual solution to the racism, sexism and homophobia they face since, "it's perfectly obvious the two of [them] can't change the world." The dangerous notion that race makes no difference in their relationship also leads them to believe that they in fact have "already ended [racism] in [their] own individual way.[38]

Both Renay and Terry come to political consciousness of homophobia and racism, respectively, within the relationship and not before it. And in order to protect the relationship, the novel has to account for Terry's position as the exemplary white person.

To some extent the novel does so by establishing Terry's innate sympathy as a fellow outsider. But there are many gay characters in the book who are racist, and only one heterosexual character who shares Terry's status as an exemplary white person. Mrs. Stilling, Terry's educated, upper-crust neighbor at the cottage in the woods, accepts Terry and Renay's relationship openly and graciously. Terry and Mrs. Stilling discuss the "race factor" in the context of the way external prejudice may infiltrate Terry and Renay's relationship. But Terry's response to the question of whether the couple might resort in anger to "ugly racial slurs . . . [like] nigger [and] honkey" is, "No, I really don't think so. I look upon her as just Renay" (1986:173). There are no overt social or cultural explanations for Terry and Mrs. Stilling's high-minded difference from other whites. But the fact that they share the same class privilege suggests that Shockley sees racism as a working-class phenomenon, and the novel does tend to project racism onto working-class characters.

Though Terry's affluent neighbors in the city force the couple to move when they discover that Renay lives in their building, the incident is precipitated by Renay's run-in with Terry's housekeeper. Finding Renay at home on the day she comes to clean, Miss Wilby first assumes that Renay can only be present in the capacity of a maid who has taken her job, and then accuses Renay of stealing when she looks for the money that Terry has forgotten to leave her. The scene implies an analysis of the economics of racism that remains undeveloped. Shockley seems aware that Renay's domesticity puts her in the traditional role of the black servant, but projects the "real" threat of racism onto her working-class counterpart. Without a more developed portrait of Miss Wilby, she seems innately racist, just as Terry and Mrs. Stilling seem innately antiracist. Positing racism and antiracism as innate predispositions allows the notion of abstract individualism to prevail over a cultural critique of racism. If Terry and Mrs. Stilling can transcend the effects of institutional racism, then some individual pathology must afflict those who fail to transcend it.

Terry's jilted lover, Jean, exemplifies how Shockley posits racism as both a working-class phenomenon and an individual pathology. Like Angela in *The Well*, Jean is not a "real lesbian," but a shallow, opportunistic blond who taps Terry for money. Jean's gold-digging behavior fits the narrative of the working-class girl with aspirations of upward mobility. Blinded by her need for companionship, Terry sees more than is there in Jean. When Jean tries and fails to seduce Terry away from Renay, she shows her true character. Calling Renay a "nigger bitch" and Terry a "Goddamn Bulldike," she declares that she prefers men to women and never loved Terry but only used her, revealing her artifice and her prejudice at the same time (1986:56–57). Jean's racism and homophobia thus seem to be character defects that coincide with her generally superficial nature. This emphasis on

the origins of racism within the individual has unexplored implications for the rhetoric of color-blindness; it suggests that racism
will inevitably persist through those who do not have the ability
to see past color.

The complication suggested here is not one that Shockley
addresses, as is evident when Renay meditates on her ability to
love a white woman. Even when she considers how her own
light skin may attest to the origins of institutional racism in
slavery, when sexual contact between blacks and whites was
frequently an enactment of violence and domination, her romance with Terry supersedes a historicized contemplation of
race relations. As she "trace[s] the whiteness of Terry's skin
with her finger," Renay thinks:

> It is amazing how I can lie here and see and feel this skin and
> not think of the awful things others of her color have done to
> us. And yet, my skin is light—tinged with the sun. Someone,
> somewhere in the past, must have done and thought and felt
> like this with another—or hated in a different and helpless
> way. (1986:100)

But the impact of the last thought weakens as the two women go
on to make love and "merge" in simultaneous orgasm. The fantasy of merging sweeps away their difference.

There is a longing for difference *as* sameness operating within
Terry and Renay's relationship from the beginning of the novel.
In the first love scene, Terry murmurs that Renay is "so golden
brown, so beautiful," while Renay explores "the white body that
was new to her—the downy hair like peach fuzz on Terry's back,
the strength of her limbs, the small firmness of her breasts which
nestled against her own like twins" (1986:27). In the image of
the twin breasts, discourses of color-blindness intersect with lesbianism, which is already determined as sameness, especially in
the way that lesbianism is so frequently equated with narcissism.
The lovers eroticize race difference but mitigate the threat of that
difference through the mirror-image of their breasts against each

other. Ultimately, then, by relying on the rhetoric of color-blindness, the novel further divests Renay of black identity without interrupting Terry's white identity.

As Ruth Frankenburg explains, the logic of color-blindness holds that "people of color are 'good' only insofar as their 'coloredness' can be bracketed and ignored, and this bracketing is contingent on the ability or the decision—in fact, the virtue—of a 'noncolored'—or white—self."[39] To posit the couples' sameness "under the skin," then, is to posit that interior sameness as white, suggesting that Renay is like Terry—and not like Jerome Lee, and most especially not like the heterosexual black women who fall for Jerome Lee—"those bawdy phantoms who drank with him and had sex with him and who, too, were shadows of him, mirroring his audacity and self-destruction" (1986:130). Though *Loving Her* aestheticizes mirroring within the lesbian relationship, it pathologizes the mirroring between Jerome Lee and his girlfriends, which is grounded in the dissoluteness of the black community.

The same fantasy of difference as sameness enacted in *Loving Her* operates on another level in Bannon's *Women in the Shadows*. *Women in the Shadows*, in fact, makes more explicit that this fantasy negates blackness through the process of integration, because it emphasizes the black character's desire for self-annihilation. On one level, Bannon is self-reflexive about constructing the mulatta as exotic Other. When Laura first meets Tris in a dress shop, the novel practically lampoons the Orientalism of erotic pulp that features the sultry mulatta. In her initial admiration of Tris's beauty, which the novel codes as Eastern through the description of Tris's "jade green eyes" and the "tiny red dot between them on her brow, Indian fashion," Laura has "a brief vision of all that creamy tan skin unveiled and undulating to the rhythm of muffled gongs and bells and wailing reeds" (1986:32).

When Tris and Laura are most closely involved, however, the novel is much more earnest in representing the interracial relationship. Within that relationship, Tris's skin registers her own sickness about the matter of sexual identity through an unhealthy change in skin color (she blanches when asked to define herself), and Laura's egalitarian attitude toward Tris's racial difference indexes her relative healthiness about the matter of sexual identity. Proving that Laura is free of the very racism that Tris has internalized, Laura's previously satirized fetishization of Tris's skin gives way to Tris's unsatirized fetishization of Laura's whiteness, which she articulates here as envy. Covered in sunscreen and sitting under an umbrella, Tris admonishes Laura, who luxuriates in the sun, that she will burn:

> "Such fair skin you have." And Laura heard the yearning in her voice. "If mine were that light I would never expose it like you do. I'd do everything to keep it as light as I could. Even bleach it. They say buttermilk works wonders." (1986:94–95)

In the course of the conversation, Tris comments on how the two look when they lie on the bed together. Here, the eroticism of racial difference gives way to a fantasy of sameness in which Laura imagines that if Tris could be physically divested of her sense of difference through the act of lovemaking, and so cured of her internalized racism, she would also be cured of her internalized homophobia:

> "Me so white and you so brown. It looks like poetry, Tris. Like music, if you could see music. Your body looks so warm and mine looks so cool. And inside, we're just the other way around . . . I'm the one who's always on fire. And you're the iceberg. . . . Maybe I can melt you."
> "Better not. The brown comes off," Tris said cynically, but her strange thought excited Laura.
> "God, what a queer idea. . . . You'd have to touch me everywhere then, every corner of me, till we were both the same color. Then you'd be almost white and I'd be almost tan—and yet we'd be the same." (1986:95)

This passage records a permutation in the relationship between knowledge and the visible mapped out earlier in the novel, when the instability of Tris's racial identity, marked by the bindi as the sign of passing, indexes the instability of her sexual identity. When we first meet Tris, we understand that if she could accept herself as black, she would also accept herself as lesbian. Here the *erasure* rather than the exposure of racial difference would lead to the affirmation of lesbianism—and to the affirmation of whiteness. For in Laura's "queer" fantasy of lesbian lovemaking, Tris would become almost, but not quite, white, and Laura would retain her whiteness, becoming not almost black, but almost "tan." The residue of racial difference contained in the "almost" would be mitigated by the fact that the two women would be the same color, and color refers to shade without signifying a specific racial identity, but an amalgamation of light skin and white skin. This fantasy of racial "indifference" (where difference is both absent and insignificant) that is central to both *Women in the Shadows* and *Loving Her*, suggests that racial difference is seen as interfering with the emergence of lesbian identity. Lesbianism, constructed as sameness, demands a form of identification in which visible difference is both fetishized and refused.

In the previous chapters I have attempted to suggest how issues of visibility and identity are linked by showing that the construction of identity relies on the repudiation of differences that have been marked as Other within economies of the visible. In some way, identification has been central to the way the texts I have read to this point reveal the imbrication of racial and sexual identities. In both the *The Well of Loneliness* and *Strange Brother*, there is a moment when, in order to reconstitute unstable boundaries between self and Other, the subject refuses identification by constructing the Other's difference as visible or marked: Stephen refuses identification with the feminine, marked by whiteness, in order to consolidate her masculine identity; Mark refuses identification with the immigrant homosexual and the fairy in order to consolidate his masculine, middle-class homosexual identity, and June guards against lesbian erotic identification by marking the black woman's femininity as performative. In *Women in the Shadows* and in *Loving Her*, identification leads to the erasure of racial difference in order to preserve the integrity of the white lesbian subject. In the next chapter, I explore the act of identification within the psychoanalytic structure of fetishism more fully, turning my attention from the moment of disavowal, where cross-racial identification is refused, to the moment of recognition, where it is desired.

Strategies of Identification in Three Narratives of Female Development

This is the vision of Jane Eyre, small and pale. She is speaking of us. We dwell in the penumbra of the eclipse. In the half-darkness. They tell us the dark and light lie beyond us. "I feel sorry for you," the dark woman said. "You don't know who you are."
—Michelle Cliff, *Claiming an Identity They Taught Me to Despise*

During the 1980s, lesbian criticism began to theorize diversity in earnest. In ground-breaking texts such as *This Bridge Called My Back: Radical Writings by Women of Color* (1981), *Home Girls: A Black Feminist Anthology* (1983), Cherríe Moraga's *Loving in the War Years* (1983), Gloria Anzaldúa's *Borderlands/La Frontera: The New Mestiza* (1987), and Audre Lorde's *Sister Outsider* (1984), women of color called attention to racism within the lesbian community, and compellingly asserted that it erased differences among women and rendered the nonwhite lesbian invisible. At the same time, there was a revaluation of identity politics, and a concept of identity as multiple, fragmented, and contradictory emerged to accommodate the subject whose movement through a complex political terrain produced repeated shifts in self-other relations.

These developments were accompanied by a renewed interrogation into what the visible signified about identity—particularly regarding the focus on skin color as a signifier of racial identity and political affiliation. The performance art of Adrienne Piper, a light-skinned black woman often mistaken for white, attests to the fact that skin color can fail to mark racial identity. Similarly, the autobiographical work of Cherríe Moraga, a light-skinned Chicana lesbian, testifies to the anguish of bearing that mark of colonial violence (light skin) when it is construed as a sign of identification with the dominant white culture.

Michelle Cliff's *Abeng* (1984) is located in the moment when issues of visibility, difference, boundaries, and hybridity emerge in lesbian fiction and criticism. It pursues the questions of identification, desire, and political affiliation that are raised in *Loving Her* and explores them more fully in the context of colonial history. This autobiographical/fictional novel tells the story of Clare Savage, a light-skinned but "not quite/not white" Creole girl coming of age in Jamaica in 1958, four years before "Independence." Focusing on Clare's romantic attachment to her darker-skinned friend Zoe, the novel examines how race, class, and gender intersect to fragment rather than consolidate Clare's identity. For Clare, identification becomes the locus of nostalgia and yearning for the black woman, and the site of erotic investiture across culturally constructed lines of race and class difference. Read as the last novel in a series that includes Charlotte Brontë's *Jane Eyre* (1847) and Jean Rhys's *Wide Sargasso Sea* (1966), *Abeng* shows that the act of identification, which is central to female subject formation in the first two novels, is both eroticized and embedded within structures of visibility that are particular to the social and material history of colonialism.

In both criticism and the classroom, *Jane Eyre,* perhaps the best-known female *Bildungsroman* in English literature, and *Wide Sargasso Sea*, which gives voice to the other woman silenced in Brontë's novel by telling the story of Bertha Mason, are commonly paired to illustrate how a feminist critique of imperialism develops in the movement from representing the British white female subject to representing the (still white female) colonized West Indian subject.[1] Cliff deliberately places *Abeng* in relation to *Jane Eyre* and *Wide Sargasso Sea*, drawing on the figures and plots of the first two novels to extend the critique of colonial patriarchy and racism. She reconstructs a narrative of lesbian sexual awakening from the earlier novels, and foregrounds alternative sexual economies and anxieties about heterosexuality that are incipient in the apparently heterosexual narratives of female development in *Jane Eyre* and *Wide Sargasso Sea*.[2] By drawing on the narrative structures of the earlier novels to write a lesbian *Bildungsroman*, *Abeng* invites a rereading of the first two novels that delineates connections between the desire for identification across boundaries of visible differences and the emergence of the "lesbian novel."

To trace the development of the lesbian narrative and the coincidental emergence of race as that which more explicitly informs the desire for identification from one novel to the next, I read the texts in chronological order, beginning with *Jane Eyre* and ending with *Abeng*, though my reading of *Wide Sargasso Sea* is partial in that it treats the novel primarily as it links *Jane Eyre* with *Abeng*. In analyzing how these three narratives of female development both carry and resist patriarchal and colonial ideologies, *Wide Sargasso Sea* is most useful for the way it shows in a relatively schematic form what I discuss more fully in the other two novels. Because both psychoanalytic and postcolonial narratives of identification inform my reading of visibility and sexual identity in these three novels, I begin with a discussion of the way these two discourses imagine female identification, in particular, as existing outside social structures of visible difference.

Identification is central to issues of visibility and identity because it is an aspect of subject formation located in the field of vision. As the mechanism that produces both self-recognition and the apprehension of "difference," it is also the point where the psychological and the social converge. Identification has particular bearing on a reading of the lesbian novel because lesbianism itself is culturally formulated as a category of resemblance and doubly coded as a trope for identification. To begin with, heteronormative culture codes homosexuality in general as the desire for sameness ("like to like"). Further, psychoanalysis theorizes homosexuality as a desire to return to the moment of primary identification, and lesbianism in particular evokes that primordial signifier of mirroring, the mother-child dyad, as a figure for resemblance, because mother and daughter are of the same sex. If identification is, as Diana Fuss puts it, "the play of difference and similitude in self-other relations," then female identification, especially between mother and daughter, represents the predominance of similitude over difference.[3]

Psychoanalytic accounts of subject formation position the girl's primary identification with her mother in the mirror-stage, prior to the oedipal narrative of subject constitution that marks the child's entrance into the realm of the social.[4] In the mirror-stage the child responds to the sense of lack that accompanies the recognition of difference by seeking an imaginary wholeness with the mother.[5] The mother-daughter dyad is especially resonant for this imaginary wholeness because the category of resemblance ostensibly structures that same-sex relationship more intensely than the mother-son relationship. Presuming that resemblance structures the mother-daughter relationship, psychoanalysis relegates the daughter's primary identification with her mother to the space of the presocial where it appears to be "completely uninflected by the cultural markers associated with secondary identification" that takes place after the child's entry into the Oedipus complex.[6]

Even in neo- and postcolonial theory that challenges psychoanalysis to account for the racial formation of subjectivity, this scene of female identification that is uninflected by racial difference grounds the analysis of colonial racism. Perhaps the best example of post-colonial criticism's reference to this gendered fiction is Homi Bhabha's reading of Franz Fanon's "primal scene" of identification. This scene, in which a white boy sees Fanon and turns to his mother, crying "Look, a Negro . . . Mama, see the Negro! I'm frightened!"[7] appears in *Black Skin, White Masks*

(1952), Fanon's analysis of the psychology—or perhaps more accurately—the pathology of colonialism. Insisting on the connection between personal and social identity, Fanon dramatizes moments of looking and being looked at that describe how the black is marked as Other within the "racial epidermal schema" of colonial racism. Illustrating the violent dislocation of the black subject's identity from the marked body, the child's gaze and words fix Fanon like "a chemical solution is fixed by a dye"[8] and Fanon and the child mirror each other in their shivering:

> The nigger is shivering because he is cold, the little boy is trembling because he is afraid of the nigger, the nigger is shivering with cold, the cold that goes through your bones, the handsome little boy is trembling because he thinks that the nigger is quivering with rage, the little white boy throws himself into his mother's arms: Mama, the nigger's going to eat me up.[9]

Subject to the gaze of the white child, who affirms his own identity by turning away from blackness, Fanon becomes nothing more than what the white child sees: the black man as cannibal.

In a fascinating misreading, Bhabha transforms the child, who is male in Fanon's essay, into a girl. Analyzing the above scene, Bhabha writes: "the girl's gaze returns to her mother in the recognition and disavowal of the negroid type. . . . In the act of disavowal and fixation the colonial subject is returned to the narcissism of the Imaginary and its identification of an ideal-ego that is white and whole."[10] In Bhabha's version of the story, which rewrites the mirror-stage as a colonial moment in which colonizer and colonized are each bound by the image and the gaze of the Other, the female child returns to an imaginary wholeness in which racial difference can be disavowed because it does not exist between mother and daughter.[11] Here, female identification might be understood to represent a fantasy of "pure identification"—a moment of identification located in a realm of visual sameness that is uninterrupted by difference. In this moment, the subject seeks alignment with a figure that, reflecting its own idealized image of itself, evokes the sensation of wholeness and plenitude.

Presumably, though, all identification is threatened by difference, because the process of identification is itself enacted precisely to refuse the sight of differences that already exist. This, after all, is Bhabha's premise when he takes the Freudian account of gender difference, which is based in the realm of the scopic, as the paradigm for the colonial stereotype as "an arrested, fetishistic mode of representation within its field of identification."[12] Bhabha's work, which very usefully reconstructs psychoanalytic narratives of identity formation in terms of racial difference, represents the girl's identification with her mother as being unmarked by the physical indices and social structures of racial difference, even as it uses the narrative of her identification to theorize that difference.

In earlier chapters, I examined how fetishism worked through a process of "disidentification," where the subject consolidates her identity in relation to the Other whose difference is refused in the case of *The Well of Loneliness* and *Strange Brother*, or whose difference is erased and absorbed in the case of *Women in the Shadows* and *Loving Her*. Although none of these texts articulate a fantasy of pure identification that is completely uninflected by difference, I would argue that such a fantasy always grounds the moment of repudiation and/or erasure, when difference disrupts identification. In other words, every moment of failed identification presumes another, contrasting moment of identification that is uninterrupted by difference. The novels do not articulate this fantasy of pure identification because it is located in the realm of sameness rather than difference, and does not evoke the issues of visibility and marking that they explore.

To a certain extent, the novels I read in this chapter follow the paradigm I outline in my analysis of Bhabha. As in psychoanalysis, female identification circles around the figure of the mother in *Jane Eyre*, *Wide Sargasso Sea*, and *Abeng*, and in provisional and unstable ways the novels do invoke the fantasy of imaginary wholeness in response to the threat of visible difference. But the novels also critique the moment that Bhabha describes, where "the subject turns around the pivot of the 'stereotype' to return to a point of total identification,"[13] because they do not represent an originary point of total identification. Replaying the scene of female identification *within* the narrative of sociosexual development, the novels interject the social into the mirror-stage, and lead us to a critique of psychoanalysis and a revised understanding of visual identity. By returning female identification to the realm of the social, the novels are able to critique the fantasy of pure identification even as they invoke it.

The three novels I read in this chapter all disrupt the daughter's primary identification with the mother by portraying the dyad as already marked by difference that is figuratively or literally represented in terms of race. In *Abeng* and *Wide Sargasso Sea* especially, the mother is neither white nor whole, and the books are about the failure of identification that the mother's already fragmented identity produces for the daughter. As a result of this traumatic fragmentation, the daughter seeks new identifications with figures of "racial" difference who visually represent lost elements of the maternal. Through these new identifications, the novels replay the scene of the mirror-stage at points chronologically later than in the psychoanalytic narrative of subject formation—first during early childhood in response to the failure of the primary mother-daughter relationship that triggers the heroine's struggle to establish her own identity, and again in response to the onset of menstruation, which marks the girl's eligibility for entrance into the heterosexual economy of adulthood, marriage, and childbearing.

In each of the novels, the onset of menstruation occurs in (or is associated with) the socialized environment of school, where

romantic friendships between women signal the daughter's transference of her desire for a sheltering relationship with the mother
to another figure when the mother refuses her, indicating a movement away from the privatized arena of the mother-daughter relationship to a more public arena of female socialization.[14]
Within the sexualized narrative pattern of the novels, then, men-
struation/school is a trope with a double valence. It signifies
pleasurable unions with other women (the romantic friendships
of adolescence) and it (re)marks the girl's sexual difference,
denoting her own potential motherhood, and therefore her eligibility to enter a heterosexual economy of marriage and reproduction. School both allows and contains the possibility of lesbianism, and because lesbianism is so overdetermined as identification, it can be the place where writers explore the desire for
identification as opposed to its refusal. And whereas psychoanalytic narratives of sexual development locate lesbianism, as an instance of primary identification, outside the realm of the social,
the novels, as I have suggested above, read the visibility of racial
difference back into female identification and also return lesbianism to the realm of the social.

The narrative of lesbian identification and the representation
of racial difference are more muted in *Jane Eyre*, which works
through a strategy of disidentification to consolidate identity,
than in the later two novels. In *Jane Eyre* "lesbianism" is present
only as romantic friendship, and racial difference is almost invisible, and is often rendered through image and metaphor rather
than signified on the body. In reconstructing *Jane Eyre* to give
voice to Bertha Mason, *Wide Sargasso Sea* places Brontë's figurative representations of racial difference and colonialism in the
context of the historical reality of race relations that *Jane Eyre*
displaces. Rather than working through a strategy of disidentification, *Wide Sargasso Sea* works through a strategy of failed
identification, showing how visible differences among women
disrupt the desire for identifications across categories of racial
identity. In Rhys's novel, the white Creole's ambiguous racial sta-

tus makes her both the figure for that desire in that she is the locus of discourses about race mixing, and the figure for the impossibility of that desire in that she is the locus of discourses about racial purity.

Rhys thus replays the scene of the mirror-stage explicitly in terms of racial difference, which will most obviously and painfully create the distance between mother and daughter in *Abeng*. *Abeng* moves to an increasingly fragmented concept of identity, but unlike *Wide Sargasso Sea*, in the postmodern novel fragmentation does not have to lead to disintegration for the heroine. In Cliff's novel, difference most clearly disrupts the heroine's identification with other women, and most clearly informs her desire for other women. In *Wide Sargasso Sea*, Tia, the most explicitly racialized figure for desire, disappears as the narrative of female development becomes more sexualized and only returns imaginatively at the end of the novel with the death of the white Creole heroine. In *Abeng*, that figure is carried through the increasingly sexualized narrative. She not only remains the figure for desire, but she becomes part of the novel's "phantasmatic" resolution to the problem of identification. If all identifications are phantasmatic in that they are "efforts of alignment, loyalty, ambiguous and cross-corporeal cohabitation" that are acts of imagination never fully achieved,[15] then *Abeng* most clearly maps out the way visibility structures the tension in all three novels between the desire for and the impossibility of identification.

Jane Eyre and the Strategy of Disidentification

Initially, *Jane Eyre* seems least likely to offer much in the way of a reading for patterns of female identification and racial identity, either within the mother-child relationship or later in the narrative of female development. Although Bertha Mason, Rochester's white Creole wife, has been read as a figure for the colonized, race is an emblematic rather than a literal mark of difference in Brontë's novel. Biological mothers are conspicuously absent from the story, and the novel seems to propel Jane toward marriage. Further, Jane's disidentification with a series of other women drives her progress toward the fulfillment of the heterosexual narrative. Traditionally *Jane Eyre* has been read as the *ur* heterosexual romance novel, and certainly the passionate intensity of Jane's relationship with Rochester appeals at the level of romantic fantasy.

However, privileging the heterosexual love story refuses other familial and erotic economies that exist in the novel—economies that are structured around female identification. This refusal is enacted most obviously in criticism that actively resists the argument represented by Adrienne Rich's essay "*Jane Eyre*: The Temptations of a Motherless Woman" (1973), which is perhaps the most famous reading of the novel by a "known lesbian."[16] Rich looks for Brontë's depiction of alternatives to enforced heterosexuality and the stereotype of female rivalry. Other critics have implied that while Rich's reading should not be ignored, it misses the primary import of *Jane Eyre* as a novel that mirrors the desire of "many readers, including feminists" for "the bubble of bliss promised by [heterosexual] romantic love."[17] Further, they suggest that Rich's "denial of centrality to the love story expresses discomfort with female [hetero]sexuality and desire."[18]

As my bracketed terms indicate, such comments equate love and sexuality with heterosexuality. These readers allow that *Jane Eyre* represents both heterosexual and alternative erotic and familial economies, but they do not go beyond conceding that there is more than one way to read a book. I would argue not only that it is possible to read the novel for those alternative economies, but also that the heterosexual plot structure of Jane's subject constitution *depends* on a counternarrative of female identification, even as it demands its expulsion in order to realize the goal of that plot: Jane's marriage to Rochester. This counternarrative has often been described as one of disidentification or negation, in which other women represent versions of femininity that Jane rejects to invent herself as the ideal British woman.[19]

This negation is played out in the field of the visible through a form of color coding: the figures that Jane refuses, including Mrs. Reed, Blanche Ingram, and Bertha are devalued not only through descriptions of their greed, superficiality, and deceitfulness, but also through racialized descriptions of their appearance as "dark," "inflated," and "blackened." In contrast, the women with whom Jane identifies in a more positive way, such as Helen Burns, Miss Temple, and the cousins at Moor House, are described in terms of their personal and physical similarity to Jane. In the reading that follows, I cover some familiar ground in outlining this racialized splitting of femininity, and I develop an analysis of the erotic element of Jane's dis/identification with her "doubles."

The structure that I have identified as being common to all three novels, in which the narratives position menstruation/ school between scenes of maternal rejection and female identification on the one hand, and enforced heterosexuality on the other hand, exists in microcosm in the very first chapters of *Jane Eyre*. The novel opens with Jane "shrined in the double retirement" of the scarlet-draped window seat with a book, sheltered from the hostile arena of the nuclear family from which she has been excluded by Mrs. Reed, who does not regard Jane as one of her children. Brontë metaphorically represents the failure of this surrogate mother-daughter relationship in terms of racial difference. Jane is "a heterogeneous thing," an "alien" whom Mrs. Reed cannot abide because Jane is "an interloper, not of her race."[20] To compensate for her ostracism, Jane recreates a sense of maternal intimacy in the curtained space of the window seat. The books she peruses remind her of Bessie, the closest thing she has to a sympathetic mother figure. Jane associates the maidservant with rare moments of feeling nurtured when Bessie tells the children her own versions of love stories taken from fairy tales and from popular novels such as *Pamela*, as she crimps lace frills. Jane's contentment is short-lived. John Reed invades her sanctuary and reclaims her book in the name of the father; he hurls it at her and strikes her head, making her bleed.

As Elaine Showalter has argued, the incident signals both the onset of menstruation and the intrusion of patriarchy into the enclosed feminine space.[21] Figurative menstruation is followed by a replay of maternal rejection as Mrs. Reed banishes Jane to the red room. Looking into the mirror, Jane does not find self-recognition, but sees Mrs. Reed's vision of her as different. Unlike Mrs. Reed's plump, hardy children, Jane looks like "one of the tiny phantoms, half fairy, half imp, [that] Bessie's evening stories represented as coming out of lone, ferny dells in moors" (2.46).

Because *Jane Eyre* resists structures of female identification, Jane's own figurative racial status shifts in relation to the characters she is defined against.[22] Throughout these opening passages Jane's status as an outsider is rendered in terms of racial difference that serve both to mark her subjection and the Reeds' oppressiveness. For example, in the opening scenes, Jane is described as sitting "cross-legged, like a Turk" in the breakfast room, having been excluded from the family circle by Aunt Reed, and as a "rebel slave" (2.44). In a later passage, Georgiana Reed's whiteness, her "pink cheeks, and golden curls" which "seemed to give delight to all who looked at her, and to purchase indemnity for every fault" (2.47–48) imply by contrast Jane's darkness as a child whom Mrs. Reed would have be "lighter, franker, more natural" (1.39). But the Reeds' tyranny over Jane is also rendered in metaphors and descriptions that cast them as racial Others, as when John Reed "sometimes reviled [his mother] for her dark skin, similar to his own" (2.47). This shifting descriptive strategy is possible because, as Susan Meyer argues, Brontë uses racial difference to signify both the oppressed and the oppressor.[23]

At this point in the novel, the reiteration of the mirror-stage does not provide Jane with a unified image of herself, but offers her an image of herself as Other that she will overcome by finding substitutes to inhabit that position for her. The opening

scenes thus anticipate the impossibility of sustaining female identification, which the demands of patriarchal culture will repeatedly interrupt. But the opening scenes also establish that there is
never an uncompromised moment of female identification that
exists prior to that interruption. Jane's relationship with Bessie is
hardly idyllic. If Jane's relationship with Mrs. Reed is metaphorically marked by racial difference, her relationship with Bessie is
marked by a more literal class conflict. Bessie is given to remind-
ing Jane of her inferior social status as a dependent in the Reed
household, and the novel will tell the story of Jane's resistance to
being designated a dependent. To identify with Bessie would be
to acquiesce to a class status that Jane will rise above in the
course of the novel.

While *Wide Sargasso Sea* and *Abeng* will show daughters
trying to form alliances across boundaries of class and racial
differences and will suggest that the failure to secure these relationships produces problems with identity formation, Jane solidifies her identity by resisting identification with women and
by defining herself in opposition to a series of female figures,
both "good" and "bad," who represent forms of economic and
sexual acquiescence that Jane will spurn. Though she will ultimately refuse identification with all these figures, those who
consolidate her identity through differentiation are visually
coded as Other, while those who consolidate her identity
through self-recognition are described in terms of similitude.
The "bad figures" who threaten Jane's desire for family, beginning with Mrs. Reed and continuing through Jane's rivals
Blanche Ingram, Blanche's mother, the Dowager Lady Ingram,
and Bertha Mason, are large and dark-skinned, with "dark and
inflated" or "Roman features."

In an immediate sense, Jane learns what not to do by reference
to the examples of Rochester's dark or foreign lovers, Céline
Varens, Blanche Ingram, and Bertha Mason. She understands
that even if she lives with Rochester in a *whitewashed* villa on
the shores of the Mediterranean, she will be marked as sexually

impure, covered with the "grimy dishonour" that Rochester attributes to his foreign mistresses. On a more ideological plane, the novel uses discourses of racial difference to develop the feminist critique of patriarchy that consolidates Jane's identity. Jane refuses to let Rochester adorn her as a sultan would adorn his "harem inmates" (24.297).[24] Metaphorically, then, racial difference reinforces Jane's disidentification with these women.

On the other hand, the women who provide Jane with familial affection and support, such as Helen Burns, Miss Temple, and Mary and Diana, are visually similar to Jane. All are fair-complected with "refined features," large, "clear fronts" and well-defined eyes that, according to nineteenth-century race science, indicate their intelligence. In keeping with the structure of resemblance that will enable moments of positive identification in the novel, physical descriptions of Jane for the most part align her with the good mothers: Helen says that she reads "a sincere nature in [Jane's] ardent eyes and on [her] clear front" (8.101); Bessie remarks that Jane is "no beauty" but looks like "a lady" (10.123); and Jane is small and pale in contrast to large dark women like Blanche and Bertha.

Ultimately, Jane's disidentification with all these women will propel her through the narrative of female subject constitution. The progress of that narrative seems to follow the itinerary of heterosexuality, and in Brontë's novel, female identification frequently implies stasis, regression, stagnation, and immersion in that it stalls the forward movement of the heterosexual narrative impetus of Jane's development.[25] However, if we study the relationship between the novel's narrative of heterosexual development and its counternarrative of female identification, it becomes apparent not only that female identification impedes the heterosexual narrative, but also that the heterosexual narrative disrupts desirable and even eroticized female identifications.

The first scene of such eroticized identification takes place at Lowood, the charity school for girls where Miss Temple and Helen Burns befriend Jane. In the Lowood scenes, identification obviously depends on resemblance: Jane clearly admires Miss Temple's manners, sympathies, and interests, and tries to model herself after Helen, who takes Miss Temple's example of Christian deportment to the extreme of martyrdom. Jane first identifies with Helen when she finds her reading in the garden during breaks from lessons. This "occupation" strikes "a chord of sympathy" with Jane, whom we first met reading to escape the oppressiveness of her family life with the Reeds. Helen's choice of reading material, Samuel Johnson's oriental tale *Rasselas*, is consistent with her obsession with the after-life and the Heavenly Father—an obsession that will mark her difference from Jane, and compel Jane to disidentify with Helen as a role model.[26] *Rasselas*, about the adventures of its eponymous hero, son of the emperor of Abyssinia, his sister Nekayah, her beloved attendant Pekuah, and the well-traveled philosopher Imlac, has been traditionally read as a religious parable whose meditations on "the choice of life" point ultimately to the "choice of eternity."[27] But I would suggest that *Rasselas* might be read in ways that show Helen to be coded more complexly than just as Christian martyr; she may also stand for the unsustainable fantasy of a women's community.

Johnson's representation of harem life and of female desire for communities of educated women provides a context for reading the Lowood episodes of *Jane Eyre* in terms of the existence of female communities as an alternative to marriage and governessing, the two main options for women in Jane's social position.[28] In particular, the passages in *Rasselas* about the marriage debates and about Pekuah's captivity in an Arab tyrant's harem might signal Brontë's interest in school as the site of an independent female community. In the marriage debates, Nekayah argues with her brother that marriage is not a means of happiness but "one of the innumerable modes of human misery."[29] The harem episodes, where Pekuah laments the undereducation of women, inform the "choices of life" that the female characters make at the end of the novel—neither of which involves marriage. Pekuah wants to be prioress of a convent and Nekayah wants to preside over a women's college. *Rasselas* appears to offer an alternative to marriage as the resolution of the female narrative of development, but finally it suspends the question of marriage when it dictates that these women's communities will not be created because none of the characters can realize their "choices of life."

Whereas *Rasselas* does not specify why the characters cannot realize their choices, *Jane Eyre* makes it clear that patriarchy controls women's relationships with each other. Like a harem, Lowood is presided over by a despotic man, Mr. Brocklehurst. But Jane discovers in Miss Temple and Helen a "sympathy," both intellectual and emotional, that is charged with maternal/erotic feeling. Miss Temple is a nurturing but distant maternal figure. As she approaches the girls one evening, she is associated with the moon, which will recur as a figure for the mother/goddess later in the novel: "[the moon's] light, streaming in through a window near, shone full both on us and on the approaching figure, which we at once recognized as Miss Temple" (8.102). Miss Temple both attends to and distances herself from her charges. Jane observes that there is about her something that "precluded deviation into the ardent, the excited, the eager: something which chastened the pleasure of those who looked on her, and listened to her, by a controlling sense of awe"—she is cold, marble (8.104).

But Helen Burns, as her name suggests, is passionate. The novel describes her intellectual/spiritual rapture in eroticized language:

> Something . . . had roused her powers within her. They woke, they kindled: first, they glowed in the bright tint of her cheek . . . then they shone in the liquid lustre of her eyes, which had suddenly acquired a beauty more singular than that of Miss Temple's—a beauty neither of fine colour nor long eyelash, nor pencilled brow, but of meaning, of movement, of radiance. Then her soul sat on her lips, and language flowed, from what source I cannot tell; has a girl of fourteen a heart large enough,

vigorous enough to hold the swelling spring of pure, full, fervid eloquence? (8.104–5)

If Miss Temple's distance precludes the kind of passion that Jane seems to yearn for, Jane does experience the physical intimacy that she craves with Helen in a scene that evokes the eroticism of the mother-daughter relationship. When Jane seeks out the tubercular Helen, she finds her in a crib close to Miss Temple's bed, "half covered with its white curtains" (9.112). She hesitates before advancing past the curtain, but on Helen's invitation, joins her in bed and wraps her arms around her neck; the two whisper before falling asleep together.

The novel underscores the impossibility of sustaining the pleasures of such intimacy, for the sleeping Jane embraces Helen only on her deathbed. School is the site of both pleasurable unions with women and of the dissemination of patriarchal ideologies. Not only is Lowood supervised by Mr. Brocklehurst, who delimits the girls' lives by demanding that any evidence of their femininity, even curls and braids, be removed, but Brontë suggests that the way to escape such patriarchal tyranny is to find what Jean Wyatt terms "a patriarch of one's own." Helen leaves Jane to go to God the Father, Miss Temple leaves Jane to marry a clergyman, and Jane will leave the school and meet Rochester.

The novel replays a structural pattern through which patriarchal control interrupts Jane's maternal/erotic identification with women around the scene of Jane's impending wedding, linking Bertha Mason, Jane's rival, and Adèle, Jane's pupil, to the series of other women who precede them in the text. Jane's relationship with Bertha is usually read as a moment of negative identification that is marked by their visible difference from each other.[30] But during the incident that occurs before Jane's wedding, in which Bertha puts on Jane's bridal veil and stands before the mirror, Bertha visually represents the identification between Jane and her dark Others that Jane herself has refused throughout the novel.[31] Further, a kind of eroticism charges this moment of identification that recalls, literally in a darker form, the rapturous, fiery intensity of Helen's face when her "powers" are "roused." In the horrified description of Bertha's physical proximity as she hovers over Jane's bed, almost in the gesture of a mother checking on a sleeping child, there is something at once nurturing and sexual, protective and threatening:[32]

> Just at my bedside the figure stopped: the fiery eyes glared upon me—she thrust up her candle close to my face, and extinguished it under my eyes. I was aware her lurid visage flamed over mine, and I lost consciousness: for the second time in my life—only the second time—I became insensible from terror. (25.311–12)

The allusion to the moonlit red room, the site of Jane's first loss of consciousness and her figurative menarche, suggests that this scene is also a moment of figurative menstruation that marks Jane's liminal position between the worlds of female community and marriage. In this socialized version of the mirror-stage, the text invokes an erotic identification between the white woman and her dark Other that threatens to collapse Jane's identity. To mitigate the threat of such an identification, the novel plays out the pattern of disidentification with the Other who is visibly different through a return to the fantasy of pure identification.

The novel acts out this scenario by taking Bertha's association with the menstrual/lunar cycle and splitting her into two figures for the mother, one light and one dark, that embody the ambivalence about the maternal and female identification that runs throughout the novel. The blood-red moon that rises on the evening of Bertha's appearance connects her with bad, dark mothers such as Mrs. Reed and Lady Ingram, whose passions are not tempered and who are greedy and sexual. Bertha represents anxieties about the violence of the mother-daughter relationship that Mrs. Reed captures when she looks on Jane as being "a compound of virulent passions, mean spirit, and dangerous duplicity"—a description that the reader understands to apply to Mrs. Reed more than to Jane (2.50). Seen in this light, the novel's ultimate expulsion of Bertha signifies the expulsion of the violent and passionate aspects of the maternal.

This expulsion of the Other coincides with the desexualization of maternal/erotic identification that we saw in the Lowood chapters, and with the manifestation of the white moon goddess to replace the bad mother associated with the red moon. Following Bertha's bedside visitation, Rochester requests that Jane spend the night with her pupil Adèle. As in Bhabha's analysis, then, Jane turns away from the specter of difference to identify with a child who now mirrors her: "She seemed the emblem of my past life; and he I was now to carry myself to meet, the dread, but adored, type of my unknown future day" (25.314). The fact that Adèle, as the daughter of Céline Varens (the French actress who was Rochester's debauched lover following the disintegration of his marriage with Bertha) is part of a series of women whose Otherness is marked by their dark and foreign looks compounds the refusal of difference enacted here. The novel must temporarily elide Adèle's status as Other in order to facilitate this idealized moment of identification.

In recasting the Lowood scene of the young girl in the older one's arms, the novel also drains the relationship between Helen and Jane of any passionate affection. Jane looks at Adèle, whom she is fond of but not strongly attached to, and sees the "slumber of childhood—so tranquil, so passionless, so innocent" (25.313). There is a tension between this representation of childhood as passionless (which seems ironic in light of the fact that Jane was all emotion as a child and Adèle is all coquette), and the scene in which Jane parts from Adèle in the morning, which represents the strength of Adèle's (even unconscious) bond with and hold on Jane:[33]

> I remember Adèle clung to me as I left her: I remember I kissed her as I loosened her little hands from my neck; and I cried

over her with strange emotion, and quitted her because I
feared my sobs would break her still sound repose. (25.314)

The discrepancy between the characterization of childhood as
passionless and the imagery of intense bonding that suffuses
Jane's regret at leaving Adèle suggests that for Brontë, the narrative of heterosexuality, represented by Jane's impending marriage, must deny or displace the erotic elements of female bonding. This is consistent with the ensuing apparition of the mother
as a ghostlike figure of the moon in "white human form" that appears to Jane in a dream on what was to have been her wedding
night and whispers to her, "My daughter, flee temptation"
(27.346). Bertha's earlier visitation is "paradoxically akin to the
mediation of [this] natural, maternal force in warning against the
impending marriage."[34] But in this apparition, Bertha is "puri-
fied"; no longer associated with the blood-red moon, she is desexualized and whitened.

Having reconstituted the threatening Other as safe by desexu-
alizing and whitening her, the explicitly racialized figure drops
out of the narrative, and the novel will maintain the category of
resemblance within female identification as it moves toward the
resolution of the heterosexual plot. The Moor House chapters
that follow Jane's flight from the bigamous marriage with
Rochester emphasize how the narrative of heterosexuality in *Jane
Eyre* demands the expulsion of female identification. Here, as in
the Lowood chapters, school signifies both the desire for a community of intellectual women and the dissemination of patriarchal ideologies. Near death after days on the moors, Jane arrives
at Moor House and peers in the window at two women reading,
a scene that recalls earlier instances of Helen and Jane reading.
Further, as Rich points out, these "unmarried bluestockings
[who] delight in learning" "bear the names of the pagan and
Christian aspects of the Great Goddess—Diana or Artemis, the
Virgin huntress, and Mary, the Virgin Mother."[35] Though the references to virginity might encode "a refusal to see maternity

linked with sexuality,"[36] they might also underscore the woman-centeredness of Jane's bonds with the sisters who embrace her, implying perhaps that we need not read the refusal of heterosexual intercourse and reproduction associated with virginity as a refusal of any or all sexuality. At this point in the narrative of Jane's subject constitution, Moor House represents an alternative to the sexual exploitation implied in Rochester's request that Jane become his mistress since he cannot have her for his wife.

Within the developing scene of the female domestic, St. John Rivers appears as the patriarch who will enforce the law, if not the romance, of heterosexuality. The language through which he tries to persuade Jane to marry him is striking in its equation of female bonding with sterility. Rivers disapproves of Jane's plans to remain at Moor House with Mary and Diana and to teach at Morton school after she receives her inheritance. He tells her that Marsh End is "not the scene of fruition," that she should "look beyond Moor House and Morton, and sisterly society and the selfish calm and sensual comfort of civilized affluence" (33.416–17), and that if she refuses to marry him she will "limit [herself] for ever to a track of selfish ease and barren obscurity" (33.434).[37] Rivers's will to domination is, as Rochester's was earlier, represented through the discourse of colonialism.[38] Rivers takes Jane away from her study of German, the language that Diana and Mary read, and makes her learn Hindustani, the language of the colonized, so that she can accompany him to India as a missionary's wife. Jane describes herself as being fettered and in his servitude.

If Brontë will redeem St. John's colonialism in her complicity with what Gayatri Spivak describes as "the unquestioned idiom of imperialist presuppositions" that underlies Jane's emergence as a heterosexual (and therefore legitimate) subject following her marriage,[39] in the Moor House chapters the ideologies of colonialism, patriarchy, and heterosexuality clearly restrict rather than enable Jane's subject constitution. It is easy to minimize the significance of the Moor House episode as a site of resistance to the heteropatriarchal order because it does, after all, end with presumably happy marriages for all three women. For example, Wyatt argues that although the episode presents an "alternative lifestyle" for Jane, one based on sisterly affection, it serves a more important function for the heterosexual plot because it alleviates anxieties about the incestuous nature of Jane's in-house relationship with the older Rochester by providing Jane with a family unit which she can then leave to marry "an exogamous lover—Rochester after all."[40] For Wyatt, "the sequence is the message": "To introduce the possibility of a community of women based on shared intellectual pleasures and mutual affection, only to reject it without question for a man, does not so much suggest an alternative as affirm the cultural myth that without a man a woman's life is incomplete."[41]

I would argue, however, that the question of whether Jane gives up the possibility of a community of women without hesitation is debatable. Even if Moor House can serve as an example of how female identification is a form of stasis for Jane, as Pauline Nestor observes, the language of attachment is strong in Jane's description of her desire to keep house with her cousins:

> Jane's cousin Diana exhorts her to "be obedient" (349), and at Moor-House Jane is once more overwhelmed by an attractive and intelligent female figure who offers her nurture and ministration. Accordingly, she finds that she takes "pleasure in yielding to an authority" (348) like Diana's, and a certain stasis overtakes her again. . . . In her clinging "tenaciously to the ties of flesh" (395) Jane forswears any determination to "go forth": "I will live at Moor-House . . . I will attach myself for life to Diana and Mary" (391). Thus, ironically, the contentment she could not muster to earn Mrs Reed's approval at the beginning of the novel, she determinedly embraces at Moor-House: "'St. John,' I said, 'I think you are almost wicked to talk so. I am disposed to be as content as a queen, and you try to stir me up to restlessness!'"[42]

Although Jane's ties here, even those "of the flesh," are not so much erotic as familial, Jane refuses without question the prospect of becoming St. John's wife rather than living "content as a queen" with her "sisters." Further, although the narrative of heterosexuality will interrupt Jane's relationship with Mary and Diana as it did earlier with Miss Temple and Helen, Jane's bond with her cousins is perhaps the only instance of identification in the novel that is unmarked by structures of opposition. Jane defines herself in sympathy with these women whom she resembles, and in whom she takes "the pleasure arising from perfect congeniality of tastes, sentiments, and principles" (30.376).

Certainly, Jane's "sympathy" or identification with her cousins is based on the conservative impulse toward class solidarity. Mary and Diana prove satisfying as companions where Mrs. Fairfax and Bessie, and even Helen and Miss Temple as women working under male authority, did not. But Jane's expression of her affinity to Mary and Diana is not characterized by the feelings of restlessness and "self-submersion" that define her friendships with other women.[43] This suggests that the Moor House episode does not propel Jane toward heterosexuality in the same way that her earlier dis/identifications with women do. Unmarked by structures of difference and erotic tension, the Moor House scene does not threaten the consolidation of Jane's identity as white, middle-class, and heterosexual. So while it does not foreclose or oppose the novel's conclusion in heterosexual romance with Rochester, it does stand as a viable alternative to the heteropatriarchal order represented by St. John.

Mirroring and Fragmentation in Wide Sargasso Sea

Like *Jane Eyre*, *Wide Sargasso Sea* begins with the failure of the mother-daughter relationship, which it articulates in terms of differences in racial identification and affiliation. The opening lines of *Wide Sargasso Sea* foreground the legacy of Jamaica's colonial history by establishing the ambiguous race and class status of white Creoles following Emancipation: "They say when trouble comes close ranks, and so the white people did. But we were not in their ranks."[44] The white Creole marks both the distinction and the collapse of distinction between black and white because she embodies the white colonist's anxieties that contact with the black slave population will threaten racial purity. Rhys marks "Bertha's" liminal status, defining her as white Creole, or at least passing for white (rather than black Creole or mulatta), but also describes her in terms of darkness and blackness, especially through her "dark, alien eyes" (1982:67). Rochester will later re-iterate the distinction that the new colonialists, who are fresh from England, maintain between themselves and the former slave holders when he says of his West Indian bride that she is "Creole of pure English descent . . . but . . . not English or European either" (1982:67). This duality allows for a shifting pattern of racial identification and the insertion of racial difference into the mother-child dyad.

For Antoinette Cosway, Rhys's reconstitution of Brontë's Bertha Mason, the changing colonial relations among the English, the white Creoles, and the former slaves destabilize the structures of identification that defined her mother's race and class affiliations. Though mother and daughter share the same racial heritage, the difference in their alliances proves problematic; Annette Cosway rejects her daughter's too-close association with black slaves because it reminds her of their ambiguous identity as white Creoles. The link between Annette's struggle to maintain her tenuous social position and her rejection of her daughter becomes clear when Antoinette appears before nouveau riche white neighbors in her black playmate Tia's dirty dress. Antoinette shames her mother by making visible the family's status as "white niggers" (1982:24) just as Annette is being courted by a newly arrived Englishman who offers her the possibility of reassimilating into the post-Emancipation white society.

At this moment, mother and daughter represent figuratively different racial and class identities, and Annette refuses the daughter's embodiment as "white nigger." Following this scene, Annette continually pushes her daughter away from her, preferring the company of her crippled son, Pierre. She clings to the mute boy as a symbol of the patriarchally structured (if now debilitated) plantation society in which her subject position was well-defined, and turns away from Antoinette, who so painfully mirrors her own sense of fragmentation.

Whereas in *Jane Eyre* maternal rejection activates Jane's solidification of her own identity in opposition to a series of other women, in *Wide Sargasso Sea* it results in an identity marked by conflict. Antoinette will alternately long to be black, fear blackness and assume white privilege, and ultimately, like her mother, she will be sacrificed to the renegotiation of colonial power between men.[45] And while *Jane Eyre* resists female identification to allow heterosexual romance to prevail, *Wide Sargasso Sea*, in which the plot of *Jane Eyre* predetermines the failed relationship between Antoinette and Rochester, focuses on the desire for identification.

Both the desire for and failure of identification across boundaries of racial difference are encapsulated in the scene in which Antoinette is faced with the irreducible differences between herself and her childhood playmate, Tia. Having been rejected by her mother, Antoinette seeks care and companionship from the people her family had formerly enslaved. She turns to Christophine, the housekeeper who remains with the family after Emancipation, for the nurturing her mother refuses her, and Christophine in turn procures Tia as a "friend" for Antoinette. The two girls spend their days at the bathing pool until Annette remarries, and she and her husband try to restore the family estate to its former prosperity. The African Caribbean community sets fire to this symbol of refurbished colonial property and watches it burn to the ground. Escaping her flaming house, Antoinette turns to Tia, who is standing in the crowd. In a moment of intense identification that is tied in with her need for her mother, she fantasizes that she can merge with Tia:

> I saw Tia and her mother and I ran to her, for she was all that
> was left of my life as it had been. We had eaten the same food,
> slept side by side, bathed in the same river. As I ran, I thought,
> I will live with Tia and I will be like her. (1982:45)

Tia and her mother stand for the unified mother-daughter dyad. In running toward "her" (the unclear pronoun referent merges Tia and her mother), Antoinette hopes to remain at the home which she associates with her mother's presence. But Antoinette's fantasy of pleasurable identification is shattered when Tia throws a stone, hitting Antoinette's head.

This scene recalls the opening chapters of *Jane Eyre*, when John Reed hits Jane with a book. Paralleling Brontë's novel, where Jane recognizes in the red room mirror the image of herself as Other, Antoinette sees herself as Other mirrored in Tia's face: "We stared at each other, blood on my face, tears on hers. It was as if I saw myself. Like in a looking-glass" (1982:45). But where *Jane Eyre* uses racial difference metaphorically to define the Reeds as the oppressors and Jane as the oppressed in a way that consolidates Jane's assumption of a unified identity, *Wide Sargasso Sea* replays the mirror-stage to emphasize the disruption of unified identity for both the black and the white child. Antoinette attempts to stabilize her own identity by fixing Tia within the imaginary wholeness of the mother-child dyad, but Tia can only mirror Antoinette's sense of difference because she is herself marked as Other.

This incident not only signals the end of Antoinette's friendship with Tia but also portends her marriage to Rochester, inscribing the connection between the maternal and the menstrual as structural narrative elements that denote the unhappy transition from the fantasy of female identification to enforced heterosexuality and colonialism. As in *Jane Eyre*, the blow that Antoinette receives causes her to bleed and faint, signaling the end of childhood and the figurative onset of menses. When Antoinette later asks if the wound left by the stone will leave a mark on her forehead, her aunt responds, "It won't spoil you on your wedding day" (1982:47), alluding to virginity as a form of unmarkedness; Antoinette's physical purity is intact. But the signifiers of racial difference and sexual status collapse here. As the figurative mark of Antoinette's relatively intimate if complicated relationships with blacks, the wound stands for a form of racial impurity that will separate her from the English Rochester. Even though the wound will appear to heal, making that impurity invisible, her difference will not only spoil her wedding day but destroy her identity.

Wide Sargasso Sea develops *Jane Eyre*'s nascent connection between the maternal, the menstrual, and the emergence of lesbian eroticism as a site of resistance to the destructive regulations of enforced heterosexuality and colonialism. Between the burning of Coulibri and Antoinette's wedding day, *Wide Sargasso Sea* describes Antoinette's adolescent years at convent school. In this all-female environment that discourages vanity and espouses chastity, the girls admire and model themselves after each other, and also eroticize each other. Tia is left behind, and the explicitly racialized figure drops out of the narrative as it becomes more sexualized. However, Antoinette's sensuous description of her schoolmate Louise de Plana, a Creole girl who reminds her of her mother, eroticizes Louise's darkness and West Indianness: "Ah but Louise! Her small waist, her thin brown hands, her black curls which smelled of vetiver, her high sweet voice, singing so carelessly in Chapel about death" (1982:55).

Louise's brown skin and black hair are the marks of the Creole woman's exoticism, and the smell of vetiver will become the signifier of the Creole woman's unrestrained sensuality by the end of the novel when Antoinette, locked in the attic at Thornfield, will find one of her favorite red dresses in a closet, faintly redolent of "vetivert and frangipanni, of cinnamon and dust and lime trees when they are flowering" (1982:185). Rhys constructs the convent school's curriculum as the vehicle for both erotic and maternal identification and the dissemination of heterosexual ideologies. Antoinette appropriates narratives of heterosexual romance from the lives of the saints, who are all "loved by rich and handsome young men" (1982:53), to recall her mother in the shape of Louise. Antoinette personifies the countries that the saints are from. Thus "France is a lady with black hair wearing a white dress because Louise was born in France fifteen years ago, and my mother, whom I must forget and pray for as though she were dead, though she is living, liked to dress in white" (1982:55). In this passage, Annette's yearning for the mother and the dark Other are brought together in the description of Louise.

Though the girls are taught to recite narratives of heterosexuality at the convent, Antoinette regards the presage of marriage in her own life as an intrusion on this sheltered female space. After a visit from Antoinette's stepfather in which she is given to understand that she will make her debut shortly, Antoinette has a dream that foreshadows how Rochester will betray her, and that recalls the imagery of nighttime, overgrown gardens, and impeded travel that haunts Jane's dreams before her first wedding day. On the verge of entering into the heterosexual economy, Antoinette fantasizes a return to the maternal. When she wakes from her nightmare, Sister Marie Augustine is standing by her bed and leads her from the dormitory so she will not disturb the other girls. Erotic overtones characterize Antoinette's desire for the intimacy of the mother's comforting bedside attentions; she wonders to herself if the Sister "will take [her] behind the mysterious curtains to the place where she sleeps" (1982:60).

The scene evokes an earlier one in the novel in which Antoinette wakes from a nightmare to find her mother beside her bed. Her mother covers her but then leaves her to go to her brother. Alone, Antoinette sees that "the light of the candle in Pierre's room [is] still there," signifying her exclusion from her mother's warmer relationship with her brother (1982:27). As in *Jane Eyre*, where Jane spends the night before her wedding with

Adèle, recalling her night with Helen in Miss Temple's bed, *Wide Sargasso Sea* positions the mother's bed as a place of comfort and enclosure that is Antoinette's last refuge before the marriage contract negotiated between her brother and Rochester will place her in a fatally heterosexual relationship.

Savage Genealogy: **Abeng**'s White Fathers and Mythic Mothers

Abeng crystallizes the incipient lesbian sexuality in *Wide Sargasso Sea* and *Jane Eyre* by rendering the maternal and the menstrual as structural elements of an explicitly lesbian narrative of female development. Of the three novels, it most clearly interrogates colonial race relations by critiquing the fiction of pure identification and by figuring lesbian sexuality as a response to the disruption of both female identification *and* racial affiliation as related aspects of subject formation. Not only do visible differences in shade literally, rather than figuratively, come between mother and daughter in *Abeng*, but the desire for the mother in the figure of the explicitly racialized Other does not drop out of the novel as the narrative of female development becomes sexualized. For Cliff's protagonist, the childhood relationship between the light-skinned girl and the black girl that disappears in *Wide Sargasso Sea* when Antoinette goes to school carries over into adolescent explorations of sexual identity. Finally, *Abeng* extends the critique of pure identification that is implied in the earlier novels. It sets the narrative of female identification against the narrative of compulsory heterosexuality and against the patriarchal imperative that demands that "white" women uphold the boundaries of racial difference. Whereas in *Jane Eyre* we have a heroine with no parents, and in *Wide Sargasso Sea* we have a heroine with a mother but no father, in *Abeng* the introduction of the assimilationist father delineates the connection between compulsory heterosexuality and discourses of racial purity. *Abeng* suggests that cross-racial, erotic identification between women threatens both race and gender privilege because it refuses to value and reproduce resemblances that ensure white superiority.

The issues of heredity, identity, and desire taken up in *Abeng* recall Michel Foucault's formulation of genealogy as a method of analysis that critiques the search for pure origins. Foucault's concept of genealogy lends itself to a reading of Cliff because it is firmly located in the scopic, the same realm that Clare, the novel's protagonist, struggles to decipher. Genealogy turns around the act of looking and "corresponds to the acuity of glance that distinguishes, separates, and disperses."[46] Genealogy's task is to read the marks of difference on the text of the body that presents the illusion of unitary identity:

> The body manifests the stigmata of past experience and also gives rise to desires, failings, and errors. These elements may join in a body where they achieve a sudden expression, but as often, their encounter is an engagement in which they efface each other, where the body becomes the pretext of their insurmountable conflict.
>
> The body is the inscribed surface of events (traced by language and dissolved by ideas), the locus of a dissociated self (adopting the illusion of a substantial unity), and a volume in perpetual disintegration. Genealogy, as analysis of descent, is thus situated within the articulation of the body and history. Its task is to expose a body totally imprinted by history and the process of history's destruction of the body.[47]

In *Abeng*, it is the "desires, failings, and errors" of colonial history that imprint Clare's body, which is the site (sight) of contradiction about her identity as a light-skinned but not white Jamaican girl. Her family history is the history of colonized Jamaica, and Clare's struggle to make sense of the disparate lineages her father and mother represent is also her struggle to locate herself amidst competing discourses about color, class, gender, and sexuality. Both Clare's parents are descendants of African slaves and European plantation owners, but her family maintains the fiction that its racial ancestry is split down maternal and paternal bloodlines. Her father's family, the Savages, self-identify as white, while her mother's family, the Freemans, self-identify as black. The family names reverse the colonialist association of savagery with blackness and freedom with whiteness, suggesting that signifiers of racial difference are arbitrary and shifting. Each parent withholds from Clare the possibility of claiming a multicultural identity. Clare, then, must take up the enterprise of the genealogist, who "sets out to study the beginning—numberless beginnings, whose faint traces and hints of color are readily seen by a historical eye."[48] Clare struggles to discover her African heritage in order to forge an identification with blackness that her light skin and hair belie.

In this task, Clare is thwarted by her father, Boy Savage, who stands for the pursuit of pure (white) origins, and constructs Clare's lightness as the "phenotype of assimilation."[49] As Boy's first name suggests, he has submitted to the values and hierarchies of colonialism. He denies his black heritage, insisting on his family's uninterruptedly white descent from a wealthy English colonist in spite of the fact that "the Savages were hard put to explain the changes in their complexions, eyes, and hair, and why so many of them had freckles."[50] Boy's concept of history also validates colonialist fictions of origin. He gives Jamaica a classical Western lineage, explaining to Clare that the West Indies are the remains of Atlantis or Crete. And he is like Foucault's philosopher, who imagines the origin of things to be "the moment of their greatest perfection, when they emerged dazzling from the hands of a creator":[51]

> Mr. Savage was fascinated by myth and natural disaster. He collected books on Stonehenge, the Pyramids, the Great Wall of China—he knew the details of each ancient structure and was convinced that all were connected to some "divine plan," he said. . . . Nothing was an achievement of human

labor. Devising arch and circle; creating brick from straw and mud and hauling stones to the site of construction. Mr. Savage was a believer in extraterrestrial life—in a mythic piece of machinery found in a bed of coal, part of a spaceship, he concluded; proof that we had been visited by beings from another planet. (1984:9)

Boy's extraterrestrial creationism is ahistorical in the extreme. His mystical view of human origins as celestial elides the histories of slavery and colonialism that Cliff foregrounds elsewhere in the novel, when the narrative voice instructs us about slavery:

Slavery was not an aberration—it was an extreme. Consider the tea plantations of Ceylon and China. The coffee plantations of Sumatra and Colombia. The tobacco plantations of Pakistan and the Philippines. The mills of Lowell. Manchester. Leeds. Marseilles. The mines of Wales. Alsace-Lorraine. The railroads of the Union-Pacific. Cape-to-Cairo. All worked by captive labor. . . . The enslavement of Black people—African peoples—with its processions of naked and chained human beings, whipping of human beings, rape of human beings, lynching of human beings, buying and selling of human beings—made other forms of employment in the upkeep of western civilization seem pale. (1984:28)

Boy likewise elides the history of slavery that produces his own family as "white." The Savages are "emphatic in their statement that James Edward Constable Savage, the puisne justice and advisor to the Crown, who had studied law at the Inns of Court, had been one of the only Jamaican landowners never to impregnate a female slave or servant" (1984:29). The colonialist defense mechanism through which Clare's father overvalues marks of whiteness and refuses marks of miscegenation to preserve the boundaries between the dominant and the oppressed makes it nearly impossible for Clare to define herself in relation to her black heritage.

Clare tries to interpret her own racial identity by asking her teacher to explain the Holocaust, which she has learned about from reading *The Diary of Anne Frank*. Struggling against the sanitized colonial version of Jamaican history taught in school, Clare's identification with Anne Frank is an effort to think through a history of racial oppression in relation to a figure that is, like herself, both marked and unmarked. According to her teachers, Jews may be light but are not white, and they are like other people of color in their "devotion to their own difference" (1984:70). As Clare's teacher explains in a comparison that replaces racial oppression with religious oppression, so calling attention to their intersection, "the suffering of the Jews was similar . . . to the primitive religiosity of Africans, which had brought Black people into slavery . . . both types of people were flawed in irreversible ways" (1984:71).

Confused by her teacher, Clare turns to her father, but Boy Savage reinforces the teacher's racist history while refusing Clare's identification with Jews as both white and not white. Boy adheres to the "one-drop rule" in answering Clare's questions about Jewish identity, explaining that being half-Jewish makes one a Jew.[52] But he creates his daughter in his own self-image, telling her that she is white in spite of the fact that her mother is colored, because as his daughter she is a Savage. The history of miscegenation that produces Clare's lightness is the very history that her father's perception of her body as white conceals. Boy's attempts to construct a unitary (white) identity that excludes the multiracial heritage represented by Clare's mother do not make sense to Clare as she looks down at her legs, awaiting her father's explanation of the Holocaust: "she was considering how she could be white with a colored mother, brown legs, and ashy knees" (1984:73).

Clare's mother, Kitty, although light-skinned herself, maintains a vexed and intensely private identification with "darkness" that she does not share with her lighter-skinned daughter.

In guarding this alliance with darkness and in letting Clare's father raise her daughter, Kitty follows the unspoken rule "that a light-skinned child was by common law, or traditional practice, the child of the whitest parent"—believing perhaps that in doing so she offers Clare the opportunity to assume the privileges of whiteness (1984:129). The patterns of maternal withholding and betrayal in Clare's family go back to Judith, Clare's great grandmother, a white woman whose parents disowned her when she ran off with one of the black servants, with whom she had five children.

Judith's ostracism by her white family illustrates the system of matrilineal filiation under slavery. But Cliff demonstrates that filiation does not necessarily produce affiliation. Judith sacrifices her black daughter to the structures of difference and oppression that her own marriage transgressed when she sends the child into the fields to cut cane. Miss Mattie, Clare's grandmother, grows distant from her white mother and closer to her father, who can affirm her black identity. But Miss Mattie repeats the pattern of maternal distancing with her own daughter, who is Clare's mother. Kitty recalls being abandoned by her mother when she was sick as a child, and her mother sent her to the charity hospital for surgery with Clary, a friend of the family, but did not accompany or visit her daughter herself. The grown-up Kitty "still wondered about the absence of Miss Mattie and the presence of Clary during those days," but "neither one, mother or daughter, ever talked about the hospital, not when Kitty was seven, not when she was thirty-five" (1984:141). Ironically, Kitty later names Clare for Clary, who offered the support that Miss Mattie was unable to provide for Kitty and that Kitty, in turn, is unable to provide for her daughter. Cliff suggests that in withholding intimacy from Clare, Kitty also withholds information that Clare needs to survive in a world structured by racism and sexism. For although Clare embodies the physical ideal of assimilation, in her need for her mother she remains tied to the fragmented racial and cultural identities produced by colonialism.

Cliff details Clare's attempts to account for her mother's failings and to refigure her as supportive by returning to the connection between the racial oppression of Jews and black Ja-
maicans. Absorbed in the story of Anne Frank, Clare cuts school
to go to the cinema where *The Diary of Anne Frank* is showing.
Through a complex play on naming, the novel connects Kitty
Savage to *The Diary of Anne Frank*, in which Anne addresses her
diary as "Kitty," and then to Kitty Hart of the Holocaust survival
narrative *I Am Alive*. Clare speculates about why Kitty Hart
lived while Anne Frank died, and decides that it has something
to do with "the remoteness of Anne's mother":

> Would Anne have lived to see her liberation if her mother had
> been different? Would Anne's mother have been different if the
> Holocaust had not happened? Where *was* the source of her
> coldness? Where did her remoteness come from? The mother
> of Kitty Hart, about whom they had not made a movie, stood
> in contrast to the mother of Anne Frank. She had fought for
> her daughter's survival. She had stolen food from the dead for
> her. She had hidden her when she was sick, so her daughter
> wouldn't be selected for death. Did Kitty survive because her
> mother had confronted the horror and taught her daughter to
> live through the days? (1984:9–80)

Here Kitty Hart's mother stands for the fantasy of the mother
who is fully present for the daughter, and the absence of a movie
about her underscores the difficulty of imagining such a mother.
The novel itself shifts between representing that to which Clare's
mother does not have access—a knowledge of racial history/lin-
eage that might provide her, and through her, her daughter, with
survival skills—and fantasizing an impossible fullness in relationship to the imaginary "good" mother.

Envisaging this mother, *Abeng* attempts to reconstruct the
body of the Other—the woman of color who has been inac-
cessible to Clare—by creating alternative genealogies to the patriarchal, colonialist ones that Boy Savage embodies. Weaving

together chapters about Clare's life with mythohistorical chapters about Clare's female ancestors, the novel portrays women who are outspoken in their allegiance to colonized races and who engender heterogeneous New World identities. They include the mythologized Nanny, the Maroon leader of the Jamaican slave rebellion who wore a necklace of white men's teeth and could "catch a bullet between her buttocks and render the bullet harmless" (1984:14); Mma Alli, a slave on Clare's grandfather's plantation who was an obeah woman "with a right breast that had never grown" and who "had never lain with a man . . . [because] she loved only women in that way" (1984:34–35); and Inez, the concubine of Clare's white grandfather, whose multicultural, aboriginal heritage linked her to the Miskito Indians and the Ashanti (1984:33).

In depicting the relationship among these three mythohistorical mother figures, *Abeng* articulates the complex intersection of lesbianism, menstruation, and the maternal. Refusing to bear a child conceived out of repeated rapes by Judge Savage Constable, Inez turns to Mma Alli, who induces an abortion with a combination of herbs that bring on contractions, and lovemaking that soothes the cramps. In the course of her relationship with Mma Alli, Inez "remembers her mother," escapes the Judge, flees to Nanny, and participates in the Maroon rebellion. Inez's abortion connects lesbianism and menstrual blood both with maternal nurture and with the refusal of motherhood when motherhood threatens to literally reproduce racist and sexist colonial systems that oppress women of color, who are forced to bear children who will also be enslaved, raped, and beaten by white masters.

By coding lesbianism and menstruation as a refusal of enforced heterosexuality and colonialism, Cliff emphasizes how, within the narrative of female development, menstruation signals both adolescence, when romantic friendships between girls are permissible, and adulthood, when girls are eligible for entrance into a heterosexual economy of marriage and childbearing that guarantees the reproduction of colonialism. Clare's friendship with Zoe, who is a literary reincarnation of *Wide Sargasso Sea*'s Tia, locates school at the center of this cusp marked by menstruation. Zoe, a dark-skinned girl growing up in the countryside, embodies those aspects of black girlhood and womanhood that Clare associates with her elusive mother. School at once allows the girls to be together and separates them from each other. On the one hand, Clare and Zoe's friendship exists because Clare has summer vacations in the country where the girls feel somewhat free of the rules that would separate them had they both gone to Clare's school in Kingston. On the other hand, the girls' friendship is limited to those two months of summer and cannot remain immune to the world represented by Clare's school in Kingston, where the boundaries of class and color that the girls cross in their friendship are enforced. For Clare, school is both that which grooms her for (white) womanhood and that which preserves her from it. While she is in school, she does not have to be married, but she learns by her teachers' example what it is to be a lady—that ladies are white, married, proper, and do not "speak in a familiar manner to people beneath their station. Those with the congenital defect of poverty—or color" (1984:99). Zoe, whose mother is a squatter on Miss Mattie's land, is marked by both those "defects" of poverty and color.

School is not only a place where normative social structures are ingrained. In *Abeng*, it also represents the possibility of other social structures, specifically ones that resist compulsory heterosexuality and colonialism. The novel establishes school as a harbor for alternative ideologies and alternative lifestyles through Mr. Powell, the schoolmaster who teaches in the country where Kitty grew up. Mr. Powell, a former member of Marcus Garvey's Universal Negro Improvement Association, supplements the British schoolbooks with poetry of the Harlem Renaissance. He is coded as gay through his acquaintance with homosexual poet Claude McKay and through his friendship with Clinton, one of *Abeng*'s two gay ("battyman") characters who commit suicide. Mr. Powell's school inspires Kitty's dreams of taking her mother's land and building a school where she will write her own manuals and "teach country children about their own island, while pretending to adhere to the teachings of the Crown . . . [and] go beyond Mr. Powell in her lessons" (1984:129). Kitty's dreams end when Boy forces his sexual attentions on her after a date. She becomes pregnant and reluctantly marries to preserve her respectability.

Like her mother, Clare dreams of setting up a country school where she and Zoe can teach together, and she will also be thwarted in this desire. Clare's fantasy of establishing a school with Zoe projects the possibility for intimacy between women beyond the end of their school days, a point that, within the heterosexual narrative of female development, should signal the end of romantic friendships. But this fantasy also elides the fact that the two girls are already divided by structures of gender, race, and class differences. In an episode in which Clare plans to hunt a wild boar that lives in the bush, Clare recognizes both the quality of her feelings for Zoe and the fact that those feelings will be censored. Dissuading Clare from the hunt, Zoe explains that killing the boar, construed as an act of white male privilege, would affect her, a dark-skinned, poor country girl, differently than it would Clare, who will return to Kingston at the summer's end. She blurts out that differences of color and class make Clare's dream of establishing a school with her unrealistic because she will not have the money to go to college and become a teacher, but will become a market woman like her mother. Reluctantly, Clare abandons the hunt and the two go swimming. But, as if naming the differences between the girls makes them material, even the apparently harmless act of swimming leads to their separation.

Clare becomes aware of the sexual nature of her feelings for Zoe as they lie naked together on the rock after swimming. Clare contemplates female spaces, both the crevices of the rock beaten smooth by washerwomen, and "the ways into their own bodies . . . through which their babies would emerge and into which men would put their thing," but which for the moment "belong to them" (1984:120). She wants "to tell Zoe what she meant to her . . . to lean across Zoe's breasts and kiss her" (1984:124). But a cane cutter who sees the girls from across the river and hollers, "Coo ya! . . . Two gals nekked pon the river-rock," interrupts Clare's reverie (1984:122). She uses her class/race position to defend her turf, slipping from patois into the King's English, invoking her grandmother's status as a property owner, and firing the rifle she had illicitly taken from the house to hunt the boar. The stray bullet kills her grandmother's bull, exposing the transgressions of gender boundaries she had enacted by planning the boar hunt.

Revealing Clare's assumption of race and class privilege and her appropriation of gendered power, this scene in which Clare accidentally kills her grandmother's bull brilliantly analyzes how the rigid boundaries of race, class, and gender work to solidify Clare's distance from Zoe. Clare plans the boar hunt as an act of rebellion against the lesson she had learned earlier in the novel at hog-killing time, "when she had been told absolutely, by the boys, by the dressed up women, by Miss Mattie . . . just who she was to be in this place" (1984:114). Here, hunting and killing are defined as a male privilege, and Clare's half-cousin and playmate, Joshua, excludes her from the male ritual of consuming the animal's penis and testicles. Leaving the scene of this feast, Clare must return to the company of her grandmother's guests, women who reflect rigid boundaries of class and color in the way they are geographically divided into groups—the wealthiest in the parlor, the poorest in the yard.

In the hog-killing episode, then, Clare realizes that being divested of gender privilege is associated with systems of race and class oppression, and this recognition leads her to plan the hunt. She imagines that by killing the wild boar, she will proclaim her strength and make a tribute and a claim to the women who are oppressed by the categories of difference, including her lost ancestors and her mother, who are mixed together in her imagination: "Kitty was in there somewhere—of course—and what Kitty would think about a daughter who could kill—and thus survive—in the wild. Kitty Hart and Anne Frank were there" (1984:115). As she and Zoe climb the hillside to find the boar, Zoe accuses Clare of fantasizing that she is a "Maroon smaddy" or a "Guinea warrior," recalling the figures of Nanny, Mma Alli, and Inez. But at the crucial moment when Clare moves to protect her claim to these women, symbolized by her relationship with Zoe, she betrays that maternal genealogy. In killing the bull, Clare effectively leaps back to the side of her white father, as her grandmother suggests when she characterizes Clare's actions as those of "a girl who seemed to think she was a boy. Or white" (1984:134).

Unlike *The Well of Loneliness*, where the assumption of masculine privilege consolidates Stephen's sexual identity, in *Abeng* it disrupts the identity Clare is trying to forge by separating her from Zoe and from her mother, who agrees with Boy that Clare should be sent to live with a friend of the family, Mrs. Phillips, an old white woman who can, in Kitty's words, teach Clare "to be a [white] lady" while she finishes school (1984:150). Thus, at the point in the narrative of female development where the girl is supposed to prepare herself for adulthood and childbearing, Cliff places the youthful fantasy of school as a site of alternative ideologies and "lifestyles" in tension with a normalizing representation of school as the institution that socializes girls to assume the roles defined for them by the ideologies of colonialism and patriarchy.

The novel remains ambivalent about the possibility of sustaining friendships across lines of class and color after the relative freedom of childhood. While Clare remains in isolation at Mrs. Phillips's house, the dream scene that closes the novel recalls the landscape of the shooting episode and rewrites the outcome of the boar hunt in connection with the onset of menses. Earlier, Clare constructs menstruation as a transitional point in her life:

Menstruation appeared to her as the culmination of the process of what was happening within and without her girl's body and she wanted to understand it for what it was—and what it would mean in her life. She had a sense of it as something which would allow no turning back—a "milestone," she called it. But she had a sense of it as a sweetness—a truly private piece of life—like the inscription in Greek on an award she had won at school: "Your possession forever." (1984:106)

Here menstruation is a source of pleasure and eroticism associated with the sensuousness of Clare's first masturbatory self-explorations. It is also associated with female friendships in that it is something that Clare has discussed with Zoe and that Kitty refers to in code language as her "friend."

At the end of the novel, Clare interprets her experiences through the lens of this eroticized concept of menstruation. Drawing on imagery from the violent scene in *Wide Sargasso Sea* where Tia throws the rock at Antoinette, *Abeng* weaves together the thematic threads of lesbianism, menstruation, and racial difference to repair Clare's disrupted identifications with other women of color:

Clare dreamed that she and Zoe were fist-fighting by the river in St. Elizabeth. That she picked up a stone and hit Zoe underneath the eye and a trickle of blood ran down her friend's face and onto the rock where she sat. The blood formed into a pool where the rock folded over on itself. And she went over to Zoe and told her she was sorry—making a compress of moss drenched in water to soothe the cut. Then squeezing an aloe leaf to close the wound. (1984:165)

Although the novel has consistently critiqued the paradigm of pure identification that is unmarked by racial difference, represented most obviously by Boy, it could be argued that at the end of the novel menstruation becomes a category of resemblance through which a feminized version of that fantasy of identification is played out, and bleeding is constructed as the constitutional link between women. The cramps of Clare's first period wake her from the dream, which the narrative voice tells us Clare is not ready to understand: "She had no idea that everyone we dream about we are" (1984:166). But it is blood/bleeding, which Clare describes to herself in words that echo her mother's description of menstruation as a "sweet pain," that connects her with a continuum of women—Zoe, Kitty, Inez, Mma Alli, and Nanny—healing the divisions between them.[53] In Clare's dream of bleeding, touching, and healing, menstruation functions as a sort of imaginary resolution to the problem of identification across boundaries of difference by presenting the fantasy of a unifying female experience that symbolically brings Clare closer to her m/Others.

I want to clarify that the novel does not represent lesbian eroticism as a form of female identification that successfully replaces or repairs failed maternal and cross-racial identifications. The rock-throwing incidents in *Wide Sargasso Sea* and *Abeng* have already associated bleeding with the reality of racial violence, and this precludes any easy resolution of difference through the eroticization of menstruation as the pretext for female identification. In fact, all the novels discussed in this chapter consistently represent identifications as failed in the sense that they can never be fully achieved.[54] Judith Butler suggests that "identifications are never fully and finally made; they are incessantly reconstituted and, as such, are subject to the volatile logic of iterability. They are that which is constantly marshalled, consolidated, retrenched, contested, and, on occasion, compelled to give way."[55]

It is this iterability around the process of identification that all three novels represent. They show how problems of identification are *phantasmically*, not actually, resolved through tropes of lesbian sexuality, menstruation, and schooling. In relocating the mirror-stage, the novels juxtapose the fantasy that female identification can protect girls from the difficulties of being socialized as Other in a patriarchal, colonial culture, with the actual intrusion of the social into the realm of the maternal/feminine. What we get in these *Bildungsromans*, then, is the fantasy of imaginary wholeness repeatedly undercut, showing how female identification is always social, always interrupted by cultural markers of difference.

As a contemporary writer who draws on postcolonial and lesbian and feminist refusals of unitary identity, Cliff is able to deconstruct fantasies of identification that are based on strategies of visibility more extensively than Brontë does, and she is able to bring same-sex desire into the foreground without replicating the phobia of novels such as *Strange Brother*. But as *Abeng* develops the narrative of fragmented subjectivity begun in *Wide Sargasso Sea*, lesbianism becomes the site of the fantasy of identification. The novel does not fully deconstruct this fantasy, even if it critiques the way it is predicated on racial resemblance. For Cliff, as for many feminists, identifications imply political alliances; *Abeng* might thus be read as an effort to imagine the emotional and psychic terms on which coalitions might be founded. As the next chapter argues, the positioning of lesbianism as an origin for political alliances occurs not only in fiction, but also in feminist theory that attempts to problematize questions of identity and affiliation, where the visible continues to ground the representation of difference.

How to Recognize a Lesbian

The Cultural Politics of Looking Like What You Are

Of course, there's a strict gay dress code no matter where you cruise. At the height of my college cruising, I was attending Take Back the Night meetings dressed in Mr. Greenjeans overalls, Birkenstocks, and a bowl haircut that made me look like I'd just been released from a bad foster home. There is nothing more pitiful to look at than a closeted femme.   —Susie Sexpert[1]

In retrospect, my own entrance into the lesbian community was remarkable more for the sense of disorientation it produced than for a strong sense of identification. That would occur and recur later, and my identifications with other women are as fraught with issues of desire, idealization, and abjection as any one else's are. My disorientation was an effect of a femme's version of gender dysphoria—that confusion we feel when we experience our bodies as incoherent in relation to a socially instituted norm of "gender intelligibility."[2] Because we often conform to normative ideas about what "real girls" should look like, femmes are not usually the subject of discussions about gender dysphoria. But the lesbian community where I came out had slightly but significantly different rules of "coherence and continuity among sex, gender sexual practice, and desire" than the heterosexual one where I fit the norm.[3]

I came out at a very small, very "politically correct" liberal arts college in the late eighties, and I dutifully tried to accommodate myself to the uniform of hiking boots, jeans, and untucked flannel shirts. This was not a look specific to lesbians; many straight women sported it too. But it was a look more expected of lesbians. While I couldn't part with all my makeup, I put away my velvet hair bows and the low black heels in which I had walked through inches of new snow more than once because I refused to be practical about the realities of winter in Ohio. The transformation was unsuccessful. As a friend pointed out, even in hiking boots and jeans, my socks matched my sweaters. I wasn't pulling off the look, and I felt like I was in drag. After about a month, I was wearing my skirts and stockings again. I had figured out what I was, even if I didn't have a name for it: a lesbian who clung to clothes that matched and pretty shoes. When I graduated from college, I graduated into red lipstick and lacquered red nails, knowing my next relationship would be with a woman, and one who appreciated the look of a well-manicured hand on her thigh.

I was not initiated into the vocabulary of lesbian sexual style until my first girlfriend, ML, did some research on my species. She came home from work one day to announce that there was such a thing as a "lipstick lesbian" and that I was probably not the only one, even though she could not acquaint me with any peers. My anomalousness became painfully obvious at the New Year's Eve party where I met her friends from the rugby team. As she requested, I wore my Christmas present from her, a vintage sweater that had belonged to her grandmother, cashmere with a mink collar and pearl clasps. A black skirt, fitted through the hips and flared at the ankles, set off the soft beige of the mink and the creaminess of the pearls. I was the only one there not dressed in flannel and jeans, except for ML, who had generously agreed to don a gold lamé shirt to make me feel less out of place. I sensed that her teammates were skeptical about me when I was introduced. They smiled quickly, shook my hand, and broke off into pairs and trios with their drinks. I mingled long enough to be informed which of the guests were ML's ex-lovers. The ice did not really break until someone suggested we play a word game. Everyone took seats and formed a circle. I chose an armchair and ML sat at my feet. In the middle of someone else's turn, ML turned and lifted the hem of my skirt to peek underneath. I smiled and lightly popped her on the head, and the rest of the women burst into laughter.

The gesture both marked and recuperated my difference in a way that eased the mistrust of women whose codes of recognition did not include the sexual style "femme," but did acknowledge, if not overtly then tacitly, the sexual style "butch"—or at least an eighties' version of it, the ubiquitous flannel-shirts-and-jeans lesbian drag. I'm still not sure exactly what made the gesture work to that effect. It plays on the heterosexual oedipal scenario in which anatomical difference figures sexual difference and then reduces it to an instance of visible perception (the little boy looking up the little girl's dress). But between women, the peeking signifies not sexual difference (assumed to be anatomical difference), but differences of gender/sexual identity[4] within the category "female," so that it becomes a joke about sameness as much as difference. Perhaps the emphasis on sameness alleviates the discomfort about differences in sexual style that initially creates suspicion. It may also be that the action, initiated by a butch woman, marks the femme as the object of sexual interest in a way that includes her in a community where she is not accepted at face value.

This chapter is about difference and recognition in contemporary feminist and lesbian theory. Aside from ML's research, the other way I began to learn the vocabulary of lesbian identity was through reading. This is not unusual behavior for someone in the process of coming out; it does seem, though, especially predictable for an academic to head to the library when faced with the prospect of exploring her sexuality. I found myself, as most of us do, unsupervised in the HQ 76 section of the stacks. The HQ section can be dangerous—if you pick up the wrong book, you can read the most condemning things about yourself. The

HQ section *looks* dangerous too. In my graduate school library, many of the actual books had been replaced by wooden blocks with the call numbers typed on slips of paper and taped to what would have been the spine. The real books, I later learned, were in "the cage," a space behind the reference desk partitioned off by a locked metal fence. The library stored "sensitive" material there—things that were liable to be stolen or vandalized, including ephemera, sheet music, racially charged nineteenth-century propaganda literature, anything with erotic or nude illustrations and photographs, and books about prostitution, homosexuality, and other forms of sexual deviance. I was once given a tour of the cage, and I learned a lot there about what literature people want enough to steal and what they hate enough to destroy.

I was fortunate in my early selections of reading material. Some of the most powerful pieces I read were nonfiction—personal and theoretical essays by women who were way ahead of me in their thinking. Their bibliographies became my study guides, and this last chapter, which is the first piece I ever wrote on lesbian identity, is very indebted to their work. In this essay, I look at how three white feminists—Donna Haraway, Sue-Ellen Case, and Judith Butler—theorize radical subjectivities that disrupt race, gender, and sexuality as stable categories which support the definition of the Western unitary subject (read white male heterosexual). Their efforts to denaturalize the categories that regulate identity are constrained at certain moments by the impulse to represent disruptive subjectivities in terms of the visible.

The readings of feminist theories that follow shift between analyses of how "woman of color" and "butch" become essentialized as authentic subaltern identities signified by their visibility as "Other,"[5] theoretical moves that lead to the displacement from the field of radical subjectivity of those who do not "look like what they are"—women of color who can "pass" for white and femme lesbians who can pass for straight. These shifts between the figures of the woman of color and the butch, which produce breaks in my argument, signal the danger for white critics of enacting race privilege when we try to negotiate a discursive multiplicity that includes race.

My readings of these writers' works are intended to question and expand rather than diminish their ideas. Feminist theorist Teresa de Lauretis suggests that

> feminist critical theory as such begins when the feminist critique of sociocultural formations . . . becomes conscious of itself and turns inward . . . to question its own relation to or possible complicity with those ideologies, its own heterogeneous body of writing and interpretations, their basic assumptions and terms, and the practices which they enable and from which they emerge.[6]

It is in this spirit that I proceed to examine the work of feminist writers whose risks have made my own work possible.

Donna Haraway's "A Manifesto for Cyborgs" has become a cult text since its initial publication in 1985.[7] The piece is radical in its adaptation of what Haraway calls "technoscience discourses" to articulate a socialist-feminist politics of identity, or perhaps more accurately a politics of identity as nonidentity. Haraway develops a political myth around the image of the cyborg, "a hybrid of machine and organism, a creature of social reality as well as a creature of fiction" (1990:174). She suggests that as a hybrid, the cyborg subverts myths of origin and unity that structure Western culture, and proposes that the construction "woman of color" might give some insight into the cyborg myth. What interests her about cyborgian hybridity is the notion of a "bastard race" as a metaphor for the transgression of boundaries that delineate race, gender, sexuality, the human body—in short, individual and social identity. Examining the writings of women of color, Haraway focuses on the Mexican history/mythology of Malinche, "mother of the mestizo 'bastard' race of the new world, master of languages, and mistress of

Cortes" (1990:199). Haraway says "the bastard race teaches about the power of the margins" (1990:200).

Haraway's essay takes part in a politics of heterogeneity that has emerged in postcolonial criticism, a politics that develops a theory of what might be termed the "liminal subject," marked by a resistance to self-identity. An example of such a subject is Chicana feminist Gloria Anzaldúa's "new mestiza," who exists between cultures, languages, races, and genders. Anzaldúa's book *Borderlands* describes a fragmented and multiple subject that strategically deploys the relationships and even the contradictions among its various parts to deconstruct Western narratives of identity based on opposition and hierarchy.[8]

Haraway borrows cultural theorist Trinh T. Minh-ha's phrase "inappropriate/d others" to further describe her boundary creatures:

> The term refers to the historical positioning of those who cannot adopt the mask of either "self" or "other" offered by previously dominant Western narratives of identity and politics. To be "inappropriate/d" does not mean "not to be in relation with"—that is, to be outside appropriation by being in a special reservation, with the status of the authentic, the untouched, in the allochronic and allotopic condition of innocence. Rather, to be an "inappropriate/d other" means to be in critical, deconstructive relationality—as the means of making a potent connection that exceeds domination.[9]

Here it is clear that Haraway is interested in undermining oppositional and hierarchical thinking by positing a subjectivity that is not unitary but multiple and shifting. But the power relations which the fragmented subject is supposed to deconstruct are sometimes replicated within the heterogeneous space of the split subject.[10] Haraway is fully aware of the potential for such replication; in essays and interviews she warns against the dangers of romanticizing and/or appropriating the standpoints of the subjugated, of building new holism out of "summing and sub-suming parts"[11] and of solidifying rather than deconstructing Western privilege in drawing on the standpoints of the subjugated.[12] Unfortunately, sensitivity to issues of dominance and subordination does not immunize us against playing out old patterns in our work; to take up those issues is to risk revealing where we are still attached to the colonizing modes of thinking which structure our society. The possibility of breaking out of those modes of thinking lies precisely in the willingness first to take the risk of revealing our links to them and then to unravel the dense configurations of discourses that form those links to begin with.

With this end in mind I want to trace the slippage between deconstructing and replaying old power relationships in "A Manifesto for Cyborgs," specifically by examining how that slippage occurs along the axis of visibility. The metaphors of racial difference that Haraway invokes to theorize the cyborg consciously problematize colonialist and racist paradigms of subjectivity. She plays on the use of those metaphors of racial difference in the work of science fiction writer Octavia Butler (*Dawn*),[13] who considers the potential for both pleasure and danger in the transgression of boundaries which define self-hood, and who is keenly aware of the imperialist power relations inherent in those transgressions.[14]

However, in playing on those metaphors, cyborgian imagery relies on constructions of identity which classify according to visual differentiation, or what socialist theorists Ernesto Laclau and Chantal Mouffe describe as "the argument from appearance." This argument runs as follows: "[E]verything presenting itself as different can be reduced to identity. This may take two forms: either appearance is a mere artifice of concealment, or it is a necessary form of the manifestation of an essence"—in other words, appearance either conceals or manifests the "essence" of its subject.[15] In Haraway's work the argument takes the latter form; the "essential difference" must present itself visibly. Although "A Manifesto for Cyborgs" revises the history that constructs the "bastard" as a negatively defined difference, it replicates normative constructions of identity by privileging visibility.

Take, for example, Haraway's description of Cherríe Moraga's relationship to writing, in which writing becomes the term that bestows upon Moraga one form of otherness—racial difference—and suppresses another form of otherness—lesbianism: "Writing *marks* Moraga's body, *affirms* it as the body of a woman of color, against the possibility of *passing* into the *unmarked* category of the Anglo father" (my emphasis).[16] On one level, this comment construes the political marking of the body as affirmative and critiques the notion of whiteness as unmarked. But in the context of the issues which Moraga raises in *Loving in the War Years*, the analysis takes on a subtly justificatory tone. One of Moraga's anxieties in *Loving* is her sensitivity to the fact that she is "la guera," fair-skinned, not visibly identifiable as a Chicana, and that she is making a "claim to color, at a time when, among white feminist ranks, it is a 'politically correct' . . . assertion to make" (1983:58). Her anxiety can be traced through the shifting "we" in the essay entitled "La Guera." Moraga uses the first person plural to refer variously to the "dyke" who looks "like a white girl" (1983:52) and the black woman, as well as to women of color, working-class women, lesbian writers, feminists, and Chicanas.

By indicating that Moraga's writing marks her (light) body and keeps her from passing into the unmarked category of the Anglo father (Moraga's father was white), Haraway appears to be absolving Moraga from the guilt she harbors for being able to pass, for not really knowing "what it feels like being shitted on for being brown" (Moraga 1983:54). This exculpating gesture draws Haraway into the discourses that establish a hierarchy of oppressions according to paradigms of visibility. The hierarchy is compounded by Haraway's oversight of Moraga's perception that it is her lesbianism that keeps her from "passing" out of her connection with other women of color in spite of her light skin.

Moraga describes how lesbianism links her to the experience of racial oppression by making her difference visible on the body:

> It wasn't until I acknowledged and confronted my own lesbianism *in the flesh*, that my heartfelt identification with and empathy for my mother's oppression—due to being poor, uneducated, and Chicana—was realized. My lesbianism is the avenue through which I have learned the most about silence and oppression. . . . What I am saying is that the joys of looking like a white girl ain't so great since I realized I could be beaten on the street for being a dyke. *If my sister's being beaten because she's Black, it's pretty much the same principle.* (1983:52, my emphasis)

Here, Moraga establishes skin color as the signifier of racial difference and oppression, and then constructs lesbianism as an analogous signifier. Arguably, both Haraway and Moraga need to perceive Moraga's body as being marked because they privilege skin color as the definitive signifier of difference. In the taxonomies of difference that they inherit through the dominant discourses on race, skin color is the most visible feature of otherness. Thus, in Moraga's work, racial difference takes priority in shaping sexual difference; lesbianism is endowed with the status of the originally and authentically oppressed by association with racial difference, which is already biologized through the visible and so constructed as a natural social category.

Haraway suppresses lesbianism and privileges racial difference even though Moraga already privileges racial difference via lesbianism. This may be because Moraga discusses lesbianism in terms of wholeness and origins, fantasizing it as a metaphoric reunion with the maternal; for Moraga, lesbianism is a linking identity that returns her to the original site of oppression, the Chicana mother. This contradicts the project of Haraway's "A Manifesto for Cyborgs," which wants to construct both the lesbian and the woman of color as fragmented identities. As Haraway writes:

> *Loving in the War Years* explores the themes of identity when
> one never possessed the original language, never told the orig-
> inal story, never resided in the harmony of legitimate hetero-
> sexuality in the garden of culture, and so cannot base identity
> on a myth or a fall from innocence and a right to natural
> names, mother's or father's. (1990:199)

But by avoiding the issue of how Moraga uses lesbianism as an
avenue to the wholeness that "A Manifesto for Cyborgs" presumes she should reject, Haraway leaves lesbianism untheorized.
Lesbianism becomes the unrepresentable, the invisible. This
leads to the return of lesbianism as an originary identity in "A
Manifesto for Cyborgs."

Though lesbianism remains suppressed in Haraway's essay, it
can be traced in an unarticulated subtext. For example, in the
section "Fractured Identities," Haraway critiques Catharine
MacKinnon for reproducing the "appropriating, incorporating,
totalizing tendencies of Western theories of identity grounding
action" (1990:183).[17] The critique implies—but never directly
states—a complaint against the heterosexism of MacKinnon's
work. Haraway says:

> MacKinnon's radical theory of experience is totalizing in the
> extreme; it does not so much marginalize as obliterate the
> authority of any other women's political speech and action.
> It is a totalization producing what Western patriarchy itself
> never succeeded in doing—feminists' consciousness of the
> non-existence of women, except as products of men's desire.
> (1990:183)

The "other woman" who is obliterated in MacKinnon's work
and marginalized in Haraway's would be, according to the logic
of Haraway's argument, the woman who is not constituted by
men's desire. In some theoretical circles, this subject position
is occupied by the lesbian.[18] de Lauretis, whose work Haraway compares favorably to MacKinnon's, has since written the

critique of MacKinnon that Haraway suggests but does not elaborate in "A Manifesto for Cyborgs." de Lauretis argues that "MacKinnon's absolutist emphasis on the (hetero)sexual monopoly of 'male power' . . . unmitigated by any possibility of resistance or agency through normative or autonomous forms of female sexuality (excessive, subversive, perverse, invert, or lesbian sexual practices), unintentionally works to recontain both feminist consciousness and female sexuality."[19]

The positioning of lesbianism as a concealed fantasy of origin in "A Manifesto for Cyborgs" is most apparent in Haraway's conclusion, which installs the lesbian writer as an unacknowledged prototype of the cyborg theorist. As it progresses, Haraway's essay becomes increasingly interested in the erotic aspects of cyborg identities. It celebrates "illegitimate fusions of animal and machine . . . the couplings which make Man and Woman so problematic, subverting the structure of desire . . . and so subverting the structure and modes of reproduction of 'Western' identity" (1990:199). Although it names the "fusions of animal and machine" as examples of couplings that will undo heterosexual structures of desire, the essay is by implication also concerned with the subversiveness of couplings between women and women. But because Haraway does not directly address the issue of lesbianism, its subversive potential is effaced; in effect, lesbianism remains outside the economy of desire as a sort of absent presence.

Haraway's interest in an eroticism that will undo the "mundane fiction of Man and Woman" (1990:203) emerges in her discussion of texts that elaborate a cyborg myth. She identifies a series of writers as "theorists for cyborgs" (1990:197), several of whom are recognized as part of a lesbian literary tradition—Joanna Russ, Monique Wittig, and Luce Irigaray—although Haraway does not identify them as lesbian. Haraway then refers to Adrienne Rich and Audre Lorde, two lesbian writers who have been important to the development of U.S. lesbian-feminist thought, in her discussion of the failure of American radical feminist ideology to theorize a cyborg myth. Against them, she positions Moraga as an author of cyborg writing. This last section of the essay might be read as an attempt to imagine a conversation among lesbian writers about the viability of the cyborg as "a myth of political identity."

I have been arguing that privileging the visible (as Haraway and Moraga do) takes part in the discourses that naturalize socially constructed categories of racial difference, and that this privileging elides other identities that are not constructed as visible (for example, lesbianism in Haraway's work), with the result that these identities remain unexamined. How the issue of visibility resonates between the identities "woman of color" and "lesbian" can be approached by reading two authors who take up the question of sexual style, namely, Sue-Ellen Case and Judith Butler. In her essay "Toward a Butch-Femme Aesthetic," Case explicitly theorizes the connection between the identities woman of color and lesbian in her indictment of the feminist community's history of racism and homophobia.[20] Butler, on the other hand, fails to address racial difference in her analysis of sexual style in *Gender Trouble*, but her final chapter on male drag and on butch and femme stances as "performative subversions" of regulatory gender identities has implications for a study of visibility that includes women of color.

Case's work is part of a fairly recent (since the early 1980s) effort to reclaim butch and femme sexual styles as a valid aspect of lesbian cultural heritage. This movement responds to the lesbian-feminist redefinition of butch and femme styles[21] as an anachronism and an embarrassment. With the rise of feminism in the 1970s, the conventions of "role-play" within the bar culture of the fifties and sixties were suppressed in favor of a more androgynous lesbian-feminist chic which, theoretically at least, refused the heterosexual roles that butch and femme styles were said to imitate. Case, along with other critics such as Judy Grahn and Joan Nestle, not only challenges the assumption that butch and femme styles are imitative of heterosexuality, but also argues that feminism's rejection of role-play is tied to issues of class and race as well as gender and is symptomatic of the tension between middle-class white feminists who historically tended not to play obvious roles and working-class women and women of color who did so more often.[22] The rejection of butch and femme styles by middle- and upper-class women was frequently tinged with the condescending implication that role-play was evidence of the backwardness, conservatism, and confusion of working-class lesbians, who were generally depicted as victims of patriarchal brainwashing.[23]

Case describes feminism's impact on the lesbian community as a "compulsory adaptation of lesbian feminist identification" to more orthodox sensibilities in which the sense of community shifted from "one of working-class, often women-of-color lesbians in bars, to that of white upper-middle-class heterosexual women who predominated in the early women's movement" (1989:285). She sets out to correct what she terms the "ghosting of the lesbian subject" in contemporary feminist criticism:

> Regard the feminist genuflection of the 1980's—the catechism of "working-class-women of color" feminist theorists feel impelled to invoke at the outset of their research. What's wrong with this picture? It does not include the lesbian position. In fact, the isolation of the social dynamics of race and class successfully relegates sexual preference to an attendant position, so that even if the lesbian were to appear, she would be as a bridesmaid and never the bride. (1989:283–84)

Case wants to dissolve the isolation of these axes of difference from one another and to correct the exclusion of sexual preference from the litany by working her way back to a historical subject that has been theorized out of existence by heterosexual feminist critics. The effort to recover that subject for lesbian culture is important because the dismissal of roles was often enabled by the class and race privilege of women who did not identify as butch or femme.

But the address of classism in Case's essay invokes less pal-pable forms of class and race essentialism than the discrimina-tion she calls attention to. In describing the operations of clas-sism, the essay sets up an opposition between middle-class and working-class lesbians that subtly bestows the working-class lesbian with an aura of authenticity that is withheld from the middle and upper classes. The construction of this authenticity can be traced through discourses of sexuality and race which, while they are not fully articulated together, intertwine to lo-cate the subject position "butch-femme." The most explicit ref-erence to the overlap of those discourses is the essay's mention of Jean Genet's play *The Blacks*, in which the artifices of camp are used to satirize the mechanisms of racism: "*The Blacks* dis-placed the camp critique from homophobia to racism, in which 'black' stands in for 'queer' and the campy queen of the bars is transformed into an 'african queen.' This displacement is part of the larger use of the closet and gay camp discourse to articu-late other social realities" (1989:289). Here camp deconstructs dominant discourses on both racial difference and homosexu-ality with a multilayered parody of the figure of the "queen" that plays on stereotypes of the "noble savage" and the "fag." Elsewhere in the essay, however, racial difference does not re-main fully inscribed in the camp discourse that liberates from "the rule of naturalism, or realism" (1989:287), but through the search for "historical specificity" and "social reality" is in-stead reconstructed to signify authenticity.

This is evident in the essay's analysis of the way that gay camp discourse has been appropriated and sanitized by straight theo-rists in whose work the nonwhite subject is positioned as a marker of authenticity:

The sirens of sublation may be found in the critical maneuvers of heterosexual feminist critics who metaphorize butch-femme roles, transvestites, and campy dressers into a "subject who masquerades," as they put it, or is "carnivalesque," or even, as

some are so bold to say, who "cross-dresses.". . . [These bor-
rowings] evacuate the historical, butch-femme couple's sense
of masquerade and cross-dressing the way a cigar-store Indian
evacuates the historical dress and behavior of the Native
American. As is often the case, illustrated by the cigar-store Indian, these symbols may only proliferate when the social reality has been successfully obliterated and the identity has become the private property of the dominant class. (1989:289)

The cigar-store Indian metaphor refers to the implementa-
tion of cultural appropriation to gain control over the colonized. Without minimizing that point, the essay's use of racial
difference as a privileged signifier of colonization bears consideration. Some connection arguably exists between the essay's
construction of authenticity and its reliance on a mystique
about ethnicity that depends on the construction of ethnicity as
a visible difference. This is apparent in the essay's positioning
of the butch and femme couple in relation to the Native American as a cultural and racial minority. The Native American
bears the weight of the analogy between the two terms by func-
tioning as a signifier of the colonization of an indigenous, original "native" population.

The cigar-store Indian represents the caricature of cultural difference on which that colonization is based by emphasizing the
symbols of "Indianness" we learn from popular culture—most
likely feathers, war paint, and brown skin. The Native American's visual signification of both cultural imperialism and authenticity is then carried over to the butch and femme couple by
comparison. Katie King describes this transference of meaning
from one sign to another as the "magical" quality of signs invested with political value: "Signs have a sort of magic attached
to them, and magic operates by contiguity, or nearness, in other
words, it works by rubbing off on you."[24] In Case's argument,
then, the association of the butch-femme couple with the Native
American brings the former even closer to "social reality," so

that the "ghosting of the lesbian subject" is corrected by "coloring" her in.

This shift toward authenticity seems at odds with the essay's interest in camp as a discourse that liberates from "the rule of naturalism, or realism" (Case 1989:287). Within the cigar-store Indian metaphor, the separation of the signifier from its original referent is construed as having a negative political value, and rightly so given the genocidal policies that produced that split. But in the context of an argument in which such splitting has a positive political value when it occurs around gender difference (as when Case playfully explains that "the female body, the male gaze, and the structures of realism are only sex toys for the butch-femme couple" [1989:297]), the repudiation of artificiality and caricature raises the issue of how discourses about race and gender/sexuality coalesce and what they reveal or conceal about each other.

In her discussion of homophobia in the black community in *Talking Back*, bell hooks argues that it is exactly the specificity of visibility to people of color that is concealed in analogies between homophobia and racism. I cite her argument not as a corrective to Case's but to expand the analysis of how visibility works in those knots where discourses about race and sexuality converge. While hooks describes how analogy reproduces rather than deconstructs oppression by emphasizing sameness, she gets caught up in the same paradigms of visibility that enable Case's Indian metaphor to begin with. hooks suggests that white lesbians and gays who attempt to "make gay experience and black experience of oppression synonymous" are in danger of "minimizing or diminishing the particular problems people of color face in a white-supremacist society."[25] She explains that "there is a significant difference that arises [between the experiences of gays and people of color] because of the visibility of dark skin. Often homophobic attacks on gay people occur in situations where knowledge of sexual preference is indicated or established—outside of gay bars, for example. While it in no way lessens the severity of such suffering for gay people, or the fear that it causes, it does mean that in a given situation the apparatus of protection and survival may be simply not identifying as gay. In contrast, most people of color have no choice."[26]

While hooks's point about not making different oppressions synonymous is well taken, her explanation of the differences between gay and black experiences of oppression conceives of the category of racial difference too narrowly in terms of the visible. In spite of the qualifier in the last sentence cited ("most" people of color), the argument does not address the situation of people of color who do "have a choice," who are light-skinned enough to pass for white. Further, it overlooks the discrimination that some members of the lesbian and gay community (and the heterosexual one, for that matter) will suffer for their nonconformity to the normative visible codes for gender identity, no matter how they "choose" to identify.[27] Some men are perceived as femme and some women are perceived as butch no matter how hard they try to conform. For hooks as for Case, there is a hierarchy of oppressions in which skin color is the privileged signifier. The complexities of passing are elided from their discussions of race and gender because they threaten the identities that the two writers define on the basis of visibility.

This elision is most conspicuous in Case's essay when she calls attention to the invisibility of working-class whites and women of color in the feminist movement. Quoting Joan Nestle's commentary on the classism of middle-class feminists, the essay glosses an overt reference to passing:

> I wonder why there is such a consuming interest in the butch-fem lives of upper-class women, usually more literary figures, while real-life, working butch-fem women are seen as imitative and culturally backward. . . . [T]he reality of passing women, usually a working-class lesbian's method of survival, has provoked very little academic lesbian-feminist interest. (1989:286)

In spite of the essay's attention to racial difference elsewhere, here there is no comment on the diverse meanings of the word "passing." The contexts in which a lesbian might pass are multiple: is she passing for a man, passing for straight, passing for white? This oversight is inconsistent with the pointed inclusion of women of color in Case's description of prefeminist lesbian identification. The question then is why she is uninterested in the issue of passing at this moment in the essay. One answer might be that if the white lesbian is authenticated through contiguity with a figure who visibly signifies racial difference, then the woman of color who can pass for white does not register as a sign. When racial difference is narrowed to the purely visible, the passing figure becomes unrepresentable.

In Case's development of "the theoretical maneuver that could become the butch-femme subject position" (1989:289), the femme can be compared to the woman of color who passes for white because she too is excluded from the paradigm of visibility. Within the butch and femme economy, the butch emerges as visible while the femme is included in the identity "lesbian" through her association with the butch. In making this comparison between the femme and the woman of color who can pass for white, my essay replicates the problematic argument by analogy that I trace in Case's essay. It also shifts from considering theory that invokes racial difference as a magical sign to considering theory that doesn't refer to racial difference, paradoxically resulting in the exclusion of women of color from my initial analysis of butch and femme sexual styles. The problematic structure of my essay and of the essays I read points to the lack of an effective theoretical apparatus with which discussions of race and gender/sexuality can be combined in ways that do not catch us up in the paradigms we attempt to deconstruct, including the enactment of white privilege.

Early in her essay Case rejects the historical stereotypes of both the butch and the femme represented in Del Martin and Phyllis Lyon's 1972 book *Lesbian/Woman*: "If the butches are savages in this book, the femmes are lost heterosexuals who damage birthright lesbians by forcing them to play the butch roles" (Case 1989:285). But as her theory of the butch-femme subject position unfolds, the association of femininity with passivity creeps back into her argument in spite of her efforts to foreground the femme's active performance of the masquerade of femininity. This is perhaps a result not so much of the essay's assumption of the femme's passivity, as of its emphasis on the visible performance of the difference between lesbian and straight sexuality. It is in the process of describing this performance that the femme is relegated to a secondary position.

For example, in its discussion of feminist theater company Split Britches' stage production of *Beauty and the Beast*, the essay observes that "the butch, who represents by her clothing the desire for other women, becomes the beast—the marked taboo against lesbianism dressed up in the clothes of that desire. Beauty [the femme] is the desired one and the one who aims her desirability at the butch" (1989:294). According to Case, this "portrayal is faithful to the historical situation of the butch role, as Nestle describes it: '[The butches I knew] did announce themselves as tabooed women who were willing to identify their passion for other women by wearing clothes that symbolized the taking of responsibility.'"[28]

In each of these passages the butch is represented as the desiring subject while the femme is represented as the object of desire. Thus, while the essay suggests that "the butch-femme couple inhabit the subject position together—'you can't have one without the other'" (Case 1989:283), it could be argued that another meaning behind the phrase is something like "a femme's not queer without her butch." While the butch can stand alone as "the marked taboo against lesbianism," the femme is invisible as a lesbian unless she is playing to a butch. JoAnn Loulan notes that this tendency to see femmes as lesbian only in relation to butches is similar to "how heterosexual women have been treated as if they have no identity apart from their husbands"

(1990:90). Joan Nestle makes a similar point in remarking that femmes are

> the victims of a double dismissal: in the past they did not appear culturally different enough from heterosexual women to be seen as breaking gender taboos, and today they do not appear feminist enough, even in their historical context, to merit attention or respect for being ground-breaking women.[29]

For good reasons, it has become pejorative to suggest any comparison of butch and femme dynamics to heterosexual ones, but Loulan's and Nestle's comments do strike a chord of recognition.

The representation of the butch as the authentic lesbian has a long tradition, characterized in literary circles by the classic representation of lesbianism in *The Well of Loneliness*, which functioned as a "coming out novel" for over forty years, from its publication in the 1920s through the fifties and sixties when pulp fiction provided women with easier access to other stories about lesbianism. Judy Grahn's history of lesbian and gay life entitled *Another Mother Tongue*, which argues for the existence of an ancient and continuous queer culture, attests to the persistent construction of the butch as "magical sign." Grahn celebrates the butch as a mythical shaman figure (here again Grahn's attribution of tribal roots to the butch constructs racial difference as marker of the butch's authenticity) who is a key member of the "core or heart group [that is] made up of the blatantly Gay, the drag queens and bulldykes."[30]

Grahn describes these figures as the culture's "historians and 'true' practitioners, its fundamentalists, traditionalists, and old-timers, the orthodox who . . . retain the culture in a continuous line from one century to another." Further, Grahn suggests that, "All other Gay people in the current culture line themselves up and measure their own behavior in relation to this core or heart group on a continuum stretching into its extreme opposite, which is assimilation or the imitation of heterosexual stereotypes for the purpose of camouflage, that is, closetry, being 'in the closet'" (1984:85). The glorification of the butch as authentic lesbian is based on her "blatant" representation of sexual deviance, and this in turn implies ambiguity and confusion around the femme's sexual identity. The femme's adaptation of what has been historically defined as a "feminine" sexual style is tacitly constructed as evidence of her desire to pass for straight and not of her desire for other women.

It is interesting that Grahn expresses a certain resistance to the insecurity of the femme's position within the lesbian community that her "continuum" of homosexuality suggests. She says that the femme role was often characterized as boring, passive, and unliberated,[31] and that she felt devalued when she played the femme herself:

> however well I imitated the butches in that particular competitive underground bar scene, I soon learned I was not going to make it as a butch, at least not all of the time. . . . I had to give in and play the femme although I much preferred being seen as a butch. I am as much a ceremonial dike as [my butch lover] was, and I resented giving up any of my hardwon subterranean status.[32]

Comments like these hint at a critique of the femme's negative or dubious status within lesbian subculture that is never elaborated in Grahn's work. Rather, Grahn implies that the problem is intrinsic to the femme "role" and not to the process by which political value is attached to some sexual styles but not others. Loulan, on the other hand, attributes the devaluation of the femme to the lesbian community's internalization of sexist mainstream values that find something abhorrent about the feminine. She argues that "femme lesbians are given little room in the lesbian-feminist community to create an open identity that is strongly lesbian—powerful, vibrant, and far from passive. Femme lesbians have to struggle to claim space within the lesbian erotic circle" (1990:88).

The conflation of sexual style with what might be termed "sexual consciousness" underlies the association of the femme with the stereotypically passive heterosexual woman. By sexual consciousness I mean the sensibilities that are ascribed to sexual identities. Again, *The Well of Loneliness* will serve as an example. Hall alludes to the special insight and sensitivities, the "super-nerves" of the butch lesbian, as opposed to her lovers, whose femininity or "normality" makes them betray Stephen.[33] The butch's sexual style is perceived as expressive of her radical lesbian consciousness. As Wittig puts it in her discussion of the lesbian in "One Is Not Born a Woman," the butch's "masculine" style "proves that she escapes her initial programming."[34] Accordingly, the femme's sexual style is perceived as expressive of her subjection to heterosexual definitions of femininity.

The conflation of sexual style with sexual consciousness assumes a natural relationship between the visible signifiers of sexual style and their signified sexual identity. This last section of my essay attempts to deconstruct that relationship by reconfiguring the lesbian femme through a reading of "Bodily Inscriptions, Performative Subversions" from Judith Butler's *Gender Trouble*. While Butler goes a long way toward denaturalizing the relationship between visible signifiers and the gendered identities they signify, her overriding focus on the body as "the site [read also "sight"] of a dissonant and denaturalized performance" (Butler 1990:146) renders the femme's challenge to the compulsory practice of heterosexuality invisible. The femme can be read as the "blind spot" in Butler's notion of gender as a performance that will "construct the illusion of a primary and interior gendered self *or* parody the mechanism of that construction" (1990:138, my emphasis). The femme might be considered the *and* that cannot be contained in Butler's either/or paradigm; she both constructs the illusion of an interior gendered self (she looks like a straight woman) and parodies it (what you see isn't what you get). Bringing the femme to the foreground elucidates the limitations of the expressive model of gender/sexual identity.

A brief summary of Butler's strategy for denaturalizing gender identity will be useful here. Butler's genealogy rests on deconstructing the normative paradigm that figures a correspondence between sex, gender, and sexuality. In turn, this rests on an inner/outer distinction that "stabilizes and consolidates the coherent subject" (1990:134). This binary locates the "self" within the body and reads the body as a reflection of the "truth" of that self. In terms of gender identity, this means that the male body should contain a masculine self and the female body a feminine self, and that each body's desires will be regulated by the compulsory practice of heterosexuality. Butler explains that the inner/outer distinction will "make sense only with reference to a mediating boundary that strives for stability" (1990:134)—the body. Her focus, then, is on the way the illusion of the inner/outer distinction, of "the regulatory fiction of heterosexual coherence," is produced on the body, and specifically on the way some bodies reveal that coherence to be illusory by refusing integration (1990:136–37).

Using drag as an example, Butler shows how the refusal of integration challenges the stability of the subject. Drag, she says, "fully subverts the distinction between inner and outer psychic space and effectively mocks both the expressive model of gender and the notion of a true gender identity" (1990:137). Her annotated citation of Esther Newton's 1972 book on female impersonation, *Mother Camp*, exemplifies how drag achieves this subversion:

> At its most complex, [drag] is a double inversion that says, "appearance is an illusion." Drag says [Newton's curious personification] "my 'outside' appearance is feminine, but my essence 'inside' [the body] is masculine." At the same time it symbolizes the opposite inversion; "my appearance 'outside' [my body, my gender] is masculine but my essence 'inside' [myself] is feminine."[35]

While Butler's analysis of drag effectively illustrates the subversion of the inner/outer distinction, her reliance on the trope of visibility becomes a limitation when she discusses butch and femme roles as sexual styles that also parody the notion of true gender identity. By focusing on the visual evidence of subversion, Butler, like Case and Grahn, is forced to privilege the butch as the figure that represents the radical discontinuity of sexual and gender identities since the femme appears to be an integrated, stable subject according to the rules of normative heterosexuality.

In a strategy of destabilization which relies on the visual performance of difference, the fact that no distinction between "inner" and "outer" identities is made visible on the surface of the femme's body as it is on the drag queen's and the butch's bodies marginalizes the femme. Even as Butler refutes the common idea that butch and femme replicate heterosexual gender role stereotyping, she flounders over how to describe the femme in relation to heterosexual constructs. At one point, she suggests that "lesbian femmes may recall the heterosexual scene, as it were, but also displace it at the same time" (1990:123), but she does not elaborate on how this displacement occurs. In Butler's only extended comment on the femme, the femme is less an object of interest in herself than an optical instrument used to look at the butch as a figure of destabilized identities. Because the femme does not present the kind of surface text that Butler wants to theorize, Butler must look through rather than at the femme:

> As one lesbian femme explained, she likes her boys to be girls, meaning that "being a girl" contextualizes and resignifies "masculinity" in a butch identity. As a result, that masculinity, if that it can be called, is always brought into relief against a culturally intelligible "female body." It is precisely this dissonant juxtaposition and the sexual tension that its transgression generates that constitute the object of desire. In other words, the object [and clearly, there is not just one] of lesbian-femme desire is neither some decontextualized female body nor a discrete yet superimposed masculine

identity, but the destabilization of both terms as they come into erotic interplay.[36] (1990:123)

Here Butler explains the femme's radical discontinuity through recourse to the presumed object of her desire—the butch, who visibly destabilizes gender categories. In framing her analysis in the context of the femme's desire, Butler invokes the terms of the inner/outer distinction that she wants to undo. The femme's radical desire is understood to offset her normative external appearance, and so that desire is produced as internal. In effect, the femme cannot be conceptualized except as part of a unit in which her desire is constructed as internal to the butch's external expression of that desire. Butler's expectation of coherence between (outer) sexual style and (inner) sexual consciousness puts her back within the framework of culturally intelligible identities which she seeks to destabilize. In the process of illustrating how the sexual styles of drag queens and butches visually denaturalize the categories of sex and gender by producing signs of their nonconformity to heterosexual norms on the body, Butler establishes them as coherent subjects in terms of political rather than gender intelligibility. That is to say, radical consciousness is ascribed to radical appearance. The flip side of this equation is that orthodox ("straight"?) consciousness is ascribed to conventional appearance.

An analysis of the femme's invisibility in theories of gender/sexual identity does have implications for lesbians of color. The movement of this essay away from issues of race as it takes up issues of sexual style signals the presumption of lesbianism as white lesbianism, a presumption that reflects my own investments along lines of race, gender, and sexuality. In different ways, each of the white critics I read in this essay also runs up against the problem of talking about several identities without privileging one over the others: Haraway foregrounds racial difference while lesbianism enters her argument as a sort of absent presence; Case speaks about both racial difference and sexuality but sometimes racial difference functions as a "magical sign" that locates sexual style in her argument, and her essay, like my own, tends to neglect racial difference as it develops an argument about butch and femme; and Butler speaks only about discourses of gender and sexual identity.

The difficulty that white critics have in maintaining a simultaneous discussion of race and lesbianism betrays two related and racist assumptions. The first is, as Ekua Omosupe puts it, the assumption of "a position of authority or the privilege to universalize lesbian experiences as white lesbian experience."[37] The second is, as Jewelle Gomez puts it, the assumption that "race, not sex or gender, [is] the predominant feature in any discussion of work by women of color."[38] Each of these assumptions contributes to the double invisibility of the lesbian of color within the white lesbian community; she is invisible first as a lesbian, and then there is no perception of her sexual style (if she claims one) within the identity "lesbian." In her essay for the *Empathy* issue on visibility and invisibility, Sharon Lim-Hing explains how, for whites, markers of racial difference are so totalizing that they preclude any recognition of the existence and individuality of nonwhite members of the lesbian and gay community: "[T]he first thing many of you would think if you walked into a room and saw me is 'Asian woman.' Not young, old, badly or well dressed, intellectual, punk, jock, diesel dyke, girlie girl, etc.—just 'Asian.' Whites get to play all the roles, while Asians are invisible or are stuck in a few stereotypes."[39] If we pursue the racist logic of this layered invisibility and add to it the invisibility of the lesbian femme, it follows that the woman of color who identifies as femme may be doubly erased. That is to say, while a butch woman of color might not be recognized as a lesbian because she is not white, she might be perceived as a lesbian because her sexual style is considered "blatant." A femme woman of color, on the other hand, will probably not be recognized as lesbian, first because she is not white and then because she is not butch.

The experience of racism complicates the perception of sexual styles for women of color. In the African American lesbian community, for example, the rejection of "role-play" is not based simply on the characterization of butch and femme styles as imitative of heterosexuality. It also includes a resistance to the homophobic stereotype of the black lesbian as "bulldagger," a pejorative term within (and outside) the black community used to signal the lesbian as a woman who wants to be a man. This means that elevation of the butch to the status of mythical figure that is prevalent in the white lesbian community is often qualified for some African American lesbians by an impulse to distance themselves from the image of the butch. Barbara Christian, for example, argues that it is by breaking the "bulldagger" stereotype that black lesbians will be seen as women.[40]

Some women also describe feeling forced into the "butch role" because they have acquired a certain toughness that is perceived as masculine in order to survive. Omosupe says that "encoded in this accusation 'women acting like men,' were many of the things that my mother had socialized into me as a way of helping to assure my survival and to minimize my defeats in a racist, sexist society."[41] This means that many black lesbians feel they are denied any presumption of a choice among roles that white women have. They adopt a stance perceived as butch out of the need for self-protection. In her "biomythographical" novel *Zami*, Audre Lorde explains that her rejection of the butch stance rose from the painful recognition of its compensatory nature for many black women. For her, it signaled rather than concealed the vulnerability of black lesbians in a racist, sexist, and homophobic society: "The Black women I saw [in the Village gay bars of the fifties] were into heavy roles, and it frightened me. This was partly the fear of my own Blackness mirrored, and partly the realities of the masquerade. Their need for power and control seemed a much-too-open piece of myself, dressed in enemy clothing. . . . we seldom looked into each other's Black eyes, lest we see our aloneness and our own blunted power mirrored in the pursuit of darkness."[42]

Within the African American lesbian community, the understanding of the way some identities mask others may also
heighten the awareness of the black femme's double jeopardy.
Again, Lorde speaks to the erasure of the femme when she recalls
her experience of role-play in the fifties bar scene as oppressive
and intimidating: "By white america's racist distortions of
beauty, Black women playing 'femme' had very little chance. . . .
There was constant competition among butches to have the most
'gorgeous femme,' on their arm. And 'gorgeous' was defined by
a white male world's standards."[43] This is not to say that black
lesbian femmes did not exist. In fact, Lorde herself portrays
Kitty, a femme that she meets at a party, with loving attention to
the details of her sexual style, lingering over the descriptions of
Kitty's clothes, hair, perfume, lipstick, and mannerisms. And
though Lorde characterizes the femme role as passive at one
point, here the power of Kitty's eroticism is emphasized by her
direct and "calmly erotic gaze," her fashionable outfit, her effortless dancing, and even the name of her lipstick, "a new Max
Factor shade called 'WARPAINT.'"[44]

While white lesbians may be oblivious to the range of sexual
styles among women of color, Lorde's work indicates that
women of color are acknowledging and theorizing butch and
femme identities as well as styles that do not fit the traditional
categories of "role-play."[45] Writings by women of color that address how issues of racism intertwine with issues of sexual style
confirm the presence of a hierarchy of visible markers of difference which radical theories of subjectivity are still unable to
evade. The need to dismantle this hierarchy forms the basis of my
critique of grounding radical political identity in the visible emblems of difference. I do not want to obscure the fact that the impulse to privilege the visible often arises out of the need to reclaim signifiers of difference which dominant ideologies have
used to define minority identities negatively. But while this strategy of reclamation is often affirming, it can also replicate the
practices of the dominant ideologies which use visibility to create

social categories on the basis of exclusion. The paradigm of visibility is totalizing when a signifier of difference becomes synonymous with the identity it signifies. In this situation, members of a given population who do not bear that signifier of difference or who bear visible signs of another identity are rendered invisible and are marginalized within an already marginalized community.

By way of conclusion, I suggest that the relationship between a visible signifier of difference and its signified identity might be complicated. I propose that more attention be paid to the differences within the identities that are the subject of theory. For example, within the community of drag queens that Judith Butler analyzes, how differently would her theory about the destabilization of culturally intelligible gender identities apply to drag queens who play up the juxtaposition of the "masculine" and the "feminine" (for example, by letting razor stubble show through their makeup) and those who mimic culturally intelligible gender identities by presenting a unified image of "woman" (for example, straight guys ask them out when they're in drag)? Following this line of thought, it seems crucial that we consider how various individuals conceptualize their positions within specific configurations of the visible. Attention to ambivalence about self-image in the context of both hegemonic and subcultural values should be particularly relevant to analyzing the politics of visibility. In taking up the issue of what I have described as privileging the visible signifier of difference, I do not mean to suggest that visibility is not an arena in which to engage questions about radical subjectivities. Rather, it is my argument that we should continue to complicate our ideas about what counts as radical self-representation for minority identities.

Epilogue

This book began with a conversation about the invisibility of the feminine lesbian. As I moved to closure on the project, I found myself having a slightly different conversation—a conversation about a term that has come into fairly common parlance, and that tells us something about the nature of the femme's increased visibility in mainstream culture. That term, "lipstick lesbian," is one that I have always rejected in favor of "femme." It's not that I minimize the significance of lipstick. I'm thinking of having my rather paltry collection of about thirty lipsticks covered on my apartment insurance: if I should lose them in a fire, it would cost almost three hundred dollars to replace the dozen or so Chanels alone. But "lipstick lesbian" reduces my entire identity to a single accessory (what about my shoes, stored in two rows of clear plastic boxes that nearly reach the ceiling? what about the pocketbook installation in my walk-in closet? what about the spools of colored ribbon I use to make my dog hair bows that coordinate with my outfits?). For me, "lipstick lesbian" is a derogatory term that conjures up an apolitical creature, a "lifestyle lesbian," a lesbian who writes "no butches" in her personal ad—a lesbian who doesn't want to be a dyke and doesn't want to be associated with dykes. If the femme has been part of the "lesbian chic" of the 1990s, she stands, as the lesbian who is interested in fashion, for the fashionability of lesbianism taken out of historical and social context and divested of political relevance.[1]

This discussion of the lipstick lesbian helped me to rethink what I hoped to achieve by taking on this project, when I had begun to question the purpose of a book about visibility and identity in the context of discussions about "postidentity" politics. It may be inevitable that in finishing a book, one looks back on it and feels that its arguments are self-evident. *Looking Like What You Are* is written in response to and is part of a critical moment that saw a flurry of books about cross-dressing, passing, and race mixing, including Richard Dyer's *White* (1997), Marjorie Garber's *Vested Interests: Cross-Dressing and Cultural Anxiety* (1992), Elaine Ginsberg's *Passing and the Fictions of Identity* (1996), Eric Lott's *Love and Theft: Blackface Minstrelsy and the American Working Class* (1993), and the publication of a number of books and essays on postmodern queer theory, including Laura Doan's *The Lesbian Postmodern*, Diana Fuss's *Inside/Out*, and Michael Warner's *Fear of a Queer Planet*.[2] All these books complicate notions of stable identity. In the wake of these examinations of boundary crossing and these poststructuralist critiques of identity discourse, don't we all know that the ethnic model of lesbian and gay identity creates the fiction of a unified lesbian and gay culture and assimilates ethnic and racial difference? That the fight for cultural visibility doesn't necessarily lead to political representation? That white is a color, that lesbians can be feminine, that the unmarked do not necessarily occupy the position of the dominant? Don't we all know that identity politics creates margins among the marginalized? And hasn't difference subverted identity in the realm of lesbian and gay politics?

Perhaps. But the analogy between race and homosexuality, which underlies the ethnic model of homosexuality and which is the basis for ongoing arguments about the nature of lesbian and gay visibility, continues to be one of the primary rubrics for talking about sexual orientation. The desire for visibility, for cultural and social recognition, still drives our political agendas even in the face of our awareness that in a consumer culture, "mainstream" visibility can be a vehicle for commodification. Whiteness is still regarded as the universal/unmarked, the authenticity of the feminine lesbian is still in question, the marginalization of the marginalized continues to frustrate efforts to build coalition politics, and difference hasn't entirely subverted identity. Indeed, those writers who are frequently cited as paving the way for a new politics of difference that revises and goes beyond a modernist politics of reclaiming the marginalized subject and restoring her to cultural visibility—Gloria Anzaldúa, Audre Lorde, Cherríe Moraga, Minnie Bruce Pratt, Barbara Smith—are all deeply concerned with claiming as well as subverting identity, and with achieving visibility even as they dispute its conditions.

My own work walks a line between celebrating and critiquing visibility politics. I have an express interest in showing that the feminine lesbian does have political relevance, that she challenges the parameters of visibility that have grounded lesbian identity. While trying not to position the femme as one whose place at the margins of lesbian visibility gives her a privileged point of view, I do assert throughout this book that studying the feminine lesbian in relation to other figures, both marginalized and dominant, reveals how the visual typification of identities often replicates the hierarchies on which identity categories are built—hierarchies of gender and racial difference in particular. Yet I would not sacrifice the pleasures and the power of identity politics or visibility politics. If the primary mode of identity politics is an insistence on the self, and the primary mode of visibility politics is a public self-fashioning, in claiming the "label" femme, I manipulate both modes, quietly believing that there is something inherent about my identity, and putting that identity on display in a way that I hope demands a rethinking of what a lesbian looks like.

I might theorize my own participation in the discourses and practices I also critique in a number of ways. I might castigate myself for my complicity with the systems of oppression I try to dismantle. I might, more gently, draw attention to how I am inevitably bound by the cultural regimes that allow me to speak and also delimit what I can say and how I can say it. I might talk about critical ambivalence—ambivalence having become a popular diagnosis of contradiction. In this case, however, I think that contradiction is the appropriate term. I live in sustained contradiction, knowing that what I think and what I act on are not always the same. The sustained contradiction is one of the threads that runs through my discussion of the way we conceptualize sexual orientation and racial identity.

Placing this book in the context of other recent arguments about the current political and cultural status of identity and representation, I would say that sustained contradiction could describe our situation: Having destabilized the unitary subject and questioned the efficacy of visibility politics, it is not yet possible to set aside our interests in identity and representation for a more sophisticated postmodern politics. Or to put it another way, postmodern politics do and must continue attending to issues of identity and representation. Using the feminine lesbian as a point of departure, I have tried to open up these issues and to raise new questions about visibility and subjectivity, hoping to encourage further questions and more conversations like those that mark the beginning and ending of this book.

Notes

Notes to the Preface

1. Pat Califia, "Clit Culture: Cherchez la Femme. . . ." *On Our Backs* 8, no. 4 (1992):10.

Notes to the Introduction

1. For a discussion of how punk style has informed queer style through radical protest movements such as Queer Nation and ACT UP, see Jeff Goldthorpe, "Intoxicated Culture: Punk Symbolism and Punk Protest," *Socialist Review* 22, no. 2 (1992):55–60.

2. Danae Clark, "Commodity Lesbianism," *Camera Obscura* no. 25–26 (1991):180–201.

3. Nancy Leys Stepan, "Race and Gender: The Role of Analogy in Science," in *Anatomy of Racism*, ed. David Goldberg (Minneapolis: University of Minnesota, 1990), 38–57.

4. Historians of sexuality have argued that the concept of homosexuality as an identity rather than a sexual act emerged at the beginning of the twentieth century, when medical science became increasingly concerned with categorizing and explaining "deviant" sexualities. Before that time, homosexual relations were thought of as localized instances of unnatural sexual behavior to which anyone might be susceptible, especially given the right circumstances. In early theories of same-sex relations, engaging in homosexual practices did not designate a distinct sexual identity, but was construed as a lapse into sinfulness or perversion. On homosexuality as a modern identity, see Michel Foucault, *The History of Sexuality,* vol. 1: *An Introduction* (New York: Vintage Books, 1980), 43; and Jeffrey Weeks, *Sex, Politics, and Society: The Regulation of Sexuality since 1800* (New York: Longman, 1981), 1–11.

5. Havelock Ellis, *Studies in the Psychology of Sex,* vol. 1 (1936. Reprint, New York: Random House, 1942), 251. Sexual Inversion was first printed in England in 1897, and reprinted in Ellis's multivolume work, *Studies in the Psychology of Sex.*

6. Ellis, *Studies,* 253.

7. Richard von Krafft-Ebing, *Psychopathis Sexualis.* Trans. F. J. Rebman. (1886. Reprint, Brooklyn, N.Y.: Physicians and Surgeons Book Company, 1932), 426.

8. Ellis, *Studies,* 222.

9. Dr. George Henry, *Sex Variants: A Study of Homosexual Patterns,* vols. 1 and 2 (New York: Paul B. Hoeber, 1941).

10. Henry, *Sex Variants,* vol. 2, 1115.

11. Krafft-Ebing, *Psychopathis Sexualis,* 340.

12. Henry, *Sex Variants,* vol. 1, xv.

13. For discussions of the medical model in America, see John D'Emilio, *Sexual Politics, Sexual Communities: The Making of a Homosexual Minority in the United States, 1940–1970* (Chicago: University of Chicago Press, 1983), especially 17–19.

14. Judith Butler, *Gender Trouble and the Subversion of Identity* (New York: Routlege, 1990), 24. For a critique of visibility politics and an analysis of Butler, see Rosemary Hennessy, "Queer Visibility in Commodity Culture," *Cultural Critique* (1994–95):31–76.

15. Judith Butler, "Critically Queer," *GLQ: A Journal of Lesbian and Gay Studies* 1, no. 1 (1993):22.

16. Carole-Anne Tyler, "Passing: Narcissism, Identity and Difference," *Differences* 6, no. 2/3 (1994):212.

17. For another discussion of the limitations of visibility politics with regard to passing, see Peggy Phelan, *Unmarked: The Politics of Performance* (New York: Routledge, 1993), 6–11.

18. Elaine Ginsberg, *Passing and the Fictions of Identity* (Durham, N.C.: Duke University Press, 1996), 2.

19. Carole-Anne Tyler, "Boys Will Be Girls: The Politics of Gay Drag," in *Inside/Out: Lesbian Theories, Gay Theories,* ed. Diana Fuss (New York: Routledge, 1991), 33.

20. Richard Dyer, "Seen to Be Believed: Some Problems in the Representation of Gay People as Typical," in his *The Matter of Images: Essays on Representations* (London: Routledge, 1993), 19.

21. Dyer, "Seen to Be Believed," 19.

22. Lisa Walker, "Embodying Desire: Piercing and the Fashioning of 'Neo-Butch/Femme' Identities," in *Butch/Femme: Inside Lesbian Gender,* ed. Sally R. Munt (Washington, D.C.: Cassell, 1998), 123–32.

23. Terry Castle, *The Apparitional Lesbian: Female Homosexuality and Modern Culture* (New York: Columbia University Press, 1993); Renee C. Hoogland, *Lesbian Configurations* (New York: Columbia University Press, 1997).

24. Hoogland, *Lesbian Configurations*, 25.

25. Toni Morrison, *Playing in the Dark: Whiteness and the Literary Imagination* (Cambridge, Mass.: Harvard University Press, 1992).

26. Ginsberg, *Passing and the Fictions of Identity*, 9.

27. Jane Gaines, "White Privilege and Looking Relations: Race and Gender in Feminist Film Theory," in *Issues in Feminist Film Criticism*, ed. Patricia Evans (Bloomington: Indiana University Press, 1990), 207.

28. For example, see Michele Wallace, *Invisibility Blues: From Pop to Theory* (New York: Verso, 1990); the special issue of *Empathy* 2, no. 2 (1990–91) on Visibility and Invisibility; Evelyn Torton Beck, "The Politics of Jewish Invisibility," *NWSA Journal* 1, no. 1 (1988):93–102; and Jewelle Gomez, "Imagine a Lesbian . . . A Black Lesbian . . ." *Trivia* 12 (1988):45–60.

29. Homi Bhabha, "Interrogating Identity: Franz Fanon and the Postcolonial Prerogative," in his *The Location of Culture* (New York, Routledge, 1986), 199.

30. Eve Sedgwick, *Epistemology of the Closet* (Berkeley: University of California Press, 1990), 75–81.

31. Ralph Ellison, *Invisible Man* (1952. Reprint, New York: Vintage Books, 1995), xv.

32. Using sexual difference as her paradigm in *Unmarked*, Peggy Phelan explains how, within the system of marking, marks of value are transformed into marks of difference that leave the dominant position unmarked:

> As psychoanalysis and Derridean deconstruction have demonstrated, the epistemological, psychic, and political binaries of Western metaphysics create distinctions and evaluations across two terms. One term of the binary is marked with value, the other is unmarked. The male is marked with value; the female is unmarked, lacking measured value and meaning. Within this psycho-philosophical frame, cultural reproduction takes she who is unmarked and re-marks her, rhetorically and imagistically, while he who is marked with value is left unremarked, in discursive paradigms and visual fields. He is the norm and therefore unremarkable; as the Other, it is she whom he marks. (1993:5)

33. *All the Women Are White, All the Blacks Are Men, But Some of Us Are Brave: Black Women's Studies,* ed. Gloria T. Hull, Patricia Bell Scott, and Barbara Smith (New York: Feminist Press, 1982). Providing readings and resources in black women's studies, the book positions itself in response to the exclusion of black women from African American Studies, which has focused primarily on male history, and from women's studies, which has been concerned primarily with white women, drawing attention to the double oppression of black women in a racist and sexist culture.

34. I borrow the phrase "critical double bind" and the opposition between downplaying epistemic violence and negating the subjectivity of the oppressed from Henry Louis Gates's reading of the standoff between Abdul JanMohamed and Homi Bhabha over their readings of Franz Fanon. See Henry Louis Gates Jr., "Critical Fanonism," *Critical Inquiry* 17 (1991):457–70.

35. On Rhys as a modernist writer, see Coral Ann Howells, *Jean Rhys* (London: Harvester Wheatsheaf, 1991). Howell argues that the modernist identity crisis is related, for Rhys, to her position as a postcolonial writer:

> Historically, Rhys belongs to the period of Empire and her own formation as a white Creole is a distinctly colonial one; yet her subversive critique of Englishness and imperialism . . . should more appropriately be described as a post-colonial impulse. (1991:20)

36. Houston Baker offers one model for a broadened definition of modernism based on historical changes in structures of identity. In *Modernism and the Harlem Renaissance* (Chicago: Chicago University Press, 1987). Baker marks the commencement of "Afro-American modernism" on September 18, 1895, with Booker T. Washington's opening address at the Negro exhibit of the Atlanta Cotton States and International Exposition. Baker argues that Washington's speech set a new direction "for a mass of black citizens who had struggled through the thirty years since emancipation" (1987:15). Historians such as Michel Foucault and Jeffrey Weeks have argued in similar vein that the late nineteenth and early twentieth centuries marked the advent of new sexual identities defining the lesbian and the homosexual as personages. Thus, during the early to mid-twentieth century changing racial and sexual identities were very much at the forefront of cultural consciousness.

Notes to Chapter 1

1. Del Martin and Phyllis Lyon dubbed *The Well of Loneliness* "the Lesbian bible" in their book, *Lesbian/Woman* (New York: Bantam, 1972), 22.

2. Throughout the chapter, I shift between the terms "invert," "mannish woman," "lesbian," "butch," and "femme." The terms "invert" and "mannish woman" refer to historically specific models of homosexual identity that Hall borrowed from sexology. "Lesbian" refers more broadly to contemporary possibilities for lesbian identity, and "butch" and "femme" refer to specifically gendered lesbian identities that properly belong to the second half of the twentieth century, but can be traced back to earlier representations of the lesbian such as Hall's.

3. For a discussion of the connection between lesbian visibility and literary style, see Leigh Gilmore's comparative reading of *The Well* and *Nightwood* in her essay, "Obscenity, Modernity, Identity: Legalizing *The Well of Loneliness* and *Nightwood*," *Journal of the History of Sexuality* 4, no. 4 (1994):603–24.

4. Catherine R. Stimpson characterizes *The Well* as a "narrative of damnation" in her influential overview of lesbian literature, "Zero Degree Deviancy: The Lesbian Novel in English," *Critical Inquiry* 8, no. 2 (1981):247.

5. Vern Bullough and Bonnie Bullough, "Lesbianism in the 1920's and 1930's: A Newfound Study," *Signs* 2, no. 4 (1977):897.

6. James Douglas, *Sunday Express*, August 19, 1928.

7. Nigel Nicholson, *Portrait of a Marriage* (New York: Athenaeum, 1973), 202.

8. Virginia Woolf, *The Letters of Virginia Woolf*, vol. 3, *1923–1928*, ed. Nigel Nicholson and Joanne Trautmann (New York: Harcourt, 1978), 563.

9. Adam Parkes, "Lesbianism, History, and Censorship: *The Well of Loneliness* and the SUPPRESSED RANDINESS of Virginia Woolf's *Orlando*," *Twentieth Century Literature* 40, no. 4 (1994):435–36.

10. Inez Martinez gives a useful synopsis of the critical discomfort with the novel:

[Feminist critics] are embarrassed by her writing style, by the suffering she portrays, and by what they deem her misogyny. Lillian Faderman and Ann Williams in "Radclyffe Hall and the Lesbian Image," Dolores Klatch in *Woman + Woman*, and Blanche Cook in "'Women Alone Stir My Imagination': Lesbianism and the Cultural Tradition," all deplore the "self-pity and self-loathing" in Hall's lesbian heroes. Jane Rule in *Lesbian Images* frankly accuses Hall of believing men superior to women and of worshiping patriarchy. . . . Both Rule and Cook ascribe this poverty of vision to Hall's reading of Karl Heinrich Ulrichs and Krafft-Ebing.

"The Lesbian Hero Bound: Radclyffe Hall's Portrait of Sapphic Daughters and Their Mothers," *Journal of Homosexuality* 8, no. 3–4 (1983):127. To this summary one might add Stimpson's "Zero Degree Deviancy," which argues that *The Well* "projects homosexuality as a sickness," and so defeats its own attack on homophobia because "it gives the homosexual, particularly the lesbian, riddling images of self-pity, and of terror—in greater measure than it consoles" (1981:248–49).

11. Esther Newton, "The Mythic Mannish Lesbian: Radclyffe Hall and the New Woman," in *Hidden from History: Reclaiming the Gay and Lesbian Past*, ed. Martin Bauml Duberman (New York: New American Library, 1989), 290.

12. Foucault argues that "through the formation of a 'reverse' discourse," "homosexuality began to speak in its own behalf, to demand that its legitimacy or 'naturality' be acknowledged, often in the same vocabulary, using the same categories by which it was medically disqualified." Michel Foucault, *The History of Sexuality*, vol. 1: *An Introduction* (New York: Vintage Books, 1980), 101. In this vein, George Chauncey argues persuasively against the notion that lesbians and gays were brainwashed by medical discourses. George Chauncey, "From Sexual Inversion to Homosexuality: Medicine and the Changing Conceptualization of Female Deviance," *Salmagundi* 58 (1982–83):115.

Critics who have made similar arguments in their readings of *The Well* are Teresa de Lauretis, "Sexual Indifference and Lesbian Representation," *Theatre Journal* 40, no. 2 (1988):155–77; Jonathan Dollimore, "The Dominant and the Deviant: A Violent Dialectic," in *Homosexual Themes in Literary Studies*, ed. Wayne R. Dynes and Stephen Donaldson (New York: Garland, 1992), 87–100; Jean Radford, "An Inverted Romance: *The Well of Loneliness* and Sexual Ideology," in *The Progress of Romance: The Politics of Popular Fiction*, ed. Jean Radford (London: Routledge and Kegan Paul, 1986), 97–111; and Sonja Ruehl, "Inverts and Experts: Radclyffe Hall and the Lesbian Identity," in *Feminist Criticism and Social Change: Sex, Class and Race in Literature and Culture*, ed. Judith Newton and Deborah Rosenfelt (New York: Methuen, 1985), 165–80.

13. Patricia Duncker is perhaps the most blunt in her assessment of *The Well*'s value as an "out" text. See her *Sisters and Strangers: An Introduction to Contemporary Feminist Fiction* (Cambridge, Mass.: Blackwell, 1992), 168. But other critics have made similar claims. Radford argues for the continued relevance of *The Well* partially on the basis that it has been and is still "read as a story for lesbians as well as a story for those who wish to understand more about women's sexuality" (1986:98); Newton argues that *The Well* "continues to have meaning to lesbians because it confronts the stigma of lesbianism—as most lesbians have had to live it" (1989:282); and Shelly Skinner says that "readers see *The Well of Loneliness* as the principal lesbian novel because it does express a lesbian experience which other writers, like Virginia Woolf, merely intimate." Shelly Skinner, "The House in Order: Lesbian Identity and *The Well of Loneliness*," *Women's Studies* 23 (1994):19.

For discussions of the notion that modernist lesbian writing is coded, see Julie Abraham, *Are Girls Necessary? Lesbian Writing and Modern Histories* (New York: Routledge, 1996); Marianne DeKoven, "Gertrude Stein and the Modernist Canon," in *Gertrude Stein and the Making of Literature*, ed. Shirley Newman and Ira B. Nadel (Boston: Northeastern University Press, 1988); Leigh Gilmore, "Obscenity, Modernity, Identity"; Elizabeth Meese, *(Sem)Erotics: Theorizing Lesbian: Writing* (New York: New York University Press, 1992); Stimpson's essays, "Zero Degree Deviancy: The Lesbian Novel in English," and "Gertrude Stein and the Lesbian Lie," in *American Women's Autobiography: Fea(s)ts of Memory*, ed. Margo Culley (Madison: University of Wisconsin Press, 1992), 152–66; and Bonnie Zimmerman, "What Has Never Been: An Overview of Lesbian Feminist Literary Criticism," in *The New Feminist Criticism: Essays on Women, Literature and Theory*, ed. Elaine Showalter (New York: Pantheon Books, 1985).

14. Abraham, *Are Girls Necessary?* 23.

15. Rita Felski, *The Gender of Modernity* (Cambridge, Mass.: Harvard University Press, 1995), 26.

16. Shari Benstock coined the term "Sapphic Modernism" in her essay, "Expatriate Sapphic Modernism Entering Literary History," in *Rereading Modernism: New Directions in Feminist Criticism*, ed. Lisa Rado (New York: Garland, 1994), 97–121.

17. For discussions of Stein's sartorial style, see Shari Benstock, *Women of the Left Bank: Paris, 1900–1940* (Austin: University of Texas Press, 1986), 177–84; and Catherine Stimpson, "The Somagrams of Gertrude Stein," in *The Female Body in Western Culture:*

Contemporary Perspectives, ed. Susan Suleiman (Cambridge, Mass.: Harvard University Press, 1986), 30–43.

18. Stimpson, "The Somagrams of Gertrude Stein," 32.

19. Catherine R. Stimpson, "Gertrude Stein and the Transposition of Gender," in *The Poetics of Gender*, ed. Nancy K. Miller (New York: Columbia University Press, 1986), 5.

20. Benstock, *Women of the Left Bank*, 165.

21. Catherine R. Stimpson, "Gertrice/Altrude: Stein, Toklas, and the Paradox of the Happy Marriage," in *Mothering the Mind: Twelve Studies of Writers and Their Silent Partners*, ed. Ruth Perry and Martine Watson Brownley (New York: Holmes and Meier, 1984), 124, 135.

22. Meese, *(Sem)Erotics*, 65.

23. Stimpson, "Gertrice/Altrude," 131.

24. Marianne DeKoven, *A Different Language: Gertrude Stein's Experimental Writing* (Madison: University of Wisconsin Press, 1983), 36–37.

25. Many biographies of Hall, including Troubridge's, discuss the relationship at length. See, for example, Michael Baker, *Our Three Selves: The Life of Radclyffe Hall* (New York: William Morrow, 1985); Sally Cline, *Radclyffe Hall: A Woman Called John* (New York: Overlook Press, 1997); Diana Souhami, *The Trials of Radclyffe Hall* (New York: Doubleday, 1999); and Una Lady Troubridge, *The Life and Death of Radclyffe Hall* (London: Hammond, 1961).

26. Stimpson, "Gertrude Stein and the Lesbian Lie," 161.

27. On Stein's appropriation of Toklas's voice, see Stimpson, "Lesbian Lie," 158–59. Other critics maintain that the autobiographies raise questions of authorship to call attention to the instability of the subject in general, and the lesbian subject in particular. See James Breslin, "Gertrude Stein and the Problems of Autobiography," in *Women's Autobiography: Essays in Criticism* (Bloomington: Indiana University Press, 1980); Leigh Gilmore, *Autobiographics: A Feminist Theory of Women's Self-Representation* (Ithaca: Cornell University Press, 1994), 199–223; and Cynthia Merrill, "Mirrored Image: Gertrude Stein and Autobiography," *Pacific Coast Philology* 20, no. 1–2 (1985), 11–17.

28. Stimpson, "Lesbian Lie," 161.

29. Stimpson, "Lesbian Lie," 161.

30. Studies of butch and femme within the twentieth century suggest that while the meanings of butch and femme change over time, the categories themselves are not specific to a single historical period. See Lillian Faderman, "The Return of Butch and Femme: A Phenomenon in Lesbian Sexuality of the 1980s and 1990s," *Journal of the History of*

Sexuality 2, no. 4 (1992):578–96; Tracy Morgan, "Butch-Femme and the Politics of Identity," in *Sisters, Sexperts and Queers: Beyond the Lesbian Nation*, ed. Arlene Stein (New York: Penguin, 1993), 35–46; Joan Nestle, "The Fem Question," in *The Persistent Desire: A Femme-Butch Reader*, ed. Joan Nestle (Boston: Alyson Publications, 1992), 138–46; and Vera Whisman, "Identity Crisis: Who Is a Lesbian Anyway?" in *Sisters, Sexperts and Queers: Beyond the Lesbian Nation*, ed. Arlene Stein (New York: Penguin, 1993), 47–60.

31. See Gilmore, *Autobiographics*, and Merrill, "Mirrored Image." Both argue that Alice is a crucial intermediary in Stein's creation of public identity and lesbian subjectivity; even here, though, Alice functions as the "mirror" through which Stein's subjectivity is created.

32. For example, Benstock quotes Stimpson's statement that "to oversimplify the Stein/Toklas marriage and menage is stupid. Toklas was also a willful woman whom Stein sought to please," but goes on to discuss the relationship as sadomasochistic. Benstock, *Women of the Left Bank*, 130, 165.

33. Criticism following Newton's essay, "The Mythic Mannish Lesbian," and Joan Nestle's 1987 essay, "Butch-Femme Relationships: Sexual Courage in the 1950's," in *A Restricted Country* (Ithaca: Fireband Books, 1987), tends to complicate the notion that butch-femme relationships were based on static roles modeled after heterosexual marriage. See Meese's discussion of the Stein/Toklas ménage in *(Sem)Erotics*, and Gilmore's discussion of the same relationship in *Autobiographics*.

34. Quoted in Joanne Glasgow, "Rethinking the Mythic Mannish Radclyffe Hall," in *Queer Representations: Reading Lives, Reading Cultures*, ed. Martin Duberman (New York: New York University Press, 1997), 25.

35. The novel also uses Christian rhetoric to defend the homosexual. For more detailed readings of religion and homosexuality, see Radford, "An Inverted Romance," and Joanne Glasgow, "What's a Nice Lesbian Like You Doing in the Church of the Torquemada? Radclyffe Hall and Other Catholic Converts," in *Lesbian Texts and Contexts: Radical Revisions*, ed. Karla Jay (New York: New York University Press, 1990). With reference to Cain specifically, Dollimore notes that "Stephen the invert is nothing less than a blend of Cain and Christ, simultaneously transgressing God's law and sacrificing herself to save an ignorant, philistine humanity." Jonathan Dollimore, *Sexual Dissidence: Augustine to Wilde, Freud to Foucault* (Oxford: Clarendon Press, 1991), 49.

36. Radclyffe Hall, *The Well of Loneliness* (1928. Reprint, New

York: Avon Books, 1982), 352–53. All further references are to the 1982 edition.

37. For more on class and gender in *The Well*, see Dollimore, who argues that the narrative voice seems unaware of the extent to which it is "class rather than nature which constructs the particular notion of masculinity being used." Dollimore, "The Dominant and the Deviant," 183.

38. The metaphor of castration (Sir Phillip's blind pencil-groping) in connection with Stephen's indiscernibility alludes to the power structures that enable marking. The indiscernible body impedes the dominant figure's ability to control the system of signification that constructs homosexual difference as otherness.

39. Lee Edelman develops the connection between writing, reading, seeing, and homosexual difference in his essay "Homographesis," *Yale Journal of Criticism* 3, no. 1 (1989):189–207. The title of the essay identifies a term that the author summarizes elsewhere as referring to "the disciplinary and projective fantasy that homosexuality is visibly, morphologically, or semiotically, written upon the flesh, so that homosexuality comes to occupy the stigmatized position of writing itself within the Western metaphysics of presence." Lee Edelman, "Tea Rooms and Sympathy, or, The Epistemology of the Water Closet," in *The Lesbian and Gay Studies Reader*, ed. Michele Aina Barale et al. (New York: Routledge, 1993), 571 n23.

40. Hélène Cixous, "The Laugh of the Medusa," in *New French Feminisms*, ed. Elaine Marks and Isabelle de Courtivron Marks (Amherst: University of Massachusetts Press, 1980), 250.

41. Judith Roof points out that Cixous's theory of writing the body also perpetuates binary gender oppositions in her representation of the lesbian by "split[ting] lesbian sexuality into two categories, phallicizing it on the one hand and making it homogeneously feminine on the other hand." Judith Roof, *A Lure of Knowledge: Lesbian Sexuality and Theory* (New York: Columbia University Press, 1991), 135. In this, perhaps, Cixous is no more successful than Hall at evading or subverting oppositional thinking.

42. Judith Halberstrom, *Female Masculinity* (Durham, N.C.: Duke University Press, 1998), 102.

43. Halberstrom, *Female Masculinity*, 106.

44. Halberstrom, *Female Masculinity*, 99.

45. Gilmore notes that for "the contemporary reader, the use of 'queer' by everyone in the household except her father to describe

Stephen is practically redundant. . . . [T]he father, a well-read person of means, does not call Stephen 'queer' because he understands more precisely what is strange about his daughter." Gilmore, "Obscenity, Modernity, Identity," 609. In her reading of Nella Larsen's *Passing*, a novel that was published the same year as *The Well of Loneliness*, Judith Butler suggests that while at the time, "'queer' did not yet mean homosexual . . . it did encompass an array of meanings associated with deviation from normalcy which might well include the sexual," and so it resonates with the term's current connotations. Judith Butler, *Bodies That Matter: On the Discursive Limits of "Sex"* (New York: Routlege, 1993), 176.

46. Gillian Whitlock, "'Everything Is Out of Place': Radclyffe Hall and the Lesbian Literary Tradition," *Feminist Studies* 13, no. 3 (1987): 563–66.

47. Whitlock, "'Everything Is Out of Place,'" 564.

48. The consolidation of the butch's masculine identity through opposition to the feminine is complicated when that masculine identity breaks down at the end of the novel. During the strange vision in which Stephen recognizes her calling as the spiritual mother and defender of the oppressed invert, effeminate hands accuse her of using them to strengthen her masculine position and then refusing them:

And these terrible ones started pointing at her with their shaking, white-skinned, effeminate fingers: "You and your kind have stolen our birthright; you have taken our strength and have given us your weakness!" They were pointing at her with white, shaking fingers. . . . "You dare not disown us!" (1982:436–37)

The boundary between masculine and feminine seems to blur as the effeminate outcasts reclaim Stephen by possessing her womb, reinscribing her masculinized body within the realm of the feminine/maternal. This apparent moment of union does not resolve but sustains the tension between the natural and the unnatural that consistently characterizes the relation between masculine and feminine, and homosexual and heterosexual in *The Well*. Stephen's body is both fruitful and sterile; she is both mother and monster: "Her barren womb became fruitful—it ached with its fearful and sterile burden" (1982:437). Here, the dialectic of desire and repulsion still circulates around the difference between the masculine body of the female invert and the feminine/maternal body.

49. At the time of the book's publication, Vera Brittain critiqued the rigidity of Hall's conception of gender roles as follows:

Miss Hall appears to take for granted that this over-emphasis of sex characteristics is part of the correct education of the normal human being; she therefore makes her "normal" woman clinging and "feminine" to exasperation and even describes the attitudes towards love as "an end in itself" as being a necessary attribute to true womanhood. Many readers will know too many happy wives and mothers for whom it is not, to take on trust Miss Hall's selection of the qualities essential to one sex or the other.

Vera Brittain, *Radclyffe Hall: A Case of Obscenity?* (London: Femina, 1968), 50.

50. Newton, "The Mythic Mannish Lesbian," 292–93.

51. See Benstock, *Women of the Left Bank*, and Karla Jay, *The Amazon and the Page: Natalie Clifford Barney and Renee Vivien* (Bloomington: Indiana University Press, 1988), for useful analyses of how Barney revised French representations of the lesbian and developed the cult of female beauty and the "religion of love." As in the discussion of sexual and literary style with regard to Stein and Hall, Benstock raises the question of why Barney, a forward-thinking lesbian feminist, wrote in "an outdated form of French prosody" rather than a "radical and unconventional form of expression" (1986:282).

52. Benstock, *Women of the Left Bank,* 281.

53. Alan Sinfeld, *The Wilde Century: Effeminacy, Oscar Wilde and the Queer Moment* (London: Cassell, 1994), offers a detailed study of how Wilde crystallized the connection between aestheticism, decadence, and homosexuality. See chapter 4, "Aestheticism and Decadence."

54. Dollimore, "The Dominant and the Deviant," 188.

55. Dollimore, "The Dominant and the Deviant," 188. Clearly, Valerie does not represent camp in the same way that Wilde does; she doesn't like the spectacle of queens in the bars, where she sits "calm and aloof" as if to say, "'Enfin, the whole world has grown very ugly, but no doubt to some people this represents pleasure'" (Hall 1982:382). This distaste, however, is a function of her Romantic aesthetics more than her refusal of superficiality. While this does not fully distance her from the camp aesthetic as Dollimore describes it, her response is more indicative of her association with decadence than with camp per se.

56. See Katie King, "The Situation of Lesbianism as Feminism's Magical Sign," *Communication* 9 (1986):65–91, for a discussion of the problematic way that a given sign, such as lesbianism, can become a "magical" site in which political identity is constructed.

57. Ruehl, "Inverts and Experts," 171.

58. Dollimore, "The Dominant and the Deviant," 188.

59. For discussions of Hall's difficulty in representing the feminine lesbian, see Alison Hennegan, "Introduction," *The Well of Loneliness* by Radclyffe Hall (1928. Reprint, London: Virago Press, 1982), xv–xvii; and Leslie J. Henson, "'Articulate Silence[s]': Femme Subjectivity and Class Relations in *The Well of Loneliness*," in *Femme: Feminists, Lesbians and Bad Girls*, ed. Laura Harris and Elizabeth Crocker (New York: Routledge, 1997), 61–67. On imperialism and Hall's representation of the feminine lesbian, see Margot Gayle Backus, "Sexual Orientation in the (Post)Imperial Nation: Celticism and Inversion Theory in Radclyffe Hall's *The Well of Loneliness*," *Tulsa Studies in Women's Literature* 15, no. 2 (1996):253–66.

Notes to Chapter 2

1. On the ethnic model of homosexuality, see Jeffrey Escoffier, "Sexual Revolution and the Politics of Gay Identity," *Socialist Review* 20, no. 82–83 (1985):119–53. On white slumming in Harlem, see Lillian Faderman, *Odd Girls and Twilight Lovers: A History of Lesbian Life in Twentieth Century America* (New York: Columbia University Press, 1991), 67–72.

2. On the use of analogy in nineteenth-century race science, see Nancy Leys Stepan, "Race and Gender: The Role of Analogy in Science," in *Anatomy of Racism*, ed. David Goldberg (Minneapolis: University of Minnesota, 1990), 38–57.

3. Homi Bhabha, "The Other Question: Difference, Discrimination and the Discourse of Colonialism," in *Literature, Politics, Theory: Papers from the Essex Conference, 1976–84*, ed. Francis Barker et al. (New York: Methuen, 1986), 161.

4. See Carroll Smith Rosenberg, "The New Woman as Androgyne: Social Disorder and Gender Crisis, 1870–1936," in *Disorderly Conduct: Visions of Gender in Victorian America* (New York: Alfred A. Knopf, 1985), 245–96.

5. "Review of *Strange Brother*," *Saturday Review of Literature*, 1931.

6. Blair Niles, *Condemned to Devil's Island: The Biography of an Unknown Convict* (New York: Harcourt, Brace, 1928), xiii.

7. Robert A. Coles and Diane Isaacs, "Primitivism as a Therapeutic

Pursuit: Notes toward a Reassessment of Harlem Renaissance Literature," in *The Harlem Renaissance: Revaluations*, ed. Amritjit Singh (New York: Garland, 1989), 3–12.

8. Niles, *Condemned*, xiii and 133.

9. Arthur O. Lovejoy, *Primitivism and Related Ideas in Antiquity* (1935. Reprint, New York: Octagon Books, 1973), 7.

10. David R. Roediger dates a form of primitivism in America from the era following the Civil War: "the growing popular sense of whiteness represented a hesitantly emerging consensus holding together a very diverse white working class . . . part of that consensus derived from the idea that blackness could be made permanently to embody the preindustrial past that they scorned and missed." His analysis of how primitivism consolidates working-class white identity suggests that the study of primitivism in America has been class-biased in its traditional focus on the primitivist aesthetic of the upper classes during the 1920s. David R. Roediger, *Toward the Abolition of Whiteness* (London: Verso, 1994), 152.

11. On the impact of Freud in the United States, see Nathan G. Hale, *The Rise and Crisis of Psychoanalysis in the United States: Freud and the Americans, 1917–1985* (New York: Oxford University Press, 1995). On Freud's visit to Clark University, see 58–59.

12. T. J. Jackson Lears, *No Place of Grace: Antimodernism and the Transformation of American Culture, 1880–1920* (New York: Pantheon Books, 1981), provides a useful study of the fear of "overcivilization" at the turn of the century. On the fear of impotency in particular, see Kevin J. Mumford, "'Lost Manhood' Found: Male Sexual Impotence and Victorian Culture in the United States," in *American Sexual Politics: Sex, Gender and Race since the Civil War*, ed. John C. Fout and Maura Shaw Tantillo (Chicago: University of Chicago Press, 1993).

13. Theodore Roosevelt, "Race Decadence" and "Women and the Home," in *Theodore Roosevelt, An American Mind: A Selection from His Writings*, ed. Mario R. Di Nunzio (New York: St. Martin's Press, 1994). For an analysis of Roosevelt's theory of "race suicide," see Thomas G. Dyer, *Theodore Roosevelt and the Idea of Race* (Baton Rouge: Louisiana State University Press, 1992), 143–67. Donna Haraway, *Primate Visions: Gender, Race and Nature in the World of Modern Science* (New York: Routledge, 1989) 29, points out that the American Museum of Natural History's Roosevelt Memorial uses the iconography of Roosevelt's journey to Africa and the Amazon to establish the "truth of manhood" to regenerate "a miscellaneous, incoherent urban public threatened with genetic and social decadence, threatened with the

prolific bodies of the new immigrants, threatened with the failure of manhood."

14. See Ellen Kay Trimberger, "Feminism, Men, and Modern Love: Greenwich Village, 1900–1925," in *Powers of Desire: The Politics of Sexuality,* ed. Ann Snitow, Christine Stansell, and Sharon Thompson (New York: Monthly Review Press, 1983), 131–52.

15. See Anthony Rotundo, *American Manhood: Transformations in Masculinity from the Revolution to the Modern Era* (New York: Basic Books, 1993), for a discussion of the changing language of effeminacy from the early nineteenth to the late nineteenth century (especially 271–72); and George Chauncey, *Gay New York: Gender, Urban Culture, and the Making of the Gay Male World, 1890–1940* (New York: Basic Books-HarperCollins, 1994) for a discussion of how the effeminate homosexual became "the primary pejorative category against which male normativity was measured" (1994:115).

16. Blair Niles, *Strange Brother* (1931. Reprint, London: Gay Men's Press, 1991), 227. All further quotations from *Strange Brother* are from the 1991 edition.

17. Chauncey, *Gay New York*, 74.

18. On the definition of masculinity at the turn of the century, see George L. Mosse, "Masculinity and the Decadence," in *Sexual Knowledge, Sexual Science*, ed. Roy Porter and Mikulas Teich (Cambridge: Cambridge University Press, 1994), 251–66.

19. See Eve Sedgwick, *Epistemology of the Closet* (Berkeley: University of California Press, 1990), 84–90, for a discussion of gender-separatist versus "integrative" paradigms of homosexual identity.

20. Havelock Ellis, *Studies in the Psychology of Sex* (1936. Reprint, New York: Random House, 1942), 21–23.

21. Christina Simmons, "Companionate Marriage and the Lesbian Threat," *Frontiers* 4, no. 3 (1979):54–59.

22. Homi Bhabha, "The Other Question: Difference, Discrimination and the Discourse of Colonialism," in *Literature, Politics and Theory: Papers from the Essex Conference, 1976–84,* ed. Francis Barker et al. (New York: Methuen, 1986), 167.

23. Ralph Ellison, "Introduction," *Invisible Man* (1952. Reprint, New York: Vintage Books, 1995), xv.

24. Peter Burton, "Introduction," *Strange Brother*, i–v.

25. Chauncey, *Gay New York*, 102–3.

26. Amy Robinson, "It Takes One to Know One: Passing and Communities of Common Interest," *Critical Inquiry* 20 (Summer 1994), 717.

27. Abdul K. JanMohamed, "Sexuality on/of the Racial Border: Foucault, Wright and the Articulation of 'Racialized Sexuality,'" in *Discourses of Sexuality: From Aristotle to AIDS*, ed. Domna C. Stanton (Ann Arbor: University of Michigan Press, 1992), 105–6.

28. Bhabha, "The Other Question," 170.

29. Marianna Torgovnick, *Gone Primitive: Savage Intellects, Modern Lives* (Chicago: University of Chicago Press, 1990), 8.

30. Eric Garber, "Gladys Bentley: The Bulldagger Who Sang the Blues," *Out/Look* (1988):54.

31. Judith Butler, *Bodies That Matter: On the Discursive Limits of "Sex"* (New York: Routledge, 1993), 162.

32. Burton, "Introduction," *Strange Brother,* iii.

33. According to Lacan, woman is said to *be* the phallus in that she appears as the phallus in order to reflect or represent masculine desire. See Judith Butler, *Gender Trouble: Feminism and the Subversion of Identity* (New York: Routledge, 1990), for her explanation of Lacan on how women represent the phallus: "To 'be' the Phallus is to be the 'signifier' of the desire of the Other and *to appear* as this signifier. In other words, it is to be the object, the Other of a (heterosexualized) masculine desire, but also to represent or reflect that desire. This is an Other that constitutes not the limit of masculinity in a feminine alterity, but the site of a masculine self-elaboration. For women to 'be' the Phallus means, then, to reflect the power of the Phallus, to signify that power, to 'embody' the Phallus" (1990:44).

34. Following Deborah McDowell's reading of *Passing* as a lesbian text, available in the "Introduction" to her edition of Nella Larsen's two novels *Quicksand and Passing* (New Brunswick, N.J.: Rutgers University Press, 1986), ix–xxxv, several critics have debated her reading of the book as a narrative of suppressed lesbianism. See Lauren Berlant, "National Brands/National Body: Imitation of Life," in *Comparative American Identities: Race, Sex and Nationality in the Modern Text*, ed. Hortense J. Spillers (New York: Routledge, 1991), 110–40; Judith Butler, "Passing, Queering: Nella Larsen's Psychoanalytic Challenge," in *Bodies That Matter*; and Anne du Cille, "The Bourgeois, Wedding Bell Blues of Jessie Fauset and Nella Larsen," in her *The Coupling Convention: Sex, Text and Tradition in Black Women's Fiction* (New York: Oxford University Press, 1993), 86–109.

35. Early criticism of the novel argued over which narrative, the racial or the sexual, the book was "really" interested in. But more recently it has been argued that the "illegibility of blackness" in the story

of passing and the "muteness of homosexuality" in the story of female friendship are interdependent. Butler, *Bodies That Matter*, 175.

36. McDowell, "Introduction," *Quicksand* and *Passing*, xxix; Butler, *Bodies That Matter*, 179.

37. Larsen, *Passing*, 237.

38. Sedgwick, *Epistemology of the Closet*, 15. Sedgwick's study of nineteenth-century English literature, *Between Men: English Literature and Male Homosocial Desire* (New York: Columbia University Press, 1985), expands on Levi-Strauss's explanation of how, in marriage, woman is an object of exchange between men, not one of the partners in the exchange. Sedgwick argues that the homosocial bonds which structured relations of exchange between men were distinguished from the taint of homosexuality by the presence of women, who functioned as a token of male heterosexuality.

39. Carole-Anne Tyler, "Boys Will Be Girls: The Politics of Gay Drag," in *Inside/Out: Lesbian Theories, Gay Theories*, ed. Diana Fuss (New York: Routledge, 1991), 57.

40. For an analysis of the white person's relationship to the minstrel show as a type of performative difference, see Eric Lott, *Love and Theft: Blackface Minstrelsy and the American Working Class* (New York: Oxford University Press, 1993).

41. Pamela S. Haag, "In Search of the 'Real Thing': Ideologies of Love, Modern Romance, and Women's Sexual Subjectivity in the United States, 1920–1940," *Journal of the History of Sexuality* 2, no. 4 (1992):547–77. Haag argues that the middle-class woman's "natural" sexual style was constructed in opposition to the commodified sexuality of the prostitute and the unrestrained sexuality of the "vulgar" classes: "the working-class girl—as defined by material status as well as by personal style—appears in a variety of discourses as the girl who cannot properly own her sexuality because she either cannot master her instincts or because she alienates and relinquishes her sexuality according to the rules of the market and economic pragmatism" (1992:551). The idea that the working-class girl relinquishes her sexuality according to the rules of the market is especially evident in Niles's representation of the girl with the handbag.

42. Karl Marx, "The Fetishism of Commodities," in *Selected Writings/Karl Marx*, ed. David McLellan (Oxford: Oxford University Press, 1977), 436.

43. Tyler explains how fantasies of identification with the Other work within the phallic economy in her reading of transvestite pornography: "What is remarkable about these fantasies is their subject's fluid

shifting not only of gender but also of racial and class identities in ways which simultaneously subvert and sustain phallic identifications complexly articulated through differences in gender, race, and class. . . . the fantasy of the 'other' as phallic Other is not necessarily radical, since s/he may be phallic in exactly those terms a sexist, racist and classist symbolic legitimates, and the fantasizing subject may identify with that position of omnipotence and omniscience, rather than imagine s/he is excluded from it." Tyler, "Boys Will Be Girls," 61–62. Tyler's analysis can also explain how June "sustains phallic identifications."

44. For an analysis of the relationship between allegory and fetishism that discusses the proliferation of contradictory images in structures of comparison, see also Christopher L. Miller, *Blank Darkness: Africanist Discourses in French* (Chicago: University of Chicago Press, 1985), 130–38.

Notes to Chapter 3

1. Barbara Grier, *The Lesbian in Literature*, 3d ed. (Naiad Press: 1981), xix. I should point out that both the novels discussed in this chapter remain in the bibliography—*Women in the Shadows* because it contains "a very substantial qua[nt]ity of Lesbian material" and *Loving Her* because it is one of the "few titles that stand out above all the rest and must properly belong in any collection of Lesbian literature." *The Lesbian in Literature*, Grier, xx. For discussions of the history of lesbian pulp, see Kate Adams, "Making the World Safe for the Missionary Position: Images of the Lesbian in Post–World War II America," in *Lesbian Texts and Contexts: Radical Revisions*, ed. Karla Jay and Joanne Glasgow (New York: New York University Press, 1990), 255–74; and two short surveys, Susanna Benns, "Sappho in Soft Cover: Notes on Lesbian Pulp," in *Fireworks: The Best of Fireweed*, ed. Makeda Silvera (Toronto: Women's Press, 1986), 60–68; and Rebecca Yusba, "Odd Girls and Strange Sisters: Lesbian Pulp Novels of the 50s," *Out/Look* 12 (Spring 1991):34–37.

2. Studies of lesbian literature and history mention Bannon's novels along with other pulp titles, but do so in order to mark their place in lesbian literary history rather than to delve into close reading. See, for example, Lillian Faderman, *Odd Girls and Twilight Lovers: A History of Lesbian Life in Twentieth Century America* (New York: Columbia University Press, 1991), 266; and Bonnie Zimmerman, *The Safe Sea of Women: Lesbian Fiction 1969–1989* (Boston: Beacon

Press, 1990), 9. Three essays that develop extended readings of Bannon's work are Michele Aina Barale, "When Jack Blinks: Si(gh)ting Gay Desire in Ann Bannon's Beebo Brinker," *Feminist Studies* 18, no. 1 (Spring 1992):533–549; Diane Hamer, "'I Am a Woman': Ann Bannon and the Writing of Lesbian Identity in the 1950s," in *Lesbian and Gay Writing: An Anthology of Critical Essays*, ed. Mark Lily (Philadelphia: Temple University Press, 1990), 47–75; and Suzanna Danuta Walters, "'As Her Hand Crept Slowly Up Her Thigh': Ann Bannon and the Politics of Pulp Fiction," *Social Text* 23 (1989): 83–101. Like sympathetic criticism on *The Well*, recent criticism on Bannon's work focuses on textual contradiction to explore how the novels construct a specifically lesbian identity.

3. Diana Frederics makes this point in her introduction to *Diana: A Strange Autobiography* (1939. Reprint, New York: New York University Press, 1995), xxiii.

4. The series includes *Odd Girl Out* (1957), which recounts Laura's love affair with her sorority sister, Beth; *I Am a Woman* (1959), which chronicles Laura's coming out in the Village after Beth breaks off their affair to marry a man, and which ends with Laura meeting Beebo; *Women in the Shadows* (1959), about the demise of Laura's relationship with Beebo; *Journey to a Woman* (1960), about Beth's failed marriage to her college sweetheart and her flight to the Village to explore her lesbianism; and finally *Beebo Brinker* (1962), which ends the series by returning to the chronological "beginning" of the narrative, telling the story of Beebo's arrival in the Village, fresh off the farm from the midwest.

5. Ann Bannon, *Women in the Shadows* (1959. Reprint, Tallahassee, Fla.: Naiad Press, 1986), 87. All further citations reference the 1986 edition.

6. Jennifer Levin, "Beebo Lives," *Harvard Gay and Lesbian Review* 2, no. 21 (1995), 54.

7. Suzanna Walters makes a compelling argument that although the novel seems torn between ideological constructions of homosexuality that are apparently at odds, these discourses are in fact part of the same narrative of determinism. She focuses on that always present facet of the nature-culture debate, the origin of homosexuality, suggesting that whether that origin is posited as biological (sexology) or psychological (Freud), there is always one deterministic and essentialist cause for homosexuality. Walters, "'As Her Hand Crept Up Her Thigh,'" 89–90.

8. Hazel V. Carby, *Reconstructing Womanhood: The Emergence of the Afro-American Novelist* (New York: Oxford University Press,

1987), 89. The figure serves a similar function, albeit to different ends, in *Women in the Shadows*.

9. Judith Berzon, *Neither White nor Black: The Mulatto Character in American Fiction* (New York: New York University Press, 1978).

10. Walters, "'As Her Hand Crept Up Her Thigh,'" 88.

11. See JR Roberts, *Black Lesbians: An Annotated Bibliography* (Tallahassee, Fla.: Naiad Press, 1981) for a review of lesbian fiction to 1981.

12. Jewelle Gomez, "A Cultural Legacy Denied and Discovered: Black Lesbians in Fiction by Women," in *Home Girls: A Black Feminist Anthology*, ed. Barbara Smith (New York: Kitchen Table: Women of Color Press, 1983), 112–13.

13. SDiane Bogus, "Theme and Portraiture in the Fiction of Ann Allen Shockley" (Ph.D. dissertation, University of Miami, 1988).

14. Arguably, *Loving Her* traces a movement from one marginal community to another—from the black community to the white lesbian community. But because the novel defines the black community as working- and underclass and associates the white lesbian community primarily with upper-class privilege and privacy, the lesbian community feels more closely aligned with the dominant culture.

15. For positive commentary on *Loving Her*, see Patricia Hill Collins, *Black Feminist Thought: Knowledge, Consciousness and the Politics of Empowerment* (New York: Routledge, 1991), 84–85; and Linnea A. Stenson, "From Isolation to Diversity: Self and Communities in Twentieth-Century Lesbian Novels," in *Sexual Practice/Textual Theory: Lesbian Cultural Criticism*, ed. Susan J. Wolfe and Julia Penelope (Cambridge, Mass.: Blackwell, 1993), 221–22.

16. Jean Cordova, review essay, "*Loving Her*," *Lesbian Tide* 4 (October 1974):18; Beverly Smith, "A Study of Black and White: *Loving Her*," *Gay Community News* 6 (November 11, 1978):4.

17. See, for example, the discussions of Shockley's work and the politics of feminist criticism in Cheryl Clarke et al., "Black Women on Black Women Writers: Conversations and Questions," *Conditions: Nine* (1983):88–137; and Caroline Streeter, "We Sisters Have a Legacy of Power," Review Essay, *Home Girls: A Black Feminist Anthology*, *Off Our Backs* 14 (1984):10–11.

18. Bogus, "Theme and Portraiture," 101.

19. In 1986, Shockley explained that she had composed *Loving Her* between 1960 and 1969. Quoted in Bogus, "Theme and Portraiture," 110.

20. Barbara Grier, "The Lesbian Paperback," *Tangents* (1966):4.

21. John D'Emilio, *Sexual Politics, Sexual Communities: The Making of a Homosexual Minority in the United States, 1940–1970* (Chicago: Chicago University Press, 1983), 142, 144.

22. Ann Allen Shockley, *Loving Her* (1974. Reprint, Tallahassee, Fla.: Naiad Press, 1986), 36–37. All further references are to the 1986 edition.

23. See chapter 9, "Civil Rights and Direct Action: The New East Coast Militancy, 1961–1965," in D'Emilio's *Sexual Politics, Sexual Communities*, for a detailed account of how civil rights activists inspired the gay rights movement during the sixties.

24. Shockley's collection of short stories, *The Black and White of It* (Tallahassee, Fla.: Naiad Press, 1987), and her latest novel, *Say Jesus and Come to Me* (Tallahassee, Fla.: Naiad Press, 1987), have been criticized for politics that are similar to if not more conservative than *Loving Her*. Most notably, see Gomez, "A Cultural Legacy Denied and Discovered," 113–15. See also Rita Dandridge, "Gathering Pieces: A Selected Bibliography of Ann Allen Shockley," *Black American Literature Forum* 21, no. 1–2 (1987):133–46, for a list of reviews through 1987. Dandridge's bibliography also provides a thorough list of Shockley's fiction and nonfiction prose since 1945.

25. For a discussion of the rhetoric of color-blindness, see Ruth Frankenberg, *White Women, Race Matters: The Social Construction of Whiteness* (Minneapolis: University of Minnesota Press, 1993), 142–49. Frankenberg describes "color-/power-evasive" discourses on race as being "organized around the desire to assert essential *sameness*," and "race cognizant" discourses as insisting on "the importance of recognizing difference" (1993:157). For a history of racial discourses in twentieth-century America, see Michael Omi and Howard Winant, *Racial Formation in the United States from the 1960s to the 1980s* (New York: Routledge and Kegan Paul, 1986).

26. For an example of this argument, see the essay, "Lesbianism among Blacks," anonymously published in 1975, the year after *Loving Her,* in the independent magazine *Brown Sister*. To examine how the notion of compulsory heterosexuality affects black lesbians in particular, the author suggests that there is an imperative in black communities to assimilate to "white norms" and argues that in order for the black lesbian to embrace her identity as a "lesbian," she has to leave the community or stay in the closet (1975:17).

27. Daniel Patrick Moynihan, "The Negro Family: The Case for National Action," in *The Moynihan Report and the Politics of Controversy*, ed. Lee Rainwater and William Y. Yancey (Cambridge, Mass.:

M.I.T. Press, 1967), 71. Jerome Lee's response to economic deprivation is also consistent with contemporaneous explanations of black male behavior in the "matriarchal household":

> Both as a husband and a father, the Negro male is made to feel inadequate. . . . To this situation he may react with withdrawal, bitterness toward society, aggression, both within the family and the racial group, self-hatred, or crime. Or he may escape through a number of avenues that help him to lose himself in a fantasy or to compensate for his low status through a variety of exploits.

Whitney Young, quoted in Moynihan 1967:34.

28. Michele Wallace, *Black Macho and the Myth of the Superwoman* (1978. Reprint, Warner Books, 1980). For commentary on Wallace's book, see bell hooks, *Ain't I a Woman: Black Women and Feminism* (Boston: South End Press, 1981), which argues that Wallace is not a feminist and that she dismisses the significance of the Black Power movement in her emphasis on black men's desire for white women (1981:11–12, 98); and Robyn Wiegman, *American Anatomies: Theorizing Race and Gender* (Durham, N.C.: Duke University Press, 1995), which points out that "Wallace inscribes an essential, natural black masculinity that even she, in the preface to the 1990 revised edition, has come to disavow" (1995:109).

29. Wallace, *Black Macho,* 26–27.

30. Frank Lamont Phillips, review essay, "*Loving Her*," *Black World* 24 (1975):89–90.

31. Imamu Amiri Baraka, *Home: Social Essays* (New York: William Morrow, 1966), 216.

32. Eldridge Cleaver, *Soul on Ice* (1967. Reprint, New York: Dell, 1968), 101.

33. Huey Newton, "A Letter from Huey to the Revolutionary Brothers and Sisters about the Women's Liberation and Gay Liberation Movements," *3d World Gay Revolution* (Gay Flames Pamphlet no. 7, 1970):1–4.

34. Cheryl Clarke, "The Failure to Transform: Homophobia in the Black Community," in *Home Girls: A Black Feminist Anthology*, ed. Barbara Smith (New York: Kitchen Table: Women of Color Press, 1983), 205. For other discussions of homophobia in the black community, see bell hooks, "Homophobia in Black Communities" in her book, *Talking Back: Thinking Feminist, Thinking Black* (Boston: South End

ress, 1981), 120–26; and Jewelle Gomez, "Imagine a Lesbian . . . A Black Lesbian," *Trivia* 12 (1988):45–60.

35. Barbara Christian, "The Rise and Fall of the Proper Mulatta," in her book, *Black Women Novelists: The Development of a Tradition, 1892–1976* (Westport, Conn.: Greenwood Press, 1982), 44.

36. Lauren Berlant, "National Brands/National Bodies: Imitation of Life," in *Comparative American Identities: Race, Sex and Nationality in the Modern Text*, ed. Hortense J. Spillers (New York: Routledge, 1991), 111.

37. Smith, *"Loving Her,"* 4.

38. While Beverly Smith laments that "Shockley does not have a lesbian feminist analysis of the lives and events she portrays," she is astute in guessing that this is probably due to the fact that "she wrote it years before anyone saw fit to publish it . . . before the development of lesbian feminist and black feminist political analyses." Smith, *"Loving Her,"* 4.

39. Frankenberg, *White Women, Race Matters*, 147.

Notes to Chapter 4

1. See the Marxist Feminist Literature Collective's "Women's Writing: *Jane Eyre, Shirley, Villette, Aurora Leigh*," in *1848: The Sociology of Literature*, ed. Francis Barker et al. (Essex Conference on the Sociology of Literature: University of Essex, 1977), 185–296; and Susan L. Meyer, "Colonialism and the Figurative Strategy of *Jane Eyre*," *Victorian Studies* 33 (1990):247–68. See Mary Poovy, "The Anathematized Race: The Governess and *Jane Eyre*," in her *Uneven Developments: The Ideological Work of Gender in Mid-Victorian England* (Chicago: University of Chicago Press, 1988), for an analysis of the novel's rags to riches plot. See Gayatri Spivak, "Three Women's Texts and a Critique of Imperialism," *Critical Inquiry* 12 (1985):243–61, for the critique of how Jane's progress follows the program of colonialism that has sparked the current wave of criticism on the novel's colonial discourses.

2. I use the terms lesbian sexuality and lesbian eroticism in my discussion of all three texts, aware of the historical problems that this poses. The term lesbian is anachronistic for a reading of Brontë's novel, given that it was not in usage until the end of the nineteenth century, and Cliff's self-identification as a lesbian, which informs her writing of the precursor texts as a lesbian novel in *Abeng*, is not in evidence for Rhys. But without reading *Wide Sargasso Sea* and *Jane Eyre* as lesbian novels

per se, I would argue two things: first, that it is the latent eroticism of
the mother-daughter relationships represented in these novels that allows Cliff to write lesbian desire into *Abeng*, and second, that this eroticism is more properly called "lesbian" than "homo" erotic, as homoeroticism is commonly associated with relationships between men.

3. Diana Fuss, *Identification Papers* (New York: Routledge, 1995), 2.

4. In Freudian theory, "primary" identification is preoedipal and
"secondary" identification postoedipal. See Diana Fuss, "Freud's Fallen
Woman: Identification, Desire, and 'A Case of Homosexuality in a
Woman,'" in *Fear of a Queer Planet*, ed. Michael Warner (Minneapolis:
University of Minneapolis Press, 1993), 53.

5. Elizabeth Grosz, *Jacques Lacan: A Feminist Introduction* (New
York: Routledge, 1990), 46–47.

6. Fuss, "Freud's Fallen Woman," 58–59.

7. Franz Fanon, *Black Skin, White Masks* (1952. Trans. Charles
Lam Markmann. Reprint, New York: Grove Press, 1967), 111–12.

8. Fanon, *Black Skin, White Masks,* 109.

9. Fanon, *Black Skin, White Masks,* 114.

10. Homi Bhabha, "The Other Question: Difference, Discrimination and the Discourse of Colonialism," in *Literature, Politics and Theory: Papers from the Essex Conference, 1976–84*, ed. Francis Barker et
al. (New York: Methuen, 1986), 163.

11. In the mirror-stage, Lacan takes the scene of the child's first
recognition of itself in the mirror as a paradigm for identification. It is
during the mirror-stage that the child first differentiates between itself
and its mother. Jacques Lacan, "The Mirror Stage as Formative of the
Function of the I," in *Ecrits, A Selection*. Trans. Alex Sherodan. (New
York: W. W. Norton, 1977), 1–7. For an analysis of the mirror-stage, see
Grosz, "The Ego and the Imaginary," in *Jacques Lacan,* 24–49.

12. Bhabha, "The Other Question," 163. As Jacqueline Rose explains in her book *Sexuality in the Field of Vision* (London: Verso,
1986), the Freudian narrative of identity formation hinges on the child's
refusal of visible difference:

Freud often related the question of sexuality to that of visual
representation. Describing the child's difficult journey into
adult sexual life, he would take as his model little scenarios, or
the staging of events, which demonstrated the complexity of an
essentially visual space, moments in which perception founders
(the boy child refuses to believe the anatomical difference that
he sees). (1986:227)

The girl's identification with the mother, while seeming to be based on their sameness, is also the result of the castration complex that is precipitated by the sight of anatomical difference.

13. Bhabha, "The Other Question," 163.

14. Lillian Faderman offers historical evidence for school as the site of homoerotic attachments when she suggests that "more than any other phenomenon, education may be said to have been responsible for the spread among middle-class women of what eventually came to be called lesbianism" because school brought women together and provided them with careers as teachers. *Odd Girls and Twilight Lovers: A History of Lesbian Life in Twentieth Century America* (New York: Columbia University Press, 1991), 13.

15. Judith Butler, *Bodies That Matter: On the Discursive Limits of "Sex"* (New York: Routledge, 1993), 105.

16. Adrienne Rich, "*Jane Eyre*: The Temptations of a Motherless Woman," in *On Lies, Secrets and Silence: Selected Prose 1966–1978* (New York: W. W. Norton, 1979), 89–106.

17. Jean Wyatt, "A Patriarch of One's Own: Oedipal Fantasy and Romantic Love in *Jane Eyre*," in her book *Reconstructing Desire: The Role of the Unconscious in Women's Reading and Writing* (Chapel Hill: University of North Carolina Press, 1990), 39.

18. Firdous Azim, *The Colonial Rise of the Novel* (New York: Routledge, 1993), 103.

19. Sandra Gilbert and Susan Gubar, "A Dialogue of Self and Soul: Plain Jane's Progress," in their book *The Madwoman in the Attic: The Woman Writer and the Nineteenth Century Literary Imagination* (New Haven: Yale University Press, 1980), 360. Rosemarie Johnstone, "*Jane Eyre* and the Invention of Femininity," *Nineteenth-Century Contexts* 16, no. 2 (1992):167–69.

20. Charlotte Brontë, *Jane Eyre* (1847. Reprint, New York: Penguin Classics, 1986), 2.44, 2.48. All further references are to the 1986 edition.

21. Elaine Showalter, *A Literature of Their Own: British Women Novelists from Brontë to Lessing* (Princeton: Princeton University Press, 1977), 113–17.

22. See, for example, Elsie B. Michie's reading of the opening passage of the novel in *Outside the Pale: Cultural Exclusion, Gender Difference, and the Victorian Woman Writer* (Ithaca: Cornell University Press, 1993), 65–66.

23. Meyer, "Colonialism and the Figurative Strategy of *Jane Eyre*," 261.

24. For an in-depth reading of how the novel uses discourses of racial difference to develop a feminist rhetoric, see Joyce Zonana, "The Sultan and the Slave: Feminist Orientalism and the Structure of *Jane Eyre*," *Signs* 18 (1993):592–617.

25. For a discussion of female identification as stasis, see Pauline Nestor, *Charlotte Brontë's "Jane Eyre"* (New York: Harvester Wheatsheaf, 1992), 40–44.

26. Typically, readings of the Lowood scenes emphasize the contrast between Jane and Helen, noting Jane's inability to conform to Christian ideals of self-denial. Certainly the passages where Jane resists Mr. Brocklehurst's accusations that she is ungrateful and a liar— "worse than many a little heathen who says its prayers to Brahma and kneels before Juggernaut" (7.98)—by imagining herself, not in the spirit of Christian acceptance but in the spirit of anger and rebelliousness as "a victim and a slave," define her in opposition to Helen. Helen chastises Jane for her rebelliousness by telling her that only "[h]eathens and savage tribes" nurse their anger and that "Christians and civilized nations disown it" (6.90). The novel (and feminist readers of the novel especially) thus represent Helen as being in many ways unsatisfying as a role model for Jane.

27. Samuel Johnson, "Rasselas," in *The Selected Writings of Samuel Johnson*, ed. Katharine Rogers (New York: Signet Classic, 1981). For a history of the criticism on *Rasselas*, see Edward Tomarken, "A History of *Rasselas* Criticism, 1759–1986," in his *Johnson, Rasselas, and the Choice of Criticism* (Lexington: University Press of Kentucky, 1989), 5–37. Gilbert and Gubar suggest that in Helen's study of *Rasselas*, she is "perhaps comparing Dr. Johnson's Happy Valley to the unhappy one in which she herself is immured" and dreaming of freedom in eternity. Gilbert and Gubar, "A Dialogue of Self and Soul," 346. I would suggest that she may also be contemplating both the inadequacies of Lowood as a female community because of the ignorance of its leadership, and the comfort of the earthly companionship of intellectual women like Miss Temple.

28. Brontë would not be unique in drawing on "feminist" images of the harem. Ali Behdad notes that "female Orientalists who depicted scenes of the harem represent it differently than male Orientalists. At least in Lady Mary Wortley Montagu's letters from Turkey . . . she even claims that oriental women are in fact freer than their counterparts in Europe, for, thanks to their veils which serve them as perpetual masks, they can go anywhere and do anything they wish." Ali Behdad, "The

Eroticized Orient: Images of the Harem in Montesquieu and His Precursors," *Standard French Review* 13 (1989):116.

Homoeroticism and images of the Orient may also inform Brontë's work in coded/unconscious ways. Behdad suggests that the fantasy/threat of women sexually pleasing themselves is part of the Orientalist discourse on harems. He points out that narratives about harems include details about "the popularity of cucumbers among members of the harem and how women are only served chopped cucumbers" (1989:112), and quotes from Chardin's *Voyage en Perse* (1689):

> Les Femmes orientales ont toujours passé pour *Tribades*. J'ai oui assurer si souvent, & à tant de gens, qu'elles le sont, & qu'elles ont des voyes de contenter mutuellent leurs passions, que je le tiens pour fort certain," or "Oriental women have always passed for lesbians. I have heard it often, and from enough people, that they are, and that they have ways of mutually satisfying their passions, that I take it to be almost certain.

Quoted in Behdad, 122 n24, my translation. See Zonana, "The Sultan and the Slave," for a more detailed reading of how the harem functions in feminism's Orientalist discourses.

29. Johnson, "Rasselas," XXVIII.212.

30. On the subject of this opposition, Meyer, among others, has written on "the *topoi of racial 'otherness'*" used to describe Bertha in this scene (1990:253).

31. See Gilbert and Gubar for a discussion of how Bertha embodies or mirrors Jane's projected anxieties about marriage (1980:360).

32. In her reading of *Jane Eyre* in "Caliban's Daughter: The Tempest and the Teapot," *Frontiers* 12 (1991):36–51, Cliff sees in Bertha the figure of the lesbian. She notes that there are masculine as well as feminine/maternal elements in the representation of her racial/sexual monstrosity. While she suggests that "Bertha's savagery originates in the forest, on the island, transfused through the bloodlines of her savage mother" (1991:41) she also focuses on Bertha's virility:

> In her descriptions of Bertha Rochester, Charlotte Brontë stresses Bertha's virility, her maleness, which are part of Bertha's monstrosity. In those passages, and in the mental images of Bertha and Grace Poole, her keeper, secreted behind a secret door, I find myself thinking of the notion of the lesbian as monster, marauder; the

man/woman in the closet. When Jane calls Bertha "the clothed hyena," I think of the common belief that the hyena is a hermaphroditic creature, capable of switching his/her dominant sexuality. In short, a sexual monstrosity. (1991:48)

33. While I read forward in the narrative from Bertha's visit to the mother-child imagery in Jane's stay with Adèle, Pauline Nestor reads backward for the same imagery in Jane's dreams of carrying the infant who clings to her neck, an infant that she drops. In interpreting the dream sequences, Nestor notes the parallel between Jane's decision to marry and Miss Temple's earlier "choice" to marry. She sees in this connection "a refusal to give priority to the claims of dependence associated with maternal protectiveness" and suggests that "the choice Jane makes for her lover" is thus radical. While I agree that Jane's dreams signify, among other things, a refusal of the maternal, Nestor's analysis privileges heterosexuality.

What is missing from the analysis is how agonized the "choice" of marriage is for Jane, and that her tearful perception of Adèle as an emblem of her past life can be read as grief over how marriage marks the end of female communities for Jane. Pauline Nestor, *Female Friendships and Communities: Charlotte Brontë, George Elliot, Elizabeth Gaskell* (Oxford: Clarendon Press, 1985), 110.

34. Pauline Nestor, *Female Friendships and Communities*, 108.

35. Rich, "*Jane Eyre*," 103.

36. Nestor, *Charlotte Brontë's "Jane Eyre*," 46.

37. This passage connects interestingly with what Elaine Miller says about Brontë's desire to set up house with Ellen Nussey. She quotes a letter from Brontë to Nussey as saying, "If we had but a cottage and a competency of our own, I do think we might live and love on till Death without being Dependent on any third person for happiness." Miller also suggests that Brontë considered marrying Ellen's brother so that she could live with Ellen. Elaine Miller, "Through All Changes and Through All Chances: The Relationship of Ellen Nussey and Charlotte Brontë," in her book *Not a Passing Phase: Reclaiming Lesbians in History 1840–1985* (London: Women's Press, 1989), 36–37.

38. For a useful analysis of the way discourses of Orientalism change the representation of colonialism, see Michie, *Outside the Pale*, 73.

39. Spivak, "Three Women's Texts," 249.

40. Wyatt, "A Patriarch of One's Own," 31.

41. Wyatt, "A Patriarch of One's Own," 35.

42. Nestor, *Charlotte Brontë's "Jane Eyre*," 45.

43. On Jane's "self-submersion" in her relationships with women, see Nestor, *Charlotte Brontë's "Jane Eyre,"* 44.

44. Jean Rhys, *Wide Sargasso Sea* (1966. Reprint, New York: W. W. Norton, 1982), 17. All further references are to the 1982 edition.

45. For an analysis of how Antoinette becomes the site of power negotiations between her brother, Rochester, and Daniel Cosway, the son of a slave woman who claims that he and Antoinette share the same father, see Moira Ferguson, *Colonialism and Gender from Mary Wollstonecraft to Jamaica Kincaid* (New York: Columbia University Press, 1993).

46. Michel Foucault, "Nietzsche, Genealogy, History," in *The Foucault Reader*, ed. Paul Rabinow (New York: Pantheon Books, 1984), 87.

47. Foucault, "Nietzsche," 83.

48. Foucault, "Nietzsche," 81.

49. Françoise Lionnet, "Of Mangoes and Maroons: Language, History and the Multicultural Subject of Michelle Cliff's *Abeng*," in *De/Colonizing the Subject: The Politics of Gender in Women's Autobiography*, ed. Sidonie Smith and Julia Watson. Minneapolis: University of Minnesota Press, 1992, 326.

50. Michelle Cliff, *Abeng* (Trumansburg, N.Y.: Crossing Press, 1984), 29.

51. Foucault, "Nietzsche," 79.

52. John G. Mencke explains the logic of the one-drop rule as follows: "By classifying as black all who had any degree of black blood—by insisting that 'one drop' of black blood was enough to make any individual a Negro—whites conveniently did away with the mulatto as an anomaly in their racial schema. If whiteness meant pure white, then those of mixed blood were, by definition, not white." John G. Mencke, *Mulattoes and Race Mixture: American Attitudes and Images, 1865–1918* (N. p.: Research Press, 1979), 20.

53. For a different interpretation of the ending, see Simon Gikandi, "Narration and the Postcolonial Moment: History and Representation in *Abeng*," in his *Writing in Limbo: Modernism and Caribbean Literature* (Ithaca: Cornell University Press, 1992). Gikandi reads the last line of the novel as "a moment of closure marked by silence and emptiness" (1992:251).

54. There are critics who disagree. Nancy Harrison, for example, reads the ending of *Wide Sargasso Sea* as a renewal of maternal and cross-racial identification. Nancy R. Harrison, *An Introduction to the Writing Practice of Jean Rhys: The Novel as Women's Text* (Chapel Hill: University of North Carolina Press, 1988). She points out that her

"interpretation differs from readings of *Wide Sargasso Sea* that analyze the relationship between Antoinette and her mother as a failure of bonding that cannot be redeemed" (1988:60), and suggests a reading of Antoinette's suicide as a moment of merging with Others through the decision to affirm the survival of all oppressed women (1988:58). I would argue that the ending of Rhys's novel, which describes Antoinette in language that recalls the description of her mother's parrot falling burning from the glacis at Coulibri in an episode that dramatizes racial division, is another instance of the failure of identification.

55. Butler, *Bodies That Matter*, 105.

Notes to Chapter 5

1. Susie Bright (Susie Sexpert, pseud.), "College Confidential," *On Our Backs* 7, no. 4 (1991):11.

2. Judith Butler, *Gender Trouble: Feminism and the Subversion of Identity* (New York: Routledge, 1990), 17.

3. Butler, *Gender Trouble*, 17.

4. I use the term "gender/sexual identity" for lack of a better one to describe the intersection of gender identity and sexual orientation that defines lesbian and gay awareness of our own identities within the framework of compulsory heterosexuality. In *Gender Trouble*, Judith Butler talks about the relationship between the categories "sex, gender, and desire," using "desire" to address the issue of sexual orientation (1990:6–7). This is a useful addition to the usual catechism of the "sex/gender system." However, it does not meet my need for a term that is parallel in grammatical usage to the term "gender identity." Further, it will become apparent that I find the term "desire" to be problematic in Butler's discussion of lesbian identity. I prefer "gender/sexual identity" as a phrase which complicates the concept of gender identity while maintaining the sense of identities as constructions.

5. In "The Situation of Lesbianism as Feminism's Magical Sign," *Communication* 9 (1986):65–91, Katie King describes this phenomenon as the reduction of whole systems of signifiers to a single privileged signifier. She gives as examples "the metonymic reduction of 'race' to 'Black,' that is, how 'Black' becomes the symbol, as a sort of part to some whole, for all consideration of racism"; the reduction of "oppression" to the oppression of women such that other forms of oppression become invisible; and the elevation of lesbianism as a symbol of feminist consciousness such that the actual "practice" of lesbianism is peripheral

to the concept that it becomes for both lesbians and nonlesbians (1986:81–83).

6. Teresa de Lauretis,"Eccentric Subjects: Feminist Theory and Historical Consciousness," *Feminist Studies* 16 (1990):138.

7. Donna Haraway, "A Manifesto for Cyborgs: Science, Technology, and Socialist Feminism in the 1980s," in *Coming to Terms: Feminism, Theory, Politics,* ed. Elizabeth Weed (New York: Routledge, 1990), 173–204.

8. Gloria Anzaldúa, *Borderlands/La Frontera* (San Francisco: spinsters/aunt lute, 1987).

9. Donna Haraway, "The Actors Are Cyborg, Nature Is Coyote, and the Geography Is Elsewhere: Postscript to 'Cyborgs at Large,'" in *Technoculture,* ed. Constance Penley and Andrew Ross (Minneapolis: University of Minnesota Press, 1991), 23.

10. For a reading of this slippage in the work of Anglo-American feminists, see Norma Alarcon, "The Theoretical Subject(s) of *This Bridge Called My Back* and Anglo-American Feminism," in *Making Face, Making Soul*, ed. Gloria Anzaldúa (San Francisco: aunt lute foundation, 1990), 346–69.

11. Donna Harraway, "Situated Knowledges: The Science Question in Feminism and the Privilege of Partial Perspective," in her *Simians, Cyborgs, and Women: The Reinvention of Nature* (New York: Routledge, 1990), 191–92.

12. Haraway, "The Actors Are Cyborg," 10.

13. Octavia Butler, *Dawn* (New York: Warner, 1987). Butler's later books in this series, called *Xenogenesis*, are *Adulthood Rites* (New York: Warner, 1988) and *Imago* (New York: Warner, 1989).

14. For a reading of Butler, see also Donna Haraway, "The Biopolitics of Postmodern Bodies: Constitutions of Self in Immune System Discourse," in her *Simians, Cyborgs, and Women: The Reinvention of Nature* (New York: Routledge, 1991), 203–30.

15. Ernesto Laclau and Chantal Mouffe, *Hegemony and Socialist Strategy: Towards a Radical Democratic Politics* (New York: Verso, 1985), 21.

16. Cherríe Moraga, *Loving in the War Years* (Boston: South End Press, 1983), 199.

17. Catharine MacKinnon, "Feminism, Marxism, Method, and the State: An Agenda for Theory," *Signs* 7, no. 3 (1982):515–44.

18. I am thinking in particular of Monique Wittig's comment that "Lesbian is the only concept I know of which is beyond the categories of sex (woman and man), because the designated subject (lesbian) is *not*

a woman, either economically, or politically, or ideologically." Monique Wittig, "One Is Not Born a Woman," *Feminist Issues* 2 (1981):53.

19. de Lauretis, "Eccentric Subjects," 127.

20. Sue-Ellen Case, "Toward a Butch-Femme Aesthetic," in *Making a Spectacle*, ed. Lynda Hart (Ann Arbor: University of Michigan Press, 1989), 282–99.

21. Throughout this essay I use the phrase "butch and femme styles" instead of the more common "butch-femme role-play." I choose not to hyphenate the terms "butch" and "femme" in order to construct them as identities that exist separately as well as in combination. To me, the hyphenated version seems to preclude considering the terms independently of one another or in other combinations (such as butch-butch and femme-femme). I will also use the term "role-play" in quotations, indicating my agreement with Joan Nestle's questioning of this term as one which implies that butch and femme are imitative of heterosexual gender roles and so denies the complexity of butch and femme experiences. See Joan Nestle, "Butch-Femme Relationships: Sexual Courage in the 1950's," in her *A Restricted Country* (Ithaca: Fireband Books, 1987), 100–109.

22. On the connections between class and butch and femme styles, see Madeline Davis and Elizabeth Lapovsky Kennedy, "Oral History and the Study of Sexuality in the Lesbian Community: Buffalo, New York, 1940–1960," *Feminist Studies* 12 (1986):7–26; Lillian Faderman, *Odd Girls and Twilight Lovers: A History of Lesbian Life in Twentieth Century America* (New York: Columbia University Press, 1991); and Joan Nestle's collection of personal narratives by butch and femme women, *The Persistent Desire: A Femme-Butch Reader* (Boston: Alyson Publications, 1992).

23. For discussions of the redefinition of butch and femme styles as an anachronism during the 1970s, see Nestle, "Butch-Femme Relationships," and Bonnie Zimmerman, *The Safe Sea of Women: Lesbian Fiction 1969–1989* (Boston: Beacon Press, 1990), 113. Lillian Faderman also discusses butch and femme styles in terms of class relations in *Odd Girls and Twilight Lovers*. Unfortunately, the tension between working-class and middle-class lesbians is replicated as well as described in her work, as when she suggests that middle- and upper-class lesbians were able to reject the "heterogenderal pattern[s] of 'roleplay' because of their ability to articulate a more feminist politics than working-class lesbians" (1991:167).

24. King, "The Situation of Lesbianism," 83.

25. bell hooks, *Talking Back: Thinking Feminist, Thinking Black* (Boston: South End Press, 1989), 125.

26. hooks, *Talking Back*, 125.

27. Here hooks invokes a rhetoric of choice which is frequently assumed around the idea of homosexuality, but which does not describe the experience of all gays. For example, JoAnn Loulan quotes Esther Newton's observation that flexibility about sexual style can become an imperative which assumes a rhetoric of choice that not all lesbians feel applies to their experience. Newton says: "What's frustrating to me is the new trend to say: 'You know, gee, I like to wear my jack boots one night and my high heels the next. Gee, I can express all these parts of me, it's kind of camp.'. . . For some of us it's not that at all! Some of us want to go deeper and deeper into one thing, and that's just as good." Quoted in JoAnn Loulan, *The Lesbian Erotic Dance: Butch, Femme, Androgyny and Other Rhythms* (San Francisco: Spinsters Book Company, 1990), 123–24.

28. Nestle, quoted in Case, "Toward a Butch-Femme Aesthetic," 294. For other perspectives on butch-femme role-play, see Amber Hollibaugh and Cherríe Moraga, "What We're Rollin Around in Bed With: Sexual Silences in Feminism," in *Powers of Desire: The Politics of Sexuality*, ed. Ann Snitow, Christine Stansell, and Sharon Thompson (New York: Monthly Review Press, 1983), 394–405. Hollibaugh qualifies the apparent passivity of the femme by asserting her sense of her own power and subversiveness. Moraga expresses her frustration with the expectation that the butch will always assume sexual responsibility, suggesting that her discomfort with her own "femininity" is perpetuated by the rigidness of traditional role-playing. See also Davis and Kennedy, "Oral History and the Study of Sexuality in the Lesbian Community." The researchers discuss the discrepancy between popular images of the "stone" butch and "passive" femme and the sexual experiences recalled by the women they interviewed. They suggest that there was a broad "range of sexual desires that were built into the framework of role-defined sexuality" (1986:19).

29. Joan Nestle, "The Fem Question," in *The Persistent Desire*, 140.

30. Judy Grahn, *Another Mother Tongue: Gay Words, Gay Worlds* (Boston: Beacon Press, 1984), 85.

31. Grahn, *Another Mother Tongue*, 157–58.

32. Grahn, *Another Mother Tongue*, 157, 159–60.

33. Radclyffe Hall, *The Well of Loneliness* (1928. Reprint, New York: Avon Books, 1982), 155, 423.

34. Wittig, "One Is Not Born a Woman," 49.

35. Newton, quoted in Butler, *Gender Trouble*, 137, Butler's interpolations. Esther Newton, *Mother Camp: Female Impersonators in America* (Chicago: University of Chicago Press, 1972).

36. Though Butler points out that there is more than one object of lesbian femme desire, she does not explore the options. This inattention reinforces my argument that, for Butler, the femme's radical discontinuity is only evident in her association with the butch. It is as if the femme has no lesbian identity outside the butch-femme economy.

37. Ekua Omosupe, "Black/Lesbian/Bulldagger," *Differences* 3, no. 2 (1991):105.

38. Jewelle Gomez, "Imagine a Lesbian . . . A Black Lesbian . . . ," *Trivia* 12 (1988):47.

39. Sharon Lim-Hing, "Dragon Ladies, Snow Queens, and Asian-American Dykes: Reflections on Race and Sexuality," *Empathy* 2, no. 2 (1990–91):21.

40. Barbara Christian, "No More Buried Lives," in *Black Feminist Criticism* (New York: Pergamon Press, 1985):200.

41. Omosupe, "Black/Lesbian/Bulldagger," 103.

42. Audre Lorde, *Zami: A New Spelling of My Name* (Trumansburg, N.Y.: Crossing Press, 1982), 224, 226.

43. Lorde, *Zami*, 224.

44. Lorde, *Zami*, 243.

45. For example, the term "ki-ki" seems to encompass a range of sexual styles that don't quite fit conventional definitions of butch or femme. In the 1950s ki-ki seems to have been used in a pejorative sense. Audre Lorde, for example, says that it was used to disparage "the 'freaky' bunch of lesbians who weren't into roleplay" and that the same name was used for lesbians who turned tricks (1982:178). Loulan explains its more current and more flattering usage as a term which "describes women who move easily from butch to femme and back again" (1990:143).

Notes to the Epilogue

1. Danae Clark's essay "Commodity Lesbianism" (*Camera Obscura* no. 25–26 [1991]:180–201) provides a useful analysis of how "lesbian chic" might be read in the context of consumerism.

2. Laura Doan, *The Lesbian Postmodern* (New York: Columbia University Press, 1994); Richard Dyer, *White* (New York: Routledge,

1997); Diana Fuss, *Inside/Out: Lesbian Theories, Gay Theories* (New York: Routledge, 1991); Marjorie Garber, *Vested Interests: Cross-Dressing and Cultural Anxiety* (New York: Routledge, 1992); Elaine Ginsberg, *Passing and the Fictions of Identity* (Durham, N.C.: Duke University Press, 1996); Eric Lott, *Love and Theft: Blackface Minstrelsy and the American Working Class* (New York: Oxford University Press, 1993); and Michael Warner, ed. *Fear of a Queer Planet: Queer Politics and Social Theory* (Minneapolis: University of Minnesota Press, 1993).

Works Cited

Abraham, Julie. *Are Girls Necessary? Lesbian Writing and Modern Histories*. New York: Routledge, 1996.

———. "Introduction." *Diana: A Strange Autobiography* by Diana Frederics. New York: New York University Press, 1995.

Adams, Kate. "Making the World Safe for the Missionary Position: Images of the Lesbian in Post–World War II America." In *Lesbian Texts and Contexts: Radical Revisions*. Ed. Karla Jay and Joanne Glasgow. New York: New York University Press, 1990.

Alarcon, Norma. "The Theoretical Subject(s) of *This Bridge Called My Back* and Anglo-American Feminism." In *Making Face, Making Soul*. Ed. Gloria Anzaldúa. San Francisco: aunt lute foundation, 1990.

Anzaldúa, Gloria. *Borderlands/La Frontera: The New Mestiza*. San Francisco: spinsters/aunt lute, 1987.

Azim, Firdous. *The Colonial Rise of the Novel*. New York: Routledge, 1993.

Backus, Margot Gayle. "Sexual Orientation in the (Post)Imperial Nation: Celticism and Inversion Theory in Radclyffe Hall's *The Well of Loneliness*." *Tulsa Studies in Women's Literature* 15, no. 2 (1996): 253–66.

Baker, Houston Jr. *Modernism and the Harlem Renaissance*. Chicago: Chicago University Press, 1987.

Baker, Michael. *Our Three Selves: The Life of Radclyffe Hall*. New York: William Morrow, 1985.

Bannon, Ann. *Women in the Shadows*. 1959. Reprint, Tallahassee, Fla: Naiad Press, 1986.

Baraka, Imamu Amiri. *Home: Social Essays*. New York: William Morrow, 1966.

Barale, Michele Aina. "When Jack Blinks: Si(gh)ting Gay Desire in Ann Bannon's *Beebo Brinker*." *Feminist Studies* 18, no. 1 (Spring 1992): 533–49.

Beck, Evelyn Torton. "The Politics of Jewish Invisibility." *NWSA Journal* 1, no. 1 (1988):93–102.

Behdad, Ali. "The Eroticized Orient: Images of the Harem in Montesquieu and His Precursors." *Standard French Review* 13 (1989): 109–26.

Benns, Susanna. "Sappho in Soft Cover: Notes on Lesbian Pulp." Pp. 60–68 in *Fireworks: The Best of Fireweed*. Ed. Makeda Silvera. Toronto: Women's Press, 1986.

Benstock, Shari. "Expatriate Sapphic Modernism Entering Literary History." In *Rereading Modernism: New Directions in Feminist Criticism*. Ed. Lisa Rado. New York: Garland, 1994.

———. *Women of the Left Bank: Paris, 1900–1940*. Austin: University of Texas Press, 1986.

Berlant, Lauren. "National Brands/National Body: Imitation of Life." In *Comparative American Identities: Race, Sex and Nationality in the Modern Text*. Ed. Hortense J. Spillers. New York: Routledge, 1991.

Berzon, Judith R. *Neither White nor Black: The Mulatto Character in American Fiction*. New York: New York University Press, 1978.

Bhabha, Homi. "Interrogating Identity: Franz Fanon and the Postcolonial Prerogative." In his *The Location of Culture*. New York: Routledge, 1986.

———. "The Other Question: Difference, Discrimination and the Discourse of Colonialism." Pp. 148–71 in *Literature, Politics and Theory: Papers from the Essex Conference, 1976–84*. Ed. Francis Barker et al. New York: Methuen, 1986.

Bogus, Diane. "Theme and Portraiture in the Fiction of Ann Allen Shockley." Ph.D. dissertation, University of Miami, 1988.

Breslin, James. "Gertrude Stein and the Problems of Autobiography." In *Women's Autobiography: Essays in Criticism*. Bloomington: Indiana University Press, 1980.

Bright, Susie. "College Confidential." *On Our Backs* 7, no. 4 (1991): 11–12.

Brittain, Vera. *Radclyffe Hall: A Case of Obscenity?* London: Femina, 1968.

Brontë, Charlotte. *Jane Eyre*. 1847. Reprint, New York: Penguin Classics, 1986.

Bullough, Vern, and Bonnie Bullough. "Lesbians in the 1920's and 1930's: A Newfound Study." *Signs* 2, no. 4 (1977):895–904.

Burton, Peter. "Introduction." *Strange Brother* by Blair Niles. London: Gay Men's Press, 1991.

Butler, Judith. *Bodies That Matter: On the Discursive Limits of "Sex."* New York: Routledge, 1993.

———. "Critically Queer." *GLQ: A Journal of Lesbian and Gay Studies* 1, no. 1 (1993):17–32.

———. *Gender Trouble: Feminism and the Subversion of Identity.* New York: Routledge, 1990.

Butler, Octavia. *Adult Rites.* New York: Warner, 1988.

———. *Dawn.* New York: Warner, 1987.

———. *Imago.* New York: Warner, 1989.

Califia, Pat. "Clit Culture: Cherchez la Femme . . ." *On Our Backs* 8, no. 4 (1992):10–11.

Carby, Hazel V. *Reconstructing Womanhood: The Emergence of the Afro-American Novelist.* New York: Oxford University Press, 1987.

Case, Sue-Ellen. "Toward a Butch-Femme Aesthetic." In *Making a Spectacle.* Ed. Lynda Hart. Ann Arbor: University of Michigan Press, 1989.

Castle, Terry. *The Apparitional Lesbian: Female Homosexuality and Modern Culture.* New York: Columbia University Press, 1993.

Chauncey, George Jr. "From Sexual Inversion to Homosexuality: Medicine and the Changing Conceptualization of Female Deviance." *Salmagundi* 58 (1982–83):114–45.

———. *Gay New York: Gender, Urban Culture, and the Making of the Gay Male World, 1890–1940.* New York: Basic Books-HarperCollins, 1994.

Christian, Barbara. *Black Women Novelists: The Development of a Tradition, 1892–1976.* Westport, Conn.: Greenwood Press, 1982.

———. "No More Buried Lives." Pp. 187–204 in her *Black Feminist Criticism.* New York: Pergamon Press, 1985.

Cixous, Hélène. "The Laugh of Medusa." Pp. 245–64 in *New French Feminisms.* Ed. Elaine Marks and Isabelle de Courtivron Marks. Amherst: University of Massachusetts Press, 1980.

Clark, Danae. "Commodity Lesbianism." *Camera Obscura* no. 25–26 (1991):180–201.

Clarke, Cheryl. "The Failure to Transform: Homophobia in the Black Community." Pp. 197–208 in *Home Girls: A Black Feminist Anthology.* Ed. Barbara Smith. New York: Kitchen Table: Women of Color Press, 1983.

Clarke, Cheryl, et al. "Black Women on Black Women Writers: Conversations and Questions." *Conditions: Nine* (1983):88–137.

Cleaver, Eldridge. *Soul on Ice.* 1967. Reprint, New York: Dell, 1968.

Cliff, Michelle. *Abeng*. Trumansburg, N.Y.: Crossing Press, 1984.

———. "Caliban's Daughter: The Tempest and the Teapot." *Frontiers* 12 (1991):36–51.

———. *Claiming an Identity They Taught Me to Despise*. Watertown, Mass.: Persephone Press, 1980.

Cline, Sally. *Radclyffe Hall: A Woman Called John*. New York: Overlook Press, 1997.

Coles, Robert A., and Diane Isaacs. "Primitivism as a Therapeutic Pursuit: Notes Toward a Reassessment of Harlem Renaissance Literature." Pp. 3–12 in *The Harlem Renaissance: Revaluations*. Ed. Amritjit Singh. New York: Garland, 1989.

Collins, Patricia Hill. *Black Feminist Thought: Knowledge, Consciousness and the Politics of Empowerment*. New York: Routledge, 1991.

Cordova, Jean. "*Loving Her*." *Lesbian Tide* 4 (1974):18.

Dandridge, Rita B. "Gathering Pieces: A Selected Bibliography of Ann Allen Shockley." *Black American Literature Forum* 21, no. 1–2 (1987):133–46.

Davis, Madeline, and Elizabeth Kennedy Lapovsky. "Oral History and the Study of Sexuality in the Lesbian Community: Buffalo, New York, 1940–1960." *Feminist Studies* 12 (1986):7–26.

DeKoven, Marianne. *A Different Language: Gertrude Stein's Experimental Writing*. Madison: University of Wisconsin Press, 1983.

———. "Gertrude Stein and the Modernist Canon." Pp. 8–20 in *Gertrude Stein and the Making of Literature*. Ed. Shirley Newman and Ira B. Nadel. Boston: Northeastern University Press, 1988.

de Lauretis, Teresa. "Eccentric Subjects: Feminist Theory and Historical Consciousness." *Feminist Studies* 16 (1990):115–50.

———. "Sexual Indifference and Lesbian Representation." *Theatre Journal* 40, no. 2 (1988):155–77.

D'Emilio, John. *Sexual Politics, Sexual Communities: The Making of a Homosexual Minority in the United States, 1940–1970*. Chicago: Chicago University Press, 1983.

Doan, Laura. *The Lesbian Postmodern*. New York: Columbia University Press, 1994.

Dollimore, Jonathan. "The Dominant and the Deviant: A Violent Dialectic." Pp. 87–100 in *Homosexual Themes in Literary Studies*. Ed. Wayne R. Dynes and Stephen Donaldson. New York: Garland, 1992.

———. *Sexual Dissidence: Augustine to Wilde, Freud to Foucault*. Oxford: Clarendon Press, 1991.

Douglas, James. *Sunday Express*, August 19, 1928.

du Cille, Anne. "The Bourgeois, Wedding Bell Blues of Jessie Fauset and

Nella Larsen." In her *The Coupling Convention: Sex, Text and Tradition in Black Women's Fiction*. New York: Oxford University Press, 1993.

Duncker, Patricia. "Writing Lesbian." In her *Sisters and Strangers: An Introduction to Contemporary Feminist Fiction*. Cambridge, Mass.: Blackwell, 1992.

Dyer, Richard. "Seen to Be Believed: Some Problems in the Representation of Gay People as Typical." In his *The Matter of Images: Essays on Representations*. London: Routledge, 1993.

———. *White*. New York: Routledge, 1997.

Dyer, Thomas G. *Theodore Roosevelt and the Idea of Race*. Baton Rouge: Louisiana State University Press, 1992.

Edelman, Lee. "Homographesis." *Yale Journal of Criticism* 3, no. 1 (1989):189–207.

———. "Tearooms and Sympathy, or, The Epistemology of the Water Closet." Pp. 553–74 in *The Lesbian and Gay Studies Reader*. Ed. Michele Aina Barale et al. New York: Routledge, 1993.

Ellis, Havelock. *Studies in the Psychology of Sex*. 1936. Reprint, New York: Random House, 1942.

Ellison, Ralph. *Invisible Man*. 1952. Reprint, New York: Vintage Books, 1995.

Empathy 2, no. 2 (1990–91). Special issue on Visibility and Invisibility.

Escoffier, Jeffrey. "Sexual Revolution and the Politics of Gay Identity." *Socialist Review* 20, no. 82–83 (1985):119–53.

Faderman, Lillian. *Odd Girls and Twilight Lovers: A History of Lesbian Life in Twentieth Century America*. New York: Columbia University Press, 1991.

———. "The Return of Butch and Femme: A Phenomenon in Lesbian Sexuality of the 1980s and 1990s." *Journal of the History of Sexuality* 2, no. 4 (1992):578–96.

Fanon, Franz. *Black Skin, White Masks*. 1952. Trans. Charles Lam Markmann. Reprint, New York: Grove Press, 1967.

Felski, Rita. *The Gender of Modernity*. Cambridge, Mass.: Harvard University Press, 1995.

———. "Modernism and Modernity: Engendering Literary History." In *Rereading Modernism: New Directions in Feminist Criticism*. Ed. Lisa Rado. New York: Garland, 1994.

Ferguson, Moira. *Colonialism and Gender from Mary Wollstonecraft to Jamaica Kincaid*. New York: Columbia University Press, 1993.

Fifer, Elizabeth. *Rescued Readings: A Reconstruction of Gertrude Stein's Difficult Texts*. Detroit: Wayne State University Press, 1992.

Foucault, Michel. *The History of Sexuality:* vol. 1: *An Introduction.* New York: Vintage Books, 1980.

———. "Nietzsche, Genealogy, History." In *The Foucault Reader.* Ed. Paul Rabinow. New York: Pantheon Books, 1984.

Frankenberg, Ruth. *White Women, Race Matters: The Social Construction of Whiteness.* Minneapolis: University of Minnesota Press, 1993.

Frederics, Diana. *Diana: A Strange Autobiography.* 1939. Reprint, New York: New York University Press, 1995.

Fuss, Diana. "Freud's Fallen Woman: Identification, Desire, and 'A Case of Homosexuality in a Woman.'" In *Fear of a Queer Planet: Queer Politics and Social Theory.* Ed. Michael Warner. Minneapolis: University of Minneapolis Press, 1993.

———. *Identification Papers.* New York: Routledge, 1995.

———. *Inside/Out: Lesbian Theories, Gay Theories.* New York: Routledge, 1991.

Gaines, Jane. "White Privilege and Looking Relations: Race and Gender in Feminist Film Theory." Pp. 197–214 in *Issues in Feminist Film Criticism.* Ed. Patricia Evans. Bloomington: Indiana University Press, 1990.

Garber, Eric. "Gladys Bentley: The Bulldagger Who Sang the Blues." *Out/Look* (1988):52–61.

Garber, Marjorie. *Vested Interests: Cross-Dressing and Cultural Anxiety.* New York: Routledge, 1992.

Gates, Henry Louis Jr. "Critical Fanonism." *Critical Inquiry* 17 (1991): 457–70.

Gikandi, Simon. *Writing in Limbo: Modernism and Caribbean Literature.* Ithaca: Cornell University Press, 1992.

Gilbert, Sandra, and Susan Gubar. *The Madwoman in the Attic: The Woman Writer and the Nineteenth Century Literary Imagination.* New Haven: Yale University Press, 1980.

Gilmore, Leigh. *Autobiographics: A Feminist Theory of Women's Self-Representation.* Ithaca: Cornell University Press, 1994.

———. "Obscenity, Modernity, Identity: Legalizing *The Well of Loneliness* and *Nightwood.*" *Journal of the History of Sexuality* 4, no. 4 (1994):603–24.

Ginsberg, Elaine. *Passing and the Fictions of Identity.* Durham, N.C.: Duke University Press, 1996.

Glasgow, Joanne. "What's a Nice Lesbian Like You Doing in the Church of Torquemada? Radclyffe Hall and Other Catholic Converts." Pp. 241–54 in *Lesbian Texts and Contexts: Radical Revisions.* Ed. Karla Jay. New York: New York University Press, 1990.

———. "Rethinking the Mythic Mannish Radclyffe Hall." In *Queer Representations: Reading Lives, Reading Cultures*. Ed. Martin Duberman. New York: New York University Press, 1997.

Goldthorpe, Jeff. "Intoxicated Culture: Punk Symbolism and Punk Protest." *Socialist Review* 22, no. 2 (1992):35–64.

Gomez, Jewelle. "A Cultural Legacy Denied and Discovered: Black Lesbians in Fiction by Women." Pp. 110–23 in *Home Girls: A Black Feminist Anthology*. Ed. Barbara Smith. New York: Kitchen Table: Women of Color Press, 1983.

———. "Imagine a Lesbian . . . A Black Lesbian . . ." *Trivia* 12 (1988): 45–60.

Grahn, Judy. *Another Mother Tongue: Gay Words, Gay Worlds*. Boston: Beacon Press, 1984.

Grier, Barbara. *The Lesbian in Literature: A Bibliography*. 3d ed. Tallahassee, Fla.: Naiad Press, 1981.

———. "The Lesbian Paperback." *Tangents* (1966):4–7.

Grier, Barbara, and Lee Stuart. *The Lesbian in Literature: A Bibliography*. 1st ed. San Francisco: Daughters of Bilitis, 1967.

Grosz, Elizabeth. *Jacques Lacan: A Feminist Introduction*. New York: Routledge, 1990.

Haag, Pamela S. "In Search of the 'Real Thing': Ideologies of Love, Modern Romance, and Women's Sexual Subjectivity in the United States, 1920–1940." *Journal of the History of Sexuality* 2, no. 4 (1992):547–77.

Halberstrom, Judith. *Female Masculinity*. Durham, N.C.: Duke University Press, 1998.

Hale, Nathan G. *The Rise and Crisis of Psychoanalysis in the United States: Freud and the Americans, 1917–1985*. New York: Oxford University Press, 1995.

Hall, Radclyffe. *The Well of Loneliness*. 1928. Reprint, New York: Avon Books, 1982.

Halley, Janet E. "'Like Race' Arguments." Pp. 40–74 in *What's Left of Theory? New Work on the Politics of Literary Theory*. Ed. Judith Butler, John Guillory, Kendall Thomas. New York: Routledge, 2000.

Hamer, Diana. "'I Am a Woman': Ann Bannon and the Writing of Lesbian Identity in the 1950s." Pp. 47–75 in *Lesbian and Gay Writing: An Anthology of Critical Essays*. Ed. Mark Lily. Philadelphia: Temple University Press, 1990.

Haraway, Donna. "The Actors Are Cyborg, Nature Is Coyote, and the Geography Is Elsewhere: Postscript to 'Cyborgs at Large.'" Pp.

21–26 in *Technoculture*. Ed. Constance Penley and Andrew Ross. Minneapolis: University of Minnesota Press, 1991.

Haraway, Donna. "The Biopolitics of Modern Bodies: Constitutions of Self in Immune System Discourse." Pp. 203–30 in *Simians, Cyborgs, and Women: The Reinvention of Nature*. New York: Routledge, 1990.

———. "A Cyborg Manifesto: Science, Technology, and Socialist Feminism in the 1980s." Pp. 173–204 in *Coming to Terms: Feminism, Theory, Politics*. Ed. Elizabeth Weed. New York: Routledge, 1990.

———. *Primate Visions: Gender, Race and Nature in the World of Modern Science*. New York: Routledge, 1989.

———. "Situated Knowledges: The Science Question in Feminism and the Privilege of Partial Perspective." Pp. 183–201 in *Simians, Cyborgs, and Women: The Reinvention of Nature*. New York: Routledge, 1990.

Harrison, Nancy R. *An Introduction to the Writing Practice of Jean Rhys: The Novel as Women's Text*. Chapel Hill: University of North Carolina Press, 1988.

Hennegan, Alison. "Introduction." *The Well of Loneliness* by Radclyffe Hall. 1928. Reprint, London: Virago Press, 1982.

Hennessy, Rosemary. "Queer Visibility in Commodity Culture." *Cultural Critique* (1994–1995):31–76.

Henry, Dr. George. *Sex Variants: A Study of Homosexual Patterns*, vols. 1 and 2. New York: Paul B. Hoeber, 1941.

Henson, Leslie J. "'Articulate Silence[s]': Femme Subjectivity and Class Relations in *The Well of Loneliness*." Pp. 61–67 in *Femme: Feminists, Lesbians and Bad Girls*. Ed. Laura Harris and Elizabeth Crocker. New York: Routledge, 1997.

Hollibaugh, Amber, and Cherríe Moraga. "What We're Rollin Around in Bed with: Sexual Silences in Feminism." Pp. 394–405 in *Powers of Desire: The Politics of Sexuality*. Ed. Ann Snitow, Christine Stansell, and Sharon Thompson. New York: Monthly Review Press, 1983.

Hoogland, Renee C. *Lesbian Configurations*. New York: Columbia University Press, 1997.

hooks, bell. *Ain't I a Woman: Black Women and Feminism*. Boston: South End Press, 1981.

———. *Talking Back: Thinking Feminist, Thinking Black*. Boston: South End Press, 1989.

Howells, Coral Ann. *Jean Rhys*. London: Harvester Wheatsheaf, 1991.

Hull, Gloria T., Patricia Bell Scott, and Barbara Smith, ed. *All the Women Are White, All the Blacks Are Men, But Some of Us Are Brave: Black Women's Studies*. New York: Feminist Press, 1982.

JanMohamed, Abdul K. "Sexuality on/of the Racial Border: Foucault, Wright and the Articulation of 'Racialized Sexuality.'" Pp. 94–116 in *Discourses of Sexuality: From Aristotle to AIDS*. Ed. Domna C. Stanton. Ann Arbor: University of Michigan Press, 1992.

Jay, Karla. *The Amazon and the Page: Natalie Clifford Barney and Renee Vivien*. Bloomington: Indiana University Press, 1988.

Johnson, Lemuel A. "A-Beng: (Re)Calling the Body In(to) Question." Pp. 111–42 in *Out of the Kumbla: Caribbean Women and Literature*. Ed. Carol Boyce Davies and Elaine Savory Fido. Trenton, N.J.: Africa World Press, 1990.

Johnson, Samuel. "Rasselas." In *The Selected Writings of Samuel Johnson*. Ed. Katharine Rogers. New York: Signet Classic, 1981.

Johnstone, Rosemarie. "*Jane Eyre* and the Invention of Femininity." *Nineteenth Century Contexts* 16, no. 2 (1992):165–75.

King, Katie. "The Situation of Lesbianism as Feminism's Magical Sign." *Communication* 9 (1986):65–91.

Krafft-Ebing, Richard von. *Psychopathis Sexualis*. 1886. Trans. F. J. Rebman. Reprint, Brooklyn, N.Y.: Physicians and Surgeons Book Company, 1932.

Lacan, Jacques. "The Mirror Stage as Formative of the Function of the I." In *Ecrits, A Selection*. Trans. Alex Sherodan. New York: Norton, 1977.

Laclau, Ernesto, and Chantal Mouffe. *Hegemony and Socialist Strategy: Towards a Radical Democratic Politics*. New York: Verso, 1985.

Larson, Nella. *Quicksand and Passing*. Ed. Deborah E. McDowell. New Brunswick, N.J.: Rutgers University Press, 1986.

Lears, T. J. Jackson. *No Place of Grace: Antimodernism and the Transformation of American Culture, 1880–1920*. New York: Pantheon Books, 1981.

"Lesbianism among Blacks." *Brown Sister*, 1975.

Levin, Jennifer. "Beebo Lives." *Harvard Gay and Lesbian Review* 2, no. 21 (1995):53–54.

Lim-Hing, Sharon. "Dragon Ladies, Snow Queens, and Asian-American Dykes: Reflections on Race and Sexuality." *Empathy* 2, no. 2 (1990–91):20–22.

Lionnet, Françoise. "Of Mangoes and Maroons: Language, History and the Multicultural Subject of Michelle Cliff's *Abeng*." Pp. 321–45 in

De/Colonizing the Subject: The Politics of Gender in Women's Autobiography. Ed. Sidonie Smith and Julia Watson. Minneapolis: University of Minnesota Press, 1992.

Lorde, Audre. *Sister Outsider: Essays and Speeches.* Trumansburg, N.Y.: Crossing Press, 1984.

———. *Zami: A New Spelling of My Name.* Trumansburg, N.Y.: Crossing Press, 1982.

Lott, Eric. *Love and Theft: Blackface Minstrelsy and the American Working Class.* New York: Oxford University Press, 1993.

Loulan, JoAnn. *The Lesbian Erotic Dance: Butch, Femme, Androgyny and Other Rhythms.* San Francisco: Spinsters Book Company, 1990.

Lovejoy, Arthur O. *Primitivism and Related Ideas in Antiquity.* 1935. Reprint, New York: Octagon Books, 1973.

MacKinnon, Catharine. "Feminism, Marxism, Method, and the State: An Agenda for Theory." *Signs* 7, no. 3 (1982):515–44.

Martin, Del, and Phyllis Lyon. *Lesbian/Woman.* New York: Bantam, 1972.

Martinez, Inez. "The Lesbian Hero Bound: Radclyffe Hall's Portrait of Sapphic Daughters and Their Mothers." *Journal of Homosexuality* 8, no. 3–4 (1983):127–37.

Marx, Karl. "The Fetishism of Commodities." Pp. 185–206 in *Selected Writings/Karl Marx.* Ed. David McLellan. Oxford: Oxford University Press, 1977.

Marxist Feminist Literature Collective. "Women's Writing: *Jane Eyre, Shirley, Villette, Aurora Leigh.*" Pp. 185–206. In *1848: The Sociology of Literature.* Ed. Francis Barker et al. Essex Conference on the Sociology of Literature: University of Essex, 1977.

McDowell, Deborah. "Introduction." *Quicksand and Passing* by Nella Larsen. New Brunswick, N.J.: Rutgers University Press, 1986.

Meese, Elizabeth A. *(Sem)Erotics: Theorizing Lesbian: Writing.* New York: New York University Press, 1992.

Mencke, John G. *Mulattoes and Race Mixture: American Attitudes and Images, 1865–1918.* N.p.: Research Press, 1979.

Merrill, Cynthia. "Mirrored Image: Gertrude Stein and Autobiography." *Pacific Coast Philology* 20, no. 1–2 (1985):11–17.

Meyer, Susan L. "Colonialism and the Figurative Strategy of *Jane Eyre.*" *Victorian Studies* 33 (1990):247–68.

Michie, Elsie B. *Outside the Pale: Cultural Exclusion, Gender Difference, and the Victorian Woman Writer.* Ithaca: Cornell University Press, 1993.

Miller, Christopher L. *Blank Darkness: Africanist Discourses in French.* Chicago: University of Chicago Press, 1985.

Miller, Elaine. *Not a Passing Phase: Reclaiming Lesbians in History 1840–1985.* London: Women's Press, 1989.

Moraga, Cherríe. *Loving in the War Years.* Boston: South End Press, 1983.

Morgan, Tracy. "Butch-Femme and the Politics of Identity." Pp. 35–46 in *Sisters, Sexperts and Queers: Beyond the Lesbian Nation.* Ed. Arlene Stein. New York: Penguin, 1993.

Morrison, Toni. *Playing in the Dark: Whiteness and the Literary Imagination.* Cambridge, Mass.: Harvard University Press, 1992.

Mosse, George L. "Masculinity and the Decadence." Pp. 251–66 in *Sexual Knowledge, Sexual Science.* Ed. Roy Porter and Mikulas Teich. Cambridge: Cambridge University Press, 1994.

Moynihan, Daniel Patrick. "The Negro Family: The Case for National Action." Pp. 39–124 in *The Moynihan Report and the Politics of Controversy: A Trans-action Social Science and Public Policy Report.* Ed. Lee Rainwater and William L. Yancey. Cambridge, Mass.: M.I.T. Press, 1967.

Mumford, Kevin J. "'Lost Manhood' Found: Male Sexual Impotence and Victorian Culture in the United States." Pp. 75–99 in *American Sexual Politics: Sex, Gender and Race since the Civil War.* Ed. John C. Fout and Maura Shaw Tantillo. Chicago: University of Chicago Press, 1993.

Nestle, Joan. *A Restricted Country.* Ithaca: Fireband Books, 1987.

———. *The Persistent Desire: A Femme-Butch Reader.* Ed. Joan Nestle. Boston: Alyson Publications, 1992.

Nestor, Pauline. *Charlotte Brontë's "Jane Eyre."* New York: Harvester Wheatsheaf, 1992.

———. *Female Friendships and Communities: Charlotte Brontë, George Eliot, Elizabeth Gaskell.* New York: Oxford University Press, 1985.

Newton, Esther. *Mother Camp: Female Impersonators in America.* Chicago: University of Chicago Press, 1972.

———. "The Mythic Mannish Lesbian: Radclyffe Hall and the New Woman." Pp. 281–93 in *Hidden from History: Reclaiming the Gay and Lesbian Past.* Ed. Martin Bauml Duberman. New York: New American Library, 1989.

Newton, Huey. "A Letter from Huey to the Revolutionary Brothers and Sisters about the Women's Liberation and Gay Liberation

Movements." *3d World Gay Revolution* (Gay Flames Pamphlet no. 7, 1970):1–4.

Nicholson, Nigel. *Portrait of a Marriage*. New York: Athenaeum, 1973.

Niles, Blair. *Condemned to Devil's Island: The Biography of an Unknown Convict*. New York: Harcourt, Brace, 1928.

———. *Strange Brother*. 1931. Reprint, London: Gay Men's Press, 1991.

Omi, Michael, and Howard Winant. *Racial Formation in the United States from the 1960s to the 1980s*. New York: Routledge and Kegan Paul, 1986.

Omosupe, Ekua. "Black/Lesbian/Bulldagger." *Differences* 3, no. 2 (1991):102–11.

Parkes, Adam. "Lesbianism, History, and Censorship: *The Well of Loneliness* and the SUPPRESSED RANDINESS of Virginia Woolf's *Orlando*." *Twentieth Century Literature* 40, no. 4 (1994):434–60.

Phelan, Peggy. *Unmarked: The Politics of Performance*. New York: Routledge, 1993.

Phillips, Frank Lamont. "*Loving Her*." *Black World* 24 (1975):89–90.

Poovy, Mary. *Uneven Developments: The Ideological Work of Gender in Mid-Victorian England*. Chicago: University of Chicago Press, 1988.

Pryse, Marjorie. *The Mark and the Knowledge: Social Stigma in Classic American Fiction*. Columbus: Ohio State University Press, 1979.

Radford, Jean. "An Inverted Romance: *The Well of Loneliness* and Sexual Ideology." Pp. 97–111 in *The Progress of Romance: The Politics of Popular Fiction*. Ed. Jean Radford. London: Routledge and Kegan Paul, 1986.

"Review of *Strange Brother*." *Saturday Review of Literature* (1931).

Rhys, Jean. *Wide Sargasso Sea*. 1966. Reprint, New York: W. W. Norton, 1982.

Rich, Adrienne. "*Jane Eyre*: The Temptations of a Motherless Woman." Pp. 89–106 in her *On Lies, Secrets and Silence: Selected Prose 1966–1978*. New York: W. W. Norton, 1979.

Roberts, JR. *Black Lesbians: An Annotated Bibliography*. Foreword by Barbara Smith. 1st ed. Tallahassee, Fla.: Naiad Press, 1981.

Robinson, Amy. "It Takes One to Know One: Passing and Communities of Common Interest." *Critical Inquiry* 20 (Summer 1994):715–33.

Roediger, David R. *Toward the Abolition of Whiteness*. London: Verso, 1994.

Roof, Judith. *A Lure of Knowledge: Lesbian Sexuality and Theory*. New York: Columbia University Press, 1991.

Roosevelt, Theodore. "Race Decadence." Pp. 339–43 in *Theodore Roosevelt, *An American Mind: A Selection from His Writings*. Ed. Mario R. Di Nunzio. New York: St. Martin's Press, 1994.

———. "Women and the Home." Pp. 314–19 in *Theodore Roosevelt, An American Mind: A Selection from His Writings*. Ed. Mario R. Di Nunzio. New York: St. Martin's Press, 1994.

Rose, Jacqueline. *Sexuality in the Field of Vision*. London: Verso, 1986.

Rosenberg, Carroll Smith. *Disorderly Conduct: Visions of Gender in Victorian America*. New York: Alfred A. Knopf, 1985.

Rotundo, Anthony. *American Manhood: Transformations in Masculinity from the Revolution to the Modern Era*. New York: Basic Books, 1993.

Ruehl, Sonja. "Inverts and Experts: Radclyffe Hall and the Lesbian Identity." Pp. 165–80 in *Feminist Criticism and Social Change: Sex, Class and Race in Literature and Culture*. Ed. Judith Newton and Deborah Rosenfelt. New York: Methuen, 1985.

Sedgwick, Eve Kosofsky. *Between Men: English Literature and Male Homosocial Desire*. New York: Columbia University Press, 1985.

———. *Epistemology of the Closet*. Berkeley: University of California Press, 1990.

Shockley, Ann Allen. *The Black and White of It*. Tallahassee, Fla.: Naiad Press, 1987.

———. *Loving Her*. 1974. Reprint, Tallahassee, Fla.: Naiad Press, 1986.

———. *Say Jesus and Come to Me*. Tallahassee, Fla.: Naiad Press, 1987.

Showalter, Elaine. *A Literature of Their Own: British Women Novelists from Brontë to Lessing*. Princeton: Princeton University Press, 1977.

Simmons, Christina. "Companionate Marriage and the Lesbian Threat." *Frontiers* 4, no. 3 (1979):54–59.

Sinfeld, Alan. *The Wilde Century: Effeminacy, Oscar Wilde and the Queer Moment*. London: Cassell, 1994.

Skinner, Shelley. "The House in Order: Lesbian Identity and *The Well of Loneliness*." *Women's Studies* 23 (1994):19–33.

Smith, Barbara, ed. *Home Girls: A Black Feminist Anthology*. New York: Kitchen Table: Women of Color Press, 1983.

Smith, Beverly. "A Study in Black and White: *Loving Her*." *Gay Community News* 6 (November 11, 1978).

Souhami, Diana. *The Trials of Radclyffe Hall*. New York: Doubleday, 1999.

Spivak, Gayatri. "Three Women's Texts and a Critique of Imperialism." *Critical Inquiry* 12 (1985):243–61.

Stenson, Linnea A. "From Isolation to Diversity: Self and Communities in Twentieth-Century Lesbian Novels." Pp. 208–25 in *Sexual Practice/Textual Theory: Lesbian Cultural Criticism*. Ed. Susan J. Wolfe and Julia Penelope. Cambridge, Mass.: Blackwell, 1993.

Stepan, Nancy Leys. "Race and Gender: The Role of Analogy in Science." Pp. 38–57 in *Anatomy of Racism*. Ed. David Goldberg. Minneapolis: University of Minnesota, 1990.

Stimpson, Catherine R. "Gertrice/Altrude: Stein, Toklas, and the Paradox of the Happy Marriage." Pp. 124–39 in *Mothering the Mind: Twelve Studies of Writers and Their Silent Partners*. Ed. Ruth Perry and Martine Watson Brownley. New York: Holmes and Meier, 1984.

———. "Gertrude Stein and the Lesbian Lie." Pp. 152–66 in *American Women's Autobiography: Fea(s)ts of Memory*. Ed. Margo Culley. Madison: University of Wisconsin Press, 1992.

———. "Gertrude Stein and the Transposition of Gender." Pp. 1–18 in *The Poetics of Gender*. Ed. Nancy K. Miller. New York: Columbia University Press, 1986.

———. "The Somagrams of Gertrude Stein." Pp. 30–43 in *The Female Body in Western Culture: Contemporary Perspectives*. Ed. Susan Suleiman. Cambridge, Mass.: Harvard University Press, 1986.

———. "Zero Degree Deviancy: The Lesbian Novel in English." *Critical Inquiry* 8, no. 2 (1981):243–59.

Streeter, Caroline. "We Sisters Have a Legacy of Power." Review essay, *Home Girls: A Black Feminist Anthology*. *Off Our Backs* 14 (1984): 10–11.

Tomarken, Edward. *Johnson, Rasselas, and the Choice of Criticism*. Lexington: University Press of Kentucky, 1989.

Torgovnick, Marianna. *Gone Primitive: Savage Intellects, Modern Lives*. Chicago: University of Chicago Press, 1990.

Trimberger, Ellen Kay. "Feminism, Men, and Modern Love: Greenwich Village, 1900–1925." Pp. 131–52 in *Powers of Desire: The Politics of Sexuality*. Ed. Ann Snitow, Christine Stansell, and Sharon Thompson. New York: Monthly Review Press, 1983.

Troubridge, Una Lady. *The Life and Death of Radclyffe Hall*. London: Hammond, 1961.

Tyler, Carole-Anne. "Boys Will Be Girls: The Politics of Gay Drag." In *Inside/Out: Lesbian Theories, Gay Theories*. Ed. Diana Fuss. New York: Routledge, 1991.

———. "Passing: Narcissism, Identity and Difference." *Differences* 6, no. 2/3 (1994):211–48.

Walker, Lisa. "Embodying Desire: Piercing and the Fashioning of 'Neo-

Butch/Femme' Identitites." Pp. 123–32 in *Butch/Femme: Inside Lesbian Gender.* Ed. Sally R. Munt. Washington, D.C.: Cassell, 1998.

Wallace, Michele. *Black Macho and the Myth of the Superwoman.* 1978. Reprint, New York: Warner Books, 1980.

———. *Invisibility Blues: From Pop to Theory.* New York: Verso, 1990.

Walters, Suzanna Danuta. "'As Her Hand Crept Slowly Up Her Thigh': Ann Bannon and the Politics of Pulp Fiction." *Social Text* 23 (1989): 83–101.

Warner, Michael, ed. *Fear of a Queer Planet: Queer Politics and Social Theory.* Minneapolis: University of Minnesota Press, 1993.

Weeks, Jeffrey. *Sex, Politics, and Society: The Regulation of Sexuality since 1800.* New York: Longman, 1981.

Whisman, Vera. "Identity Crisis: Who Is a Lesbian Anyway?" Pp. 47–60 in *Sisters, Sexperts and Queers: Beyond the Lesbian Nation.* Ed. Arlene Stein. New York: Penguin, 1993.

Whitlock, Gillian. "'Everything Is Out of Place': Radclyffe Hall and the Lesbian Literary Tradition." *Feminist Studies* 13, no. 3 (1987): 555–82.

Wiegman, Robyn. *American Anatomies: Theorizing Race and Gender.* Durham, N.C.: Duke University Press, 1995.

Wittig, Monique. "One Is Not Born a Woman." *Feminist Issues* 2 (1981):48–54.

Woolf, Virginia. *The Letters of Virginia Woolf.* Vol. 3, *1923–1928.* Ed. Nigel Nicholson and Joanne Trautmann. New York: Harcourt, 1978.

Wyatt, Jean. *Reconstructing Desire: The Role of the Unconscious in Women's Reading and Writing.* Chapel Hill: University of North Carolina Press, 1990.

Yusba, Rebecca. "Odd Girls and Strange Sisters: Lesbian Pulp Novels of the 50s." *Out/Look* 12 (Spring 1991):34–37.

Zimmerman, Bonnie. *The Safe Sea of Women: Lesbian Fiction 1969–1989.* Boston: Beacon Press, 1990.

———. "What Has Never Been: An Overview of Lesbian Feminist Literary Criticism." Pp. 200–224 in *The New Feminist Criticism: Essays on Women, Literature and Theory.* Ed. Elaine Showalter. New York: Pantheon Books, 1985.

Zonana, Joyce. "The Sultan and the Slave: Feminist Orientalism and the Structure of *Jane Eyre.*" *Signs* 18 (1993):592–617.

Index

Fictional works are listed as topics in the index as they are treated in the text. Characters are listed by first name under the novel in which they appear.

About the Author

Lisa Walker is assistant professor of English at the University of Southern Maine.